# RECKLESS!

ALSO BY SENATOR BYRON L. DORGAN

*Take This Job and Ship It*

# RECKLESS!

• • •

*How Debt, Deregulation, and*

*Dark Money Nearly Bankrupted America*

*(And How We Can Fix It!)*

•

## SENATOR BYRON L. DORGAN

*Thomas Dunne Books*

*St. Martin's Press* 𝕸 *New York*

THOMAS DUNNE BOOKS.
An imprint of St. Martin's Press.

www.thomasdunnebooks.com
www.stmartins.com

ISBN 978-0-312-38303-9

First Edition: June 2009

10  9  8  7  6  5  4  3  2  1

# CONTENTS

CONTENTS

# ACKNOWLEDGMENTS

To Kim, Brendon, Haley, Scott, Denise, Madison, Mason, and a generous family filled with endless patience.

To my friend, editor, and collaborator, Tony Bender, for his contributions.

To Thomas Dunne, Wayne Kabak, and Mel Berger, who felt I had something to say that was worth writing and reading.

Thanks to all of you for the time, the opportunity, and the inspiration for me to write another book that will contribute to the discussion about the future of our country.

And a special thanks to the people of North Dakota, who provide me the opportunity to serve in the U.S. Senate.

# PREFACE

In the summer of 2007 I started writing a book about the state of our economy because I was convinced that we were heading straight toward a cliff at a dangerous speed. I figured if enough of us sounded the alarm, we could head off an economic disaster.

But by February 2009, when the book was finished, our economy was already in crisis. Millions of people had lost their jobs, millions had lost or were threatened with losing their homes, and those with retirement plans had lost a substantial portion of their savings. Many had just plain lost hope.

Some of America's largest financial institutions were teetering on the brink of collapse as a consequence of what we now know was their almost unbelievably reckless behavior. The Federal Reserve Board, the Treasury Department, and Congress were in a frenzied race to bail out the big financial institutions deemed to be "too big to fail."

When I started this book, I was focusing on the larger economic issues that I felt had damaged our economy. But the more research I did, the more convinced I became that although the big economic issues set us up for a fall, the trip lever for collapse was something that in the old days was called bank robbery. I know that's a harsh term. But when you learn what some did to rob our largest financial institutions of their financial strength, you'll see it fits.

We all know a little something about robbing banks. I guess the most famous bank robber was Jesse James. When the Jesse James gang pulled the bank heist in Northfield, Minnesota, he was already famous. He robbed banks the old-fashioned way—with a six gun and a fast horse. And he became a notorious criminal.

But oh, how bank robbery has changed.

Today's bank robbers wouldn't have bothered with places like Northfield, Minnesota. They've spent the last decade robbing the biggest banks in the country—from the inside. And they don't pack guns. They wear expensive suits, fly in private jets, and for all the world look like respectable businessmen. But they are real bank robbers, sure enough.

They stole the people's money, and they did it quietly. There was no violence, but the result is the same. They emptied out the bank vaults and left with their pockets full.

They loaded up their banks with debt-financed risky assets that undermined these institutions' safety. Sure, they showed big yearly profits and collected big bonuses each year. But their actions robbed the companies they were running of their financial health. And the American taxpayers were then called on to bail them out.

And it wasn't just the bankers. They had accomplices: some of the ratings agencies, mortgage bankers, brokers, derivatives traders, hedge funds, and others who were anxious to be the lookouts and share the wealth. There were some who refused to be involved . . . but far too few.

How much money? Nobody really knows.

By January 2009, over $8 trillion of the taxpayers' money had been guaranteed to help the big financial institutions, and yet the U.S. credit markets were still largely frozen and the economy was continuing to plunge.

The panic began late in the summer of 2008 when the White House, Congress, Treasury, and the Federal Reserve Board were in Code Blue mode, rushing, day to day, to announce experimental and expensive programs to try to restart the country's economic engine.

In the fall of 2008, after months of insisting that the economy was just experiencing some hiccups, and that the fundamentals were sound, Treasury Secretary Hank Paulson and Fed Chairman Ben

Bernanke paid a Friday visit to Congress and admitted that the U.S. economy was in crisis. Moreover, they claimed that Congress had to pass a three-page piece of legislation (written by Paulson) in three days, or the economy could experience a complete collapse. The three-page bill they proposed would have given the Treasury Secretary an eye-popping $700 billion with which to bail out the big banks.

It was late September and Congress was about to break for the 2008 elections, but the urgency expressed by Paulson and Bernanke hit home. Congress resisted for a week or two, but finally wrote a longer piece of legislation and passed something called TARP (Troubled Assets Relief Program), which gave the Secretary what he wanted. It gave him $350 billion immediately and made provisions to grant him another $350 billion when he asked for it, unless Congress enacted legislation prohibiting it. (Since the President could veto that legislation, the Secretary was virtually guaranteed to get the money.)

I voted against the $700 billion because I didn't think the Treasury Secretary had the foggiest idea of what he was going to do with the money. That turned out to be the case.

In a matter of weeks in what must surely have been one of the biggest bait and switch operations in government history, the Treasury Secretary changed his mind after he got the money. Instead of buying "troubled assets" from financial institutions, he decided he would use the money to invest capital in banks. And he doled out the money with no strings attached. There was no requirement that the banks use the funds to expand lending. And there was no prohibition on the use of the money for executive bonuses. It made no sense that he would pour money into the big banks without requiring some increase in their lending. But he did.

During that period, some of the same financial institutions were busy paying big bonuses just as if nothing had happened to the economy, for example the bonuses reportedly paid by Merrill Lynch just one month before it was acquired by Bank of America in January 2009. It was reported that Merrill Lynch lost $27 billion in

2008, yet gave out $3.6 billion in bonuses, including more than $1 million each to 694 employees, and $250 million to the top fourteen executives. Remember, this was happening just prior to Bank of America receiving $20 billion in TARP funds with a portion of those funds being attributable to its takeover of Merrill Lynch. It looks to me like the taxpayers ended up financing the big bonuses! And it seems that the bonuses were accelerated to happen just prior to the takeover. And by the way, aside from the fact that it looks to me like the taxpayers got stuck paying for those bonuses, why were these firms rewarding business failure?

If this type of behavior makes your blood boil, that's the right reaction. And this is just the tip of the iceberg. What has been happening in recent years at the top of the financial food chain is scandalous.

During the period when Secretary Paulson was in his crisis mode, he came to the Capitol one day to make the case for the bailout funds he said he needed. As he was leaning on the lectern explaining to the Senators the sophisticated financial information he was privy to that persuaded him emergency action was needed, I thought about a small news story I had read the previous week that was probably just as accurate a "leading economic indicator" as the data the Secretary had.

It was a news story about Spam. That's right, the famous canned meat produced by Hormel. You know, the luncheon meat that contains all of the things that are left over after the meat processor has used almost everything else. The news story said that Spam sales were soaring and Hormel employees were working overtime to meet demand. The story speculated that as the economy worsened, more people were turning to lower-cost food products like Spam to meet their family budgets.

As Paulson was telling us about the need to bail out the big financial institutions, I wondered whether Paulson had ever eaten Spam. I figured somebody who had earned millions on Wall Street the year before probably wasn't in the market for low-cost luncheon meat.

Following the Paulson bank bailout in late 2008, Wall Street financial institutions reported their year-end results: losses of $35 billion. But they also reported paying $18 billion in bonuses to their executives. Wait a minute! They pay bonuses for losing money? They don't teach that in business school. Even in a crisis, Wall Street was paying big bonuses. The American people were furious. And rightly so! (Later, when Barack Obama assumed the presidency, he declared that any financial company that benefited from the bailout program could not compensate their top executives more than $500,000 a year.)

In the middle of the economic crisis, on January 20, 2009, Barack Obama took the oath of office to become President of the United States. At that moment he inherited the biggest economic mess since FDR, with a financial system that had been looted and an economy that was in free fall. We were in a deep recession that was growing worse, with expanding unemployment, record home foreclosures, and frozen bank lending.

President Obama immediately proposed an economic recovery program that he and his advisors said was necessary to jumpstart the economy and put people back to work. Three weeks later, on February 13, the Congress passed an economic recovery plan that cost $789 billion.

The stimulus plan was widely criticized by Republican opponents as just another big spending plan by Democrats. Inexplicably, the Republicans in the Senate offered a substitute plan that cut taxes by $2.5 trillion in ten years. It was apparently lost on them that theirs was a nearly identical strategy that helped steer us toward the big federal deficits in the first place. Remember, the Bush administration had inherited a large budget surplus and immediately put in place, with Republican support, very large tax cuts tilted toward the wealthiest Americans. That turned budget surpluses into budget deficits in a big hurry.

The 2009 economic recovery plan proposed by the new President was just the latest attempt to try to rescue an economy in deep trouble. And while I voted for it because I thought on balance we

needed to use the federal government to try to jumpstart the economy, no one can guarantee that this or any other strategy is sure to
work. Still, all of us have to believe that our country has the collec-
tive wisdom and the courage to take actions to restore economic
health.

Much of what we need to do is just common sense:

- We have to rein in federal spending and begin to balance our
  federal budget. That means fixing the longer-term financing
  problems with Medicare and Social Security as well.
- Our $700-billion-a-year trade deficit has to be reduced. No
  country can run a large long-term trade deficit without serious consequences to its economy.
- Government regulators must be held accountable. The free
  market works, but it needs referees in the form of regulators.
- We need to revisit and reinstate some of the postdepression
  laws that prohibited banks from being involved in the kinds of
  investments that caused their collapse. That means separating
  fundamental banking functions from the risks of securities and
  real estate speculation.

We can do all of these things. It has been a hard time both in the
United States and around the world as the economic crisis spreads
throughout the global economy, and our optimistic American spirit
is being tested. But we will learn from this, and I know our country
will emerge wiser, stronger, and, in the end, greater.

In historical terms, our nation is young—a prodigy, to be sure—
but with stunning potential to be much more. America, unlike any
other place on earth, is still where Hope meets Promise. Even in tough
times, we know and understand the potential of our country to unite
and prevail. We've done it before, and will do it again now.

It's not just something I believe. It's something we all know!

# RECKLESS!

# INTRODUCTION

. . .

## *The Way We Were*

I'T'S THE ECONOMY, STUPID!

That was the sign in the war room of the 1992 Clinton presidential campaign office. It was a reminder that the major concern of the American people during that campaign was jobs and what was happening to their families as a result of a sluggish economy.

Fast-forward to 2008: although the sign wasn't there on the wall in the campaign offices, both presidential candidates understood that the campaign was once again all about the economy.

The financial crisis put jobs and retirement savings at risk, and it focused, like nothing else could, the attention of the voters on what the candidates were proposing to do to put the economy back on track.

The American people were anxious and angry watching the greed and incompetence of some of the country's biggest financial institutions steer the economy into a ditch. They wanted action, and they wanted change.

The Wall Street financial meltdown in 2008, with the resulting dramatic increase in unemployment, bankruptcies, and home foreclosures, was unnerving to the American people. Most of the news was about the collapse of some of America's biggest banks and the steep drop in the stock market. The speculation and debt that caused some of America's largest financial institutions to fail were nearly unprecedented.

BUT THE REAL crisis was playing out daily in the homes of families all across the nation. It was manifested in the wrenching family discussions about the loss of a job, home, or small business.

The economic tailspin did major damage to the entire country. The daily investigative reports of the underhanded business practices that had created the crisis diminished the trust and faith people had in their stocks, their banks, and their government.

And all of this followed on the heels of a decade of news lauding some of the very CEOs and business leaders who were making record incomes while turning a part of the American financial system into a casino.

It wasn't always this way.

In times past, conservative values and common sense taught us to be wary of the "get rich quick, borrow and gamble" crowd. We knew better.

And America's small businesses and small-town banks knew better, too.

It's not surprising that they weren't a part of the problem that created the current financial crisis. The men and women who go to work every morning with such high hopes for the businesses they own are the real heroes of our economy. Their approach to business is probably considered old-fashioned by those at the top of the financial food chain who have been busy creating high-risk new financial instruments that promise big benefits in a hurry.

But, in the wake of the financial mess that has now visited our country, it's clear that the "old-fashioned" approach to business should be celebrated.

I salute the men and women who are out there every day, competing, creating jobs, and selling products and services that the American people want and need. The same can be said about the small community banks around the country. Even while the 2008 headlines were screaming that another big bank was either in trouble or failing, most local community banks were doing just fine. They didn't get involved in the high-flying, risk-taking investments that so many of the big banks couldn't resist.

THIS FINANCIAL FAILURE has been a long time brewing. In recent years we've watched the growth of an economy that rewarded debt over savings and investment. It rewarded self-interest over the public interest. It produced stratospheric incomes for the people at the top while the people at the bottom struggled.

Nearly every day we read of another CEO receiving a golden parachute worth tens of millions or even hundreds of millions while the working class saw their paychecks shrink and their health and retirement benefits disappear at the same time that their work productivity was increasing.

Over the past several decades, culminating in the dramatic crisis in September and October 2008, our country was gearing up to march off a financial cliff by caving in to some high pressure from big economic interests. The government had given a green light to some of our biggest financial firms to engage in highly speculative products and pass them off as reasonable investments.

Even the big regulated banks supposedly under the eye of the Federal Deposit Insurance Corporation (FDIC) got into the act, behaving in some cases like casino customers rather than conservative businessmen.

When the speculation in subprime mortgages and all of the new, exotic financial products, including derivatives and swaps, turned sour, the American taxpayers were told that there was an urgent crisis and it was time for them to pay the bill. And guess who got paid and who got the bill? That's right. The government helped the big companies that steered us into this mess, and the beleaguered taxpayers were told they should pay up. Truly a shameful period in American finance!

ALTHOUGH THESE PROBLEMS had been brewing for over two decades, I believe that one of the worst decisions that contributed to this period of reckless finance was made in 1999 when the Financial Services Modernization Act was passed by Congress and signed by President Clinton.

That legislation reversed the protections put in place after the Great Depression and allowed the largest financial firms to create big financial holding companies and merge banking with the riskier activities in securities and real estate. They could just as well have built a casino in their lobby.

The Wall Street crowd had chafed for decades under the restrictions put on their activities after the depression. So they mounted an effort that led Senator Phil Gramm and others to enact legislation allowing them to begin doing the very things that got banks in trouble during the 1920s. I was strongly opposed to that legislation and fought against it on the Senate floor. "If you want to gamble, go to Las Vegas," I said during Senate debate. Nevertheless, the legislation passed easily, with only a handful of us voting against it. It was a mistake of monumental proportions.

Following its enactment, President Bush assumed office and hired federal regulators who were content to be willfully blind for eight years. They boasted that they really didn't believe in regulation. They preached something they called self-regulation.

The chief evangelist was Alan Greenspan, then chairman of the Federal Reserve Board. But he was joined by a choir of like-sounding regulators, starting with some in the Clinton administration and continuing even more aggressively throughout the Bush administration.

It became a wide-open field of opportunity of eight years of excess for investment banks, hedge funds, and others who wanted to get in on the game. They behaved like sweaty gamblers at the craps table. They were all fat and happy, making incomes never before seen in our country.

Even as all of this was going on in the executive suites, things were tough at the bottom. The working families were losing ground. And they were steamed when reading the stories of dramatic incomes being earned by the people at the top.

During this period, the inequality of income in the United States grew to its worst level since the Great Depression.

In short, it was an ugly period of nearly unparalleled greed. We've all read about the Gilded Age, the Gay Nineties, and the Roaring Twenties. All were symbols of the worst in a society where private interests trumped the public good. The past couple of decades, especially the past eight years, will take their place on that list. It was a period when the growth of what I call dark money filled every crevice of the financial world. Outside of public view, the financial engineering of bizarre new risky, complex products grew and grew. It became a house of cards that was destined to collapse. And it did in 2008! No, it wasn't a "correction." It was a real, big-time collapse.

## REPAIRING A BROKEN TRUST

As this book was being completed in early 2009, the damage from the economic collapse continued to affect both the U.S. and world economies. And there remained much uncertainty about the future.

I am convinced that our economy and our country will recover. We are a resilient people. And we will rebuild both this economy and people's confidence.

But even as we repair the broken trust caused by this carnival of greed in recent years, it is important to remember that this period has been an aberration and not the norm.

Things haven't always been this way.

There have been periods in our history when the American

people understood that sometimes private gain should be balanced with the public good. That ethic seemed to have vanished for the highfliers who steered this country into a ditch in 2008 and the years leading up to it.

We know that when all of us pull together, our strength is far greater than when we work only for our personal well-being. In other words, here in the United States we all do owe something to the country, which has given us the opportunity to succeed.

## STANLEY NEWBERG WAS GRATEFUL . . .

The story of a man named Stanley Newberg is a perfect representation of that belief.

The small headline in *The New York Times* simply read: "Grateful Man Leaves Estate to the U.S." The story told of a man who, in his will, had left his entire estate of $5.6 million to the government of the United States. I wanted to know more about that unusual act. So I did a little research and found out about a man named Stanley Newberg.

I never met Stanley, but I wish I had. His was an American success story.

It turns out he was an immigrant who came to America from Austria with his family to flee the persecution of the Jews. They landed here with nothing, but his dad got a job peddling fruit on the Lower East Side in New York City. As a young boy, Stanley trailed along with his dad as he sold wares. Then Stanley went to school, and he did well. When he finished high school, his parents scraped and saved and sent him to college to get a law degree. After college he had a successful career running an aluminum company. His company made money. Finally he retired. And later, he died.

When attorneys opened Stanley Newberg's will, they discovered something very unusual.

Stanley had written a provision into his will requiring that $5.6 million of his estate was to be paid to the United States of America "as a thank-you to the country" that took his family in.

In his will Stanley wrote, "It is my expression of deep gratitude for the privilege of residing and living in this kind of government—notwithstanding many of its inequities."

Whenever I think of that story, I am inspired all over again. Without knowing Stanley Newberg, I can only guess at the feelings about America that persuaded him to leave his legacy to our nation. He must have had a unique perspective about a country that allowed everyone, including a young immigrant boy, the freedom and opportunity to succeed.

And at the end of his life he must have decided that he wanted to give something back. It was more than the money. In that simple, extraordinary act was a powerful example for us all—and, maybe, a reminder of just how blessed we are to live here.

And yes, he said "notwithstanding . . . its inequities." He knew, and so do we, that this is a great place, but it isn't perfect. It's still a work in progress. There are some things that need correcting.

Stanley Newberg's simple, unselfish act demonstrated his understanding that American citizenship brings with it an obligation to contribute to the public interest, the public good. Stanley obviously had a great appreciation for the life he had lived under the Stars and Stripes.

And more and more I wonder what happened to that appreciation for the public interest in the rest of us.

Each day's headlines bring us more news of self-interest trumping the public good. And we hear story after story about decisions by people in our big institutions—both government and business—who seem oblivious to the greater good.

I know it is the case that most of the information we receive every day is about something negative. That's just the way the news works. Crime, car accidents, and stories of scandal always lead—good news doesn't sell very well.

But it isn't just the news. There really is something off course in our country. Mammoth executive salaries, escalating health-care costs, war profiteering, media concentration, the subprime loan scandal . . . All of it seems to fit a new mold of private interest always trumping the public good. Greed and excess seem to be celebrated while old-fashioned values are scoffed at.

Contrast Stanley Newberg's message with all of the negative stories of those among us who these days want to take advantage of all that America has to offer but want none of the obligations that come with citizenship. We should expect better.

## STORM CLOUDS AHEAD

I wonder what has gone wrong, and can it be fixed? I think back to a simpler and different time far from Washington and long ago.

I think about where I am from, the northern plains, where when you drive across them you can see so far it is almost like seeing the future. You get an unobstructed view when the billowing black storm clouds start brewing above. In cities the tall buildings block the view, but not on the open plains. There you can watch a storm churning for miles. You can measure its ferocity and direction. Funnel clouds might emerge. Hail might flatten the landscape. Pelting rain driven by a strong wind makes a noise you won't forget. Sometimes, it's wise just to pull over on the side of the highway beneath an overpass and take stock.

In many ways that's a metaphor for our nation in these times. There are plenty of storm clouds all around. The financial collapse of 2008 was an example of the storm clouds that had been building but were ignored for more than a decade. The resulting massive cost to the taxpayers describes the danger of ignoring these warnings.

I have a deep-seated belief that anything and everything is possible for us as Americans if we set our minds to it. But it requires us to call on that deep reservoir of common sense that has for too long been ignored. Where I come from, farmers and ranchers respect the power of the storms, but they also know that the storms are part of the natural cycle and the rains they bring restore the soil, invigorate the crops, and fill the potholes, nurturing all the creatures of the prairie. And so it is in a democracy. Just as the rains bring a revolution of new growth, so can a revolution of new ideas and fresh resolve invigorate our country.

Americans can look at these storm clouds with the same understanding. We can shrink from them or rise to them. We can use these challenges to make our lives better, as our forefathers did.

Today, our nation seems to be teetering at a precipice. There's a hard climb to better times ahead. It's a long fall if we fail. How, I wondered, as I approached the introduction to this book, can I underscore the seriousness of our problems without contributing to the "things are going to hell in a handbasket" crowd who almost always sees every glass as half-empty and believes nearly everything is destined to fail.

Then I remembered Thomas Wolfe's assessment of America's resilience in his book *You Can't Go Home Again*. He wrote:

> It is a curious paradox about Americans that these same men who stand upon the corner and wait around on Sunday afternoons for nothing are filled at the same time with an almost quenchless hope, an almost indestructible belief, an almost boundless optimism that something good is bound to happen. This is a peculiar quality of the American soul.

That "peculiar quality of the soul" describes the relentless optimism that has existed in our country since its beginning. And in many ways, it is what has made us unique. Ours has been a country that has always felt it could do anything. We rolled up our sleeves and took care of business. We believed anything and everything was possible.

In a lightning flash of time, America has done some astonishing things. We have built the strongest economy in the world. Scientists have reached into the universe and touched other planets. Terrible diseases have been cured and there is hope and progress in the fight against cancer and AIDS. We are living longer, better lives. We have been generous, reaching out to help the sick and the poor in many nations. Communication and information are instant. We know much more about our planet's past, and that gives us opportunity for a better future. We have all the tools we need to become greater than ever. So, there is cause for great optimism. My God, we decided to go to the moon, and in eight years—*eight years*—we planted an American flag on the lunar surface.

And it's important to understand that over many years the entrepreneurs who started and managed small and large businesses have created jobs and contributed to building the strongest economy in the world. They did it not by taking shortcuts or searching for money that didn't connect effort and reward. Rather, they did it through innovation, hard work, and a willingness to take risks to succeed. My hat is off to them. That is such a contrast to what we are reading about these days, when some of the big economic interests have wanted to take all they can from our economy while giving nothing back to their country.

So much time and so many resources have been wasted in just the past decade on a behavior that is at odds with our past. Arrogance, avarice, bickering, and dishonesty have become a detour from what we know America has always stood for. But every detour leads back to the main road. And this one will as well.

## RECAPTURING THAT AMERICAN SPIRIT

It's not surprising that the optimism that almost always characterized life in this country has been shaken in recent years.

When asked, people say they are not sure that their children will have better lives than they have had. That is a very different attitude than has usually existed in our country. Many say they are worried about the future and what it holds. Their jobs are not as secure in a global economy, and they are profoundly aware of the growing divide between the rich and poor. As Billie Holiday once sang, "Empty pockets don't ever make the grade."

And one more point about this issue of income. There are some great Americans who have amassed large fortunes through invention, innovation, hard work, and/or taking risks at the right time on the right thing. They deserve these fortunes. They contributed to our country and they made their money the old-fashioned way. They earned it. Warren Buffett and Bill Gates come to mind. And there are so many others whose business and investment skills have both enriched them and helped build a bigger and stronger economy. So don't confuse my vigorous criticism in this book of those who have absconded with a fortune while steering our country into a ditch with my admiration for those business leaders who have contributed to our country's growth.

But what has been happening in our country in recent years is way outside of the norm. People are steamed. They see a country moving in the wrong direction. They feel like they are being left behind while the big interests are wallowing in privilege. They see the big financial interests go belly-up and get bailed out by the government, while they struggle every day with personal financial emergencies, but the government doesn't rush to help them.

Many also believe that their government no longer tells them the truth. Matters from the financial wreckage to the war in Iraq have been described in less than honest terms by their government. In short, the American people are angry, impatient, and want change.

This book takes a critical look at those things that I believe have undermined the faith people used to have in their government. It tackles the issues that are having and will continue to have an impact on the lives of ordinary people. It asks the question, on a series of important issues, what ever happened to common sense?

- Who allowed the big financial institutions to turn their exotic high-finance activities into a cesspool of speculation and then have the federal government bail them out with taxpayer funds when it all turned sour?

- How did the previous administration get away with hiring some big favored contractors who got fat, no-bid Iraq war contracts that resulted in the largest amount of waste, fraud, and abuse in American history? And why did Congress offer little or no oversight while the taxpayers were being fleeced?
- Why did the President, Congress, and the federal regulators walk us back into the sinkhole of massive federal deficits?
- Why did the President decide to fight a war with borrowed money while pushing big tax cuts for the wealthy?
- And which federal regulators put their hands over their eyes while the subprime loan scandal played out right in front of them?
- Why do the CEOs of major corporations now make over four hundred times the yearly income of the average worker in their companies? How is a hedge fund manager justified in earning over $3 billion in a year? And why do executives who fail still get paid tens of millions of dollars as they are ushered out the door? Isn't this greed run amuck?
- Who supports a tax system that allows the world's richest man to pay a lower tax rate than the receptionist in his office? And why would a U.S. corporation buy a German sewer system?
- When did the OPEC countries and the big oil companies put a drill bit in your bank account? What can we do about it?
- Why do we call it a health-care system when it is really a sick-care system? It costs less to keep people well than to treat them after they become sick. So how do we change the system to make that happen?
- How did we allow our country to become dependent on foreign countries for over two-thirds of the oil we need to run our economy? And how do we fix that vulnerability?

- Will we ever know the real story about the false intelligence information that led our country to go to war in Iraq? Who was responsible for the false intelligence? Was it deliberate? How do we make sure this never happens again?

These are just a few of the issues this book explores as it ponders why common sense seems lacking in so many of our public policies.

As the American people get up and go to work in the morning, they have a right to wonder who is looking out for their interests. The same is true of a lot of small-business owners who unlock their doors every morning and work hard to succeed.

We were raised to believe that there was a connection between effort and reward, and yet while productivity is up, wages are stagnant. The rewards go to the big shots. Americans have always had an innate sense of fairness, and they know full well they have been on a tilted playing field for quite some time.

Our health-care system is priced out of reach for tens of millions of Americans. School classrooms where our children spend most of their day are, in many cases, too crowded and in need of attention. Our big institutions, including both big business and big government, seem to be bloated, out of control, and too often motivated by greed or ignorance. Our infrastructure is suspect and our personal and national debt loads crushing.

## REASON FOR HOPE

Still, we can recapture the spirit that has always guided our country if we look at all that has happened and is happening from the perspective of what we know about ourselves and our country. This grand expanse of towering cities and mountains, fertile plains, forests, and valleys is a place of remarkable abundance, with more opportunity than any other place on earth. If we can regain our perspective, we can regain our sense of optimism.

It is said that we inherit our country from our parents and we borrow it from our children. If so, we should ask ourselves now, are we honoring our parents' sacrifice and meeting our responsibilities to our children? If not, we need a profound change both in public policy and in attitude.

The forces of greed and self-interest are formidable opponents. However, they are not insurmountable. But to prevail, we need resolve and leadership. Optimism must push cynicism aside even as we keep our eyes and ears wide open to the truth.

If America is to continue to be a dominant force for good in the world, we have to tackle the tough and urgent issues of energy, corruption, health care, education, the environment, fiscal policy, and much more. And, for once, we have to insist that we do it in a way that balances the common good with private gain.

We can balance our commitment to a better future with a healthy perspective about all that is good in our country and us. Stanley Newberg did that in his will. We can celebrate the goodness of America by the way we conduct our own lives every day.

It is easy to fear the future and to romanticize the past. The writer Griff Niblack once said of nostalgia, "If you're yearning for the good old days, just turn off the air conditioning." Then there was Will Rogers, who observed, "Things ain't what they used to be and probably never was."

But the fact is, all of us are destined to live in the future. So, we've got work to do. Decisions we make now will have a profound influence on what kind of country we hand over to our children. In our economic system it is expected that we all work to improve ourselves and pursue opportunities for success. But along with that, our democracy also requires obligations of citizenship. The basics such as voting, serving on the local school board, being part of a volunteer fire department, paying taxes, they are all the things we do to contribute to our country—to the public good.

You see, the silver lining in the ominous storm clouds I spoke of earlier in this introduction is that more so than any other place on earth we have the tools to rebuild ourselves. We have a Constitution and a Bill of Rights. We have freedoms that are the envy of the

world. We have the opportunity to speak out and speak up in support of change. And we not only choose our leaders; we can also
choose to become leaders. That is the nature of this long-running
experiment in self-government.

I believe that change is in the air. And we will pull together to
put America back on track. In this book, I describe the strategies
that will allow us to do that. We have all of the tools. Now we just
have to muster the will.

# CHAPTER I

...

# *The Good Old Days:*
# *I Remember When...*

THERE'S AN OLD story about the drunk who came before the judge charged with setting a mattress on fire. He said, "Judge, that bed was on fire when I got in it!"

Right!

It's a silly thought. But I'll bet there are a fair number of young people in our country who look at what has happened and what is happening in our country in just the past decade and make the same point: "Hey, that was happening when I showed up on the scene."

Remember, those graduating from high school this year were in first grade when the Monica Lewinsky sex scandal enveloped the Clinton administration. They were in fourth grade when we were attacked on 9/11. They were in fifth grade when President George W. Bush started making plans to invade the country of Iraq. They listened all through high school to a U.S. President insist that our country had the right to torture certain prisoners who might be terrorists. They heard their President claim he had the right to order wiretapping on telephone conversations in our country in order to protect us from these terrorists.

They were in grade school when Enron collapsed and we found out that one of the largest energy companies in the United States was also, in part, a criminal enterprise making money the underhanded way—by cheating its customers. And they would have seen the television commercials advertising home mortgages to people who had bad credit and couldn't pay their bills. They may not have known how out of line that was as compared to a time when their grandparents and great-grandparents saved up to buy things and knew that keeping their financial house in order was essential.

They have, during their school years, attended class about 12,000 hours and watched about 20,000 hours of television. They have been fed a steady diet of sex and violence on television since they were first able to handle a remote control.

And in 2008 they saw the meltdown of the stock market and an economic crisis unparalleled since the 1930s.

In short, those graduating from high school this year have in their brief lives seen, heard, and experienced so much in this age of instant communication.

Even in the middle of an economic crisis and cultural change, I know there are plenty of positive things in their young lives as well, starting with computers and the Internet, which brings that ability to communicate with the world to their fingertips in just a nanosecond.

Still, it's probably not surprising that, having grown up in the past decade of these strange times, young Americans, especially, seem determined to change things. And they are deciding to get involved in politics. That is a healthy sign. For the first time in many decades, the 2008 political campaign was marked by an outpouring of energy and commitment by young people. They were demanding change.

And, not surprisingly, in the 2008 campaign candidates from both major parties called for change. *Change.*

But "change" is just a word. What exactly needed to change?

In a word, I think the issue was trust. The American people had lost faith in their government's ability to tell the truth and to lead.

By mid-2008, President Bush's approval rating had dropped to a historic low of 26 percent. No institution can survive long without confidence in both the honesty and leadership of those in charge.

Frankly, while some in politics might cheer the sinking poll ratings of a President of the other party, it gives me no pleasure. It hurts our country when the American people have lost confidence in their leadership. But the American people have a right to demand change when they feel our country is off track.

Clearly, many of our problems have been brewing for some time. But the flaws of the past administration have on nearly every issue, from budget deficits, the war, and torture to the economy, the environment, and more, shaken the faith of those who long to respect and trust their government.

I have learned that sometimes government is able to move forward despite itself, but it rarely moves very far without the push of the people behind it. America cannot advance if its citizens do not have the information and the will to do so. The purpose of this book is to provide a measure of both. Nothing happens without you.

It seems as if we are in this big boat together and, though there is some splashing going on, we are not rowing together, and it is unsettling to note that for too long no one appeared to be steering!

When government is unable or unwilling to effectively lead, it is the place *and the duty* of its people to lead government. Not only do you have a right to be heard, but you also have an obligation to speak out when America takes a wrong turn.

But as I pointed out in my introduction, let's not lose sight of the many things that are right about America even as we address the things that are not.

## AN ANGRY OLD MAN

It was at a town meeting I was holding in a small North Dakota town one evening that a thin old man got to his feet shouting, "Our government is worthless! There isn't one damn thing it can do right." The veins in his neck bulged and his red face and narrow eyes made it clear that this anger wasn't just for effect.

I know that government sometimes does things that make our blood boil. So I wasn't surprised by the passion shown by the old man. But I was curious what prompted his anger.

Following the meeting, as people were filing out of the hall, an elderly gray-haired woman came up to me and said, "Don't mind Ernie! He just had open-heart surgery and he gets pretty upset and emotional about a lot of things these days."

Interesting, I thought. This old guy must have had his heart surgery paid through the Medicare insurance program. So I went over to him as he was headed out the door and said, "Thanks for giving me your opinion. Let me ask you, do you have Medicare?"

"Yup," he said. "I just had heart surgery with my Medicare plan."

"So, you must think at least that one government program works?" I asked.

"Medicare ain't government, it's Medicare!" he snorted as he stomped off into the night muttering to himself.

Well, in these situations you win some and you lose some. Of course, Medicare *is* a government program. And it *does* work. Not perfectly, and not without modifications from time to time, but time and time again it outperforms private health care when it comes to cost and efficiency. But in the years since then I have thought a lot about that old man and his anger about government and what it means for our country.

While skepticism is required of citizens these days, the loss of trust between Washington, D.C., and people like Ernie is troubling. Government has long been a target of critics and comedians, and I believe this is not only often well deserved but also healthy. But it is easy to lump all of it into one mass of human incompetence. And believe me, I have seen plenty of government waste and incompetence and spent much of my time in Congress trying to stamp it out. But I have also seen so many examples of people working together through government to move our country forward.

Our 24/7 media and talking-head culture help reinforce the

notion of government's incompetence. However, life is never as black and white as it seems. Gray areas abound.

When have you ever heard the evening newscast begin with a positive story about a government program that worked to help a family get through tough times with food stamps or unemployment benefits? Have you heard a news story about the young man or woman who was able to go to college only because there was an opportunity for a Pell Grant from the government? Or perhaps the government researcher at the National Institutes of Health who makes a breakthrough discovery of a vaccine that provides a cure for a disease? No. Good news doesn't sell. The evening news largely reports accidents, crime, scandal, incompetence, and what doesn't work. I understand that it is all news, but it leaves the impression that everything is wrong and nothing is right. And, of course, that is not accurate.

Skepticism in America is necessary. But if we allow it to destroy our capacity for optimism, we cannot maintain any measure of greatness. I am not speaking about false optimism. I'm talking about the enlightened involvement by the people of this nation that I believe offers nearly unlimited potential. My belief has never changed. But after these years in the U.S. Congress I understand more than ever that our government has a lot of work to do to regain people's trust and help restore that optimism.

And in 2008, when the American people most needed a government they could trust and leaders they could count on to steer us through the economic and financial crisis, the distrust in government undermined the ability of the government to lead.

For the sake of our country, this has to change. And it starts with each of us. It is our job to create a government we can trust and rely on to represent the real "public interest."

## MY JOURNEY TO THIS PLACE

Let me share with you just a portion of my journey from a town of three hundred people in rural North Dakota to the U.S. Senate. It has been one that helped form my values and passions about public service and public policy.

When I left my small hometown to go off to college and then left my home state to get a graduate degree, a political career was the last thing on my mind. I grew up in a family with a progressive philosophy rooted in the Farmers Union movement. And while in college and in graduate school I became increasingly interested in government policies—especially prompted by the controversial debates about the war in Vietnam.

It was for that reason I moved back to my home state at age twenty-five and accepted an offer to work in state government with a new, interesting thirty-eight-year-old Harvard Law graduate who had just been elected State Tax Commissioner (an elective office in my state). He was from a small town of eighty people in northwestern North Dakota. He had gone off to study at Harvard and had come back determined to make a difference for our state, and when invited by him, I decided to move back and become a part of that effort as his deputy in a sizable agency in the State Capitol Building.

During the following year and a half, we became good friends as we worked together on tax and economic policies. I admired him a great deal.

A phone call I received early one morning changed everything for me. It was a call from the tax commissioner's father asking me to check to see if his son was in his capitol office. He had been staying temporarily at his parents' home because of some marital difficulties and his father said he had not returned home the past evening. I told his father I doubted he was in, because his office lights were not on. But I would check.

As I unlocked his office door in the State Capitol Building that morning at about eight o'clock, I sensed something was wrong. I could not possibly have known how what I was about to discover would change my life for decades to come.

I was stunned by a sight that took my breath away. My boss, my friend, was slumped over his desk with his hand on the telephone. I could tell immediately that he was dead. And I could tell by other things in the room that he had taken his own life.

I was devastated.

First, and foremost, he was my friend. And I was filled with grief.

We had over a hundred people in the State Capitol Building office that morning, and I knew as his deputy I had responsibilities to find a way to take care of things in the middle of what was sure to become a shocking, sensational statewide news story. I was twenty-six years old at the time. When it was all over, I felt a whole lot older.

Medical teams and people from law enforcement and, finally, the coroner's office converged on the eighth floor of the State Capitol. I called the Governor, and he and I called the employees of the agency together to tell them of the tragedy. It was one of the saddest, most chaotic, and tragic mornings of my life.

Six weeks later, the Governor called me to his office and asked me to accept an appointment to fill the vacancy as state tax commissioner.

It was both an unexpected and bittersweet opportunity, born of sorrow at the loss of a friend. But I hope my years of public service are recognized to be an extension of the work of both my friend the tax commissioner as well as the Governor who gave a very young man a chance.

In the ensuing years, I stood successfully for election as state tax commissioner. Then I ran successfully for the U.S. House and finally for the U.S. Senate, pinching myself along the way to make sure it was all real.

The memories I have of the man I succeeded under those tragic circumstances serve as a reminder to me that an elected position makes one neither greater nor less human and vulnerable.

While the majority of my compassion is reserved for the people I represent, I save some for my colleagues and opponents whose work is not easy or often appreciated. I try not to lose sight of the fact that most of us want what is best for the country. We just don't always agree on the method.

## THE UNSHAKABLE FAITH IN THE FUTURE OF OUR FOREFATHERS

My roots in a small farming community have also been a steadying force in my public service in the intervening years. I learned a lot even if I did not realize it at the time. Almost all of my public service has been informed and influenced by the culture I grew up in.

I realize now that although the immigrants who came to settle the northern Great Plains had faced much harder times than most of us, they possessed an unshakable optimism about this young country. Those pioneers who came to the prairies to raise a family and work a farm as a result of the Homestead Act had to fight hard to overcome the challenges of the weather and the elements. But they also had to battle the big banks, the railroads, and the large grain companies that wanted to overcharge and underpay them. It wasn't a fair fight, but as long as they felt there was someone else fighting for them, they trusted that things would work out in the end.

One of the populist political warriors in the early part of my state's history was Governor "Wild Bill" Langer, who later in life became a U.S. Senator. He was born in the culture of those who homesteaded the land and struggled to make ends meet against the efforts of the bigger economic interests that sought to take advantage of them. Legend has it that he would travel around the state giving speeches, raising his fist in the air, shouting, "If you put a lawyer, a banker, and an industrialist in a barrel and roll it down a hill, you'll always have a son of a bitch on top."

It was a passionate and clever way to describe the adversaries faced by family farmers who were engaged in a mighty struggle to stay on the land during tough times. His description of the big interests was a reference to the understanding in a farm state that the

big grain millers, the big bankers, the railroads, and the industrialists in the east (that used to mean Minneapolis in the old days)
were economic predators taking everything they could from farm
families . . . just because they had the economic power to do it.

I grew up in, and was molded by, that populist movement and
tradition. No, I don't think the big economic interests are "sons of
bitches" as Langer used to declare. But I think some of them always
have and still do try to take advantage of those who have less economic power than them.


## THE FREE MARKET NEEDS REFEREES

There are times when we are required to challenge the big interests
to make sure the public is being served. Teddy Roosevelt, North
Dakota's adopted son, was fearless in taking on the entrenched economic powers.

As both business and government become bigger and stronger it
is critical that government enforces the rules that give everyone a
fair opportunity in our country.

The past eight years, and further back in some cases, have been
an experiment in nonregulation, or what the Bush administration
called self-regulation. I hope this book will expose the results of this
folly—although given what we have been through in 2008, it hardly
needs exposure to the American people.

It all comes back to trust. Americans have lost trust in their government to rein in corporate abuse. For too long they were witnesses to administrations driving the getaway car for bad behavior.

I recognize the frustration the American people have with the
intrusions of both government and business into their lives. But
sometimes there is a need for government to take on the excesses in
the private sector when individuals cannot do it themselves. I am a
Democrat, and I think my political party gets a bad rap on this
point. We don't want a bigger government. We just want a *better*

government . . . one that stands up for the interests of average Americans. When the big interests pervert the rules and regulations to take advantage of others, it is the government's responsibility to intervene.

In recent years, when war profiteering and high finance and oil market manipulations have screamed out for oversight, Republicans blocked efforts to hold these cheats and lawbreakers accountable. And even when the Democrats regained control of Congress, an obstructionist minority party fought tooth and nail for the status quo.

Some of that blame must be shared by Democrats who were no bargain during much of it. Too many of them were willing to accommodate their friends in high finance. But the facts are quite simply the facts. The Republicans were the ones who have long felt that the term "regulation" was a four-letter word.

While Congress has an obligation to expose fraud and waste, we must also sweep our own dirty little corners in government, if we are to regain the trust of the people. These corners include Congress!

The fact is, the federal government has become big and bloated. And that is another reason people have lost confidence in their government. The big federal agencies just keep getting bigger and more bureaucratic, and every attempt to cut the agencies back to size is met with charges that it is an attempt to cut programs that help people. That's nonsense.

We need government to administer necessary programs and to regulate where needed. But we also need to understand the American people are sick and tired of dealing with a larger and larger government that seems unresponsive to its citizens.

There has never been a time when some people didn't harbor frustration and distrust about their governments, but the difference in America has always been that citizens have had a certain confidence that they could change things. That attitude made America special because people truly believed they had a voice. They did. And they still do.

# WE THE PEOPLE

For many immigrants who came to make their home in "the new country," it was the first time that they were going to be able to be involved in the decisions of their government. And that ability gave them a stake in defining their future through government. They would have a voice on issues big and small, from decisions at their local schools and town councils to the national decisions about priorities, and because they were stakeholders in decisions about their future it gave them faith that better times were ahead.

My great-grandmother Caroline was a wonderful example of that faith. She was married in Norway to a man named Otto, and they came to the new country, settled in Minnesota, and had six children. But when Otto died, Caroline gathered her six children and took the train to western North Dakota to homestead. She pitched a tent on the prairie, and then in the years after she built a home, raised a family, and ran a farm. She had nothing but hope, but against all odds she was convinced she could do it. She had faith in the government promise in the Homestead Act that if she settled on 160 acres of land and improved it, she could own it. What a marvelous, generous government policy that offered so much to immigrants who had so little! When I see the vast expanses of wheat or the cattle herds on the very same ground that today help feed a hungry world, it is proof enough to me that government can work in magnificent fashion.

Because of the opportunity provided by the Homestead Act, I believe those pioneers generally developed a positive view of their government. They had a sense that policies were designed to help them get ahead. And they knew they could have a voice in public offices.

In those days, the institutions in the lives of people, such as business and government, were smaller and less intrusive. State and local governments, and the federal government as well, were not so large, and America for the most part was still a nation of shopkeepers and businesses that, with a few exceptions, were small and family owned. That meant that people could have a more personal relationship with both their government and the businesses that they patronized.

But over time that changed. Both government and business grew large and powerful, with the potential to have more of an impact on people, creating a sense of estrangement between ordinary citizens and these growing institutions.

As business and government grew, conflicts between self-interest and the public good more often were resolved in favor of the big interests. In recent decades self-interest has grown far more powerful, with government and big business now, in ways large and small, eroding the freedoms of individuals.

## TIME AGAIN FOR REFORM

Maybe it's just human nature. But society and government have always provided a counterweight to greed—society through peer pressure, morals, and celebration of philanthropy and government through laws, which generally aimed to keep things as fair as possible. But today private industry and government too often seem like co-conspirators, celebrating the triumph of self-interest.

Government policies seem tilted toward the powerful. Businesses have grown bigger and more powerful and have a greater ability to affect workers and consumers in ways designed to benefit the businesses and/or upper-income Americans. Political debates about things like who benefits from tax cuts have become a staple of political campaigns as government policies exacerbated the inequality of income in recent years.

In the past two decades the wealthy were accumulating more wealth at a dizzying pace. Meanwhile, most Americans were struggling just to keep up with inflation.

In the first half of this decade the income for most American workers was smaller than five years before. In 2005 the average income was 1 percent below the average income in 2000. But that

wasn't true for all income earners. The growth in incomes was concentrated among those on the upper rungs of the income ladder,
those making at least $1 million a year. The top .25 percent of
income earners managed to capture nearly *one-half* of the income
gains during that same five-year period, even as the average worker
was losing ground.

The Bush tax cuts were generous contributions to those in the
upper income class. It was reported that nearly 30 percent of the tax
savings as a result of the Bush capital-gains tax cut went to taxpayers
who made $10 million or more. On average, each of these some
eleven thousand taxpayers saved $1.9 million. Yes, that is a tax cut of
$1.9 million for *each* of them. At the same time, nearly 90 percent of
the American income earners received only 5 percent of the benefit
from the capital-gains tax cuts. And these cuts were advertised as
being aimed at ordinary American taxpayers.

The assertions by the Bush/Cheney administration about its family-
friendly tax cuts remind me of something Will Rogers once said:
"It's not what he knows that bothers me. It's what he says he knows
for sure that just ain't so."

From the tax code where wealthy folks who get their income
through dividends pay just a fraction of the taxes that working
people do, to the speculative and sometimes predatory financial
ventures on Wall Street, to the nearly unbelievable escalation of executive compensation while workers at the bottom are losing
ground—all of this cries out for reform and change. And I believe
change is coming.

In farm country, we have a weed called leafy spurge that has
proved almost impossible to kill, yet if farmers don't control it, it
will strangle their crops. So, with timely application of herbicides
and introduction of spurge-eating beetles, we have learned to control
it. There is a lesson here for the garden that is America. Pulling
weeds is something that is necessary from time to time. Weeds will
always exist in our system; it's our job to identify them and keep
them under control.

In recent decades there has been an exhausting parade of shady deals and shady characters that have blurred the line between big business and big government. I explored a great deal of that corruption as it relates to the exploitation of trade and labor with my first book, *Take This Job and Ship It*, and there will be more to come in this book.

Every day we see energy speculators, war profiteers, managed health-care providers, media propagandists, and/or financiers given some unfair advantage over the average consumers and taxpayers, and the cumulative effect of the American people watching selfishness prevail over the public interest has been an undermining of the public's trust in government.

This "anything goes" approach to capitalism has injured the very economy we have aspired to create. It is a philosophy that corporations and markets can be counted on to police themselves. Who needs pesky regulations?

This claptrap has long been the game plan in neocon circles in industry and government. It is easy to see the results as U.S. jobs have been outsourced and low-wage workers "imported" to fill other jobs. And small businesses are unable to compete with the big interests that utilize predatory business practices.

This is nothing new. As I said, it is the nature of the beast. While many people refer to the olden days with fondness, those were also a time of exploitation of workers and the abuse of women and children in the workplace.

But fortunately, those dark days were followed by days in which labor laws protected workers and set basic compensation standards and allowed a middle class to grow and a real working democracy to take root. The two Roosevelt presidencies demonstrated how to take on the monopolies and how to empower workers. Teddy Roosevelt took on the role of a trustbuster to end the monopolies that were hurting American families and crushing small business. Franklin Roosevelt gave to workers the legal tools needed to organize and fight back. Things started changing for the better. For these actions we still remember the two Roosevelt administrations. And some still despise them for it.

Consider this. After World War II, the biggest economic boom in history—the expansion of the middle class—was not born of trickle-down economics! It was a time when government helped provide a climate in which small businesses and the ordinary worker could thrive, and it percolated up. . . . That's right; prosperity percolated up!

I'm a big fan of the free-market system. I don't know of any better method of allocating the goods and services. But in a free-market economy it is not unusual to see the big interests pitted against the little guy. When they are allowed to run unchecked or to rig the system, the big interests have the potential to drag down the very economy they need to remain stable and healthy. That is why it is so important we fight for a new era of reform and change to put our country back on track—giving working people and small businesses the voice and the power to make the changes necessary.

This is not about a liberal or conservative philosophy. It is about making sure our economy and the free-market system work for everybody.

Every business ought to embrace this, because the strength in our economy is measured not only in dollars and cents but also in the confidence of the people.

# CHAPTER 2

• • •

# *A Financial House of Cards*

IN 1999 MY advice for the nation's financial gurus who were pushing something they called modernization for our financial system was simple. I said, "If you want to gamble, go to Las Vegas."

I had no idea how close I had been in describing the reckless behavior of some of the executives of big financial firms. Although their titles included the word "bank," for some it could just as well have been "casino."

Will Rogers never had much of an appetite for all of the high-finance kingpins on Wall Street. He was said to call them shysters. Rogers looked at all of the fancy financial transactions they were involved in, like short selling, puts, and futures contracts, and he saw it as just trading paper rather than buying and selling products. He described the participants as "people who are buying things they'll never get from people who never had it."

Rogers said he learned about buying stock from his dad. Will said his dad told him to buy stock. Then hold it until it goes up. Then sell it. "And if it doesn't go up, don't buy it."

Sounds simple, and funny. But what happens in the financial

markets on Wall Street is serious business for the well-being of all Americans.

And given what has happened recently, old Will Rogers must be rolling over in his grave. The shysters have been back in business in a big way. The financial crisis that consumed the end of 2008 was eerily similar to what took place nearly eighty years ago.

In early October 2008, the financial house of cards collapsed and the stock market took a plunge of historic proportions, losing 25 percent of its value in less than two weeks' time. In fact, the week of October 6 through 10, the U.S. stock market logged its worst week in seventy-five years.

That was on top of an already long, slow slide the market had taken throughout 2008 as people lost confidence in the economy and their government. Trillions of dollars of value in both the stock market and real estate was lost in the blink of an eye, and people's confidence in the future suffered a serious blow.

A financial house of cards had been created over the years by a lot of highfliers who had loaded up with debt and made big wagers with other people's money. Not surprisingly, when it collapsed it caused massive economic damage here and around the world.

We couldn't see it clearly until the collapse because so many of the sophisticated financial instruments that were being bought and sold were unregulated and beyond the vision of regulatory authorities. But now we know how we were all taken to the cleaners by some financial predators who created bad products and got rich trading and selling them until it brought down our economy.

When the economic crisis hit, we finally saw the nearly unbelievable greed and excess that had permeated our financial system, starting right at the top with some of the biggest financial companies in the world and eating away at the core of some of the banking institutions that were supposed to have been walled off from that kind of risk.

There was a lot of finger-pointing about what caused the crisis. And it wasn't just one thing. Over several decades the big business interests had pressed hard to eliminate regulations and get rid of oversight so they could expand into new areas. And the financiers began to create fancy, complicated financial products that were hard to understand but very profitable to buy and sell. But it couldn't last forever.

It turns out it was a big Ponzi scheme.

## THE FINANCIAL SERVICES MODERNIZATION ACT

Of all the shortsighted, greedy, and downright ignorant actions that helped create the economic collapse, none was more pronounced than the action of Congress and President Clinton to repeal the banking protections that were put in place after the bank failures of the 1930s. That action came in 1999 in the form of the Financial Services Modernization Act, which breezed through Washington, D.C., greased by some of the largest financial institutions in America.

It was U.S. Senator Phil Gramm of Texas, joined by Congressman Tom Bliley and Congressman Jim Leach, who created the legislation called the Financial Services Modernization Act. And the legislation garnered widespread bipartisan support.

That legislation, among other things, repealed a law called the Glass-Steagall Act, which was a postdepression statute designed to protect our banks from risky investments. It also allowed the creation of large financial holding companies to create "one-stop shopping" in the financial sector. For many of the big financial firms, this turned out to be a step toward bankruptcy.

One of the important lessons of the bank failures during the Great Depression was that banks had taken on substantial risks by investing in securities and real estate that brought many of them down when the investments went sour. So the Glass-Steagall Act was created to prevent that kind of speculation by banks from ever happening again. Those protections served this country well for nearly seventy years.

But Senator Gramm and others (especially the influential high-fliers on Wall Street) chafed under the restrictions of the Glass-Steagall Act, and they wanted it repealed. In November 1999 they succeeded. It was like removing the traffic lights from a busy inter-section, and it was just a matter of time before there was a big crash.

The vote in the U.S. Senate was 90 to 8. I was one of eight Senators who aggressively opposed it and voted against the bill. When it was debated on the Senate floor I made the following state-ments in opposition:

> It will fuel the consolidation and mergers in the banking and financial services industry. . . . The bill will raise the likeli-hood of future massive taxpayer bailouts. . . . We will look back in ten years' time and say: we should not have done that because we forgot the lessons of the past.
>
> Fusing together the idea of banking, which requires not just the safety and soundness to be successful but the percep-tion of safety and soundness, with other risky, speculative ac-tivity is, in my judgment, unwise. . . . I say to the people who own banks, if you want to gamble, go to Las Vegas. If you want to trade in derivatives, God bless you. Do it with your own money. Do not do it through the deposits that are guar-anteed by the American people and by deposit insurance.

I wish I hadn't been right, but actions of the past decade prove how this legislation pulled the rug out from under the American economy.

The vote on the measure was a runaway! They had it all wired, and they didn't even work up a light sweat in rolling over the eight of us in the Senate who opposed the plan.

I don't take pleasure that I was proved right. But when Congress passed the 1999 legislation (signed by and supported by President Clinton) it gave a green light to the growth of the big financial hold-ing companies and the merging of risky investments with banking.

It was a boneheaded thing to do and Congress should have known better. So should have President Clinton and his team at the Treasury Department who supported it. But the Clinton financial gurus largely came from Wall Street and they knew the sermon by heart. Build bigger financial institutions with the ability to become one-stop shops for all of the financial needs of the American people and America would be a better place. That was their chant. But it was wrongheaded. It was a strategy that concealed a recklessness and risk taking that we had long ago determined to prevent. And more important, it was a major contributor to the financial collapse of 2008.

The Clinton administration and the Republican supporters in Congress argued that they needed to do this in order to compete in the global economy. That argument was bogus, but Congress swallowed it hook, line, and sinker.

Following the enactment of the Financial Services Modernization Act, which gave the big financial players a lot more running room, President Bush came to town preaching the doctrine of "less government regulation." It was just what we didn't need. The President appointed regulators who were "business friendly," which was code for regulators who would be likely to be willfully blind. It turns out that the real business-friendly approach would have been to have regulators who did their job.

But the combination of the enactment of the new rules under the so-called Financial Services Modernization Act and the arrival of President George W. Bush with his agenda of deregulation set our country and our economy up for a crash.

And so it was in 2008 that the house of cards that had been built during the past couple of decades began to collapse.

In 2007 when the economy began to take a nosedive, Henry "Hank" Paulson was the Secretary of the Treasury. Interestingly, before he was appointed Treasury Secretary by President Bush, he had been the chairman of Goldman Sachs and had earned a healthy $38 million in 2005, his last year of employment there. Just over $30 million came from restricted stock awards. According to CNN, his Goldman holdings were worth about $700 million at the end of 2005.

Paulson was a Wall Street insider who, in fact, was an active participant in the go-go world of high finance during a period when
the U.S. financial system careened out of control. And he made a lot
of money doing it.

In 2004 Hank Paulson's investment banking firm and four other
investment banks petitioned the Securities and Exchange Commission to exempt the large investment banks from the regulation that
limited the amount of leverage to equity that their banks could assume. If they could get the SEC to agree, it would allow billions of
dollars their brokerage units were required to keep as reserves in
case of investment losses to be used instead by the holding companies to invest in other exotic investment products surrounding
mortgage-backed securities. Paulson was chairman of Goldman Sachs
at the time.

Representatives of the large investment banks met in a basement
conference room at the SEC where they presented their proposal to
the commissioners. Only one newspaper covered the proceeding.

When the investment bankers left the hearing, they had successfully managed to convince the SEC, with little discussion and by a
unanimous vote, to allow them to substantially increase their leverage. Translated into English, it meant the bankers could reduce the
reserves they were carrying to cover any future losses and use the
money instead to increase their profits by moving money up through
their holding company in search of other investments.

That SEC decision allowed the largest investment banks to increase their leverage and their risk from, in some cases, twelve times
their capital to over thirty times their capital. If you think that is
nuts, so do I. But the story illustrates the culture and the relationship
between the SEC and those they were charged with regulating. It
was the story of sympathetic regulators pretending to do their job
even though their role was reduced to one of holding a green light
for Wall Street firms that were looking for more profits even if it
meant more risk.

The irony is that one of the people who convinced the SEC to
take this boneheaded step was Hank Paulson, who two short years

later would become U.S. Secretary of the Treasury. He would have to try to rescue the economy from the very excess leverage and business practices that he himself had previously encouraged.

But Paulson wasn't the only one who sat atop the world of high finance and appeared to forget all of the lessons we'd learned in the seventy-five years since the Great Depression. In fact, Paulson had maintained a good enough reputation to be confirmed as Treasury Secretary. But that was before the financial collapse.

During that time almost all of the big financial interests in our country participated in an unprecedented orgy of greed in search of profits and bonuses. They created a house of cards with unsound investments and massive leverage. And ultimately it came crashing down around them.

Many of the best-known names in high finance who helped create this house of cards escaped with their millions and even billions of dollars intact. But many others lost their shirts.

It was a story of greed that will be told and retold in our business schools for decades to come. But rather than analyzing and correcting the abuses that caused the financial crisis, the government spent most of 2008 trying to prevent a complete collapse of our financial system.

After sitting idly by while the fast-buck artists were speeding major U.S. corporations toward a financial cliff, the Federal Reserve Board and the Treasury Secretary, late in 2008, took action to try to provide a safety net. No, it wasn't for the regular folks. It was a safety net for the financial companies and reckless speculators that had been gambling with your money. However, not surprisingly, it was described as action designed to help you. But the stock market and the banks and investors were spooked and continued to drive down the market, freeze credit, and paralyze the economy.

The business and banking failures in 2008 were spectacular failures of companies that were household names in the United States. In the blink of an eye some of America's biggest financial companies went belly-up, were purchased, or were bailed out.

Bear Stearns, an investment bank that experienced a run on their assets and came up short, was purchased by JPMorgan Chase, another investment bank. The Federal Reserve in an unprecedented action pledged nearly $30 billion of the government's money to offset the risks of the assets JPMorgan was buying from Bear Stearns.

Then the Fed, for the first time in history, announced that it would lend money directly to investment banks to stem the panic in the financial markets resulting from the scandal over subprime mortgages. The Fed has always allowed borrowing by federally insured, regulated banks. But this decision allowed uninsured and unregulated investment banks to borrow directly from it.

Fannie Mae and Freddie Mac, two big organizations that were supposedly government-sponsored enterprises but were run like other big corporations, had to be taken over by the federal government and put in a conservatorship because of the large percentage of nonperforming mortgages on their books. They have a lot to answer for. That takeover loaded substantial additional future liability on the back of the government.

Bank of America stepped in and purchased Merrill Lynch when it appeared that there would be a run on the Merrill Lynch holdings because of their investments in toxic assets. The Federal Reserve Board decided to lend $85 billion to bail out AIG, one of America's largest insurance companies, when it was discovered that AIG had massive exposure for tens and tens of billions of dollars on credit default swaps that threatened to bring the entire company down. Following that, the Federal Reserve Board announced it would have to put another $38 billion into AIG. And it still wasn't done. More money was needed later. A small group of several hundred employees in a London office was involved in credit default swaps that without a bailout would have destroyed America's largest insurance company. Again, who was supposed to be regulating that bizarre behavior?

Lehman Brothers, an investment bank since the mid-1800s, filed for bankruptcy. A portion of that company was purchased by Barclays of London. And by the way, just prior to Lehman's filing for bankruptcy several departing executives were awarded over $20 million in bonuses. And the CEO of Lehman, it was disclosed, had earned $22 million in 2007 and $480 million over the past nine years.

Wachovia Bank was set to go under when it announced that it would be purchased by Wells Fargo. That acquisition was later contested by Bank of America, which also wanted to purchase Wachovia. Bank of America won that battle, and now one federally insured bank will take over another federally insured bank that had gambled and lost. And by the way, with the takeovers and combinations, we have ended up with only four major banks (Bank of America, JP-Morgan Chase, Citigroup, and Wells Fargo) controlling nearly one-third of all bank deposits in the United States.

But at the close of 2008, Citigroup was reeling from the weight of toxic assets. The FDIC and the U.S. Treasury agreed to back $306 billion in toxic assets and provide another $20 billion in funding to Citigroup over and above the $25 billion the bank received from the original $700 billion bailout package. Finally, the sum total of the Citigroup bailout was $45 billion in direct cash and a government guarantee of $306 billion in toxic assets they had on their balance sheets. And by the way, the executives at Citigroup whose irresponsible behavior allowed this to happen are still there. The Treasury Secretary bailed them out without requiring any accountability or change in management.

Seattle-based Washington Mutual Bank had $53 billion in risky option adjustable rate mortgages and $16 billion in loans made to subprime borrowers. The FDIC seized the bank and orchestrated a takeover by JPMorgan Chase. By the way, the CEO of Washington Mutual was paid $14 million in 2007.

The bottom line was, the Fed and the President took aggressive action in late 2008 to pledge American taxpayers' dollars to shore up the big investment banks because they said these banks were "too big to fail."

It begs a question from ordinary people. *If these companies were too big to fail, why in the hell weren't they big enough to regulate?*

The answer is simple. While the big operators in the financial world were making fortunes creating new speculative products and taking on new risk that they were able to obscure, they operated under the wing of a business-friendly administration and Federal Reserve Board that put its total faith in the market. Self-regulation, they called it. And although the deregulation frenzy was most pronounced during the eight years of the Bush administration, it is worth noting that the Clinton administration was no bargain on this score. They weren't exactly overly aggressive in making sure the big financial interests were regulated. The Clinton administration's Treasury Department was foursquare behind most of the financial modernization and opposed to the regulation of derivatives and hedge funds.

But the deregulation mania took on new energy when George W. Bush took office. And Congress deserves its share of the blame. Too many in Congress were cuddling up to the same big financial firms that caused the problem.

Congress, the President, and the Federal Reserve Board had the philosophy that the market would effectively require these companies to self-regulate. But it was absurd. The Fed and the Bush administration should be ashamed that they sat by quietly while they could both see and hear the wild financial speculation that put our entire country at risk. In October of 2008 former Fed chairman Alan Greenspan was called on the carpet during congressional hearings and finally admitted he had been wrong not to aggressively regulate the companies and activities that caused this financial wreckage. He said he felt they would regulate themselves. Sure, and the moon is made of green cheese!

As of December 2008, the Treasury Secretary and the Federal Reserve Board chairman had pledged over $8 trillion of public assets to try to shore up the economy. Almost all of that money went to the big financial firms who had caused the wreck in the first place.

But the big scandal that finally collapsed the house of cards in 2008 was the home mortgage meltdown, which is a story that encompasses nearly all of the worst features of a behavior that seemed more like the Wild West than thoughtful financing. It demonstrated all of the underhanded tactics that characterized this age of excess and greed.

## DON'T ASK, DON'T TELL:
## THE HOME MORTGAGE SCANDAL

The past decade has seen almost unparalleled financial scandals in both the public and private sectors. But the hood ornament for ignorance and greed has to be the so-called subprime lending scandal, because it welds together nearly every level of the worst instincts of greed with big interests trying to prey on the little guy, and it caused a major meltdown of the American economy.

Home ownership is part of the American dream. So, those involved in helping families purchase their homes have always been considered the white hats. And there are plenty of good people working today to help those who want to borrow money to purchase a home.

The housing industry is an important barometer of the nation's well-being because it is one of the most important generators of new jobs in our economy. It not only creates employment when the new home is being constructed, but it also stimulates jobs in other areas, such as furniture and appliance manufacture.

Since most families don't have the cash to pay the total cost of a home when they purchase it, the home mortgage industry is essential to allow families to finance their home purchases. For many decades the home mortgage industry was typically run by good people working every day to do the right thing in helping families buy their dream house. But in recent years that industry had also spawned a new breed of get-rich-quick interlopers who were willing to take advantage of borrowers along the way.

In the good old days, borrowing money for a home was a serious and thoughtful process where the lenders and the borrowers wanted to be sure the borrowers were qualified and could make the payments. The lenders were doing what was called underwriting the loan. And the borrowers wanted to make sure they could trust the lenders to offer an honest deal without hidden costs or undisclosed provisions that would come back and bite the borrowers later.

Things were changing in the home loan industry in the late 1990s and it gathered steam as the Bush administration took office in 2001. The sleepy, time-honored activity of writing home mortgages turned into an industry on steroids, with big money to be made.

Pumped full of helium by the housing bubble (a bubble also fed by the new subprime mortgages) and assisted by an administration that did not believe in regulation, the home mortgage companies changed and morphed into financial betting parlors operating at warp speed in search of big profits, often at the expense of both home owners and investors.

Under the "if it feels good, do it" mantra of the day, the term "subprime mortgages" entered the public lexicon. As the housing bubble began to expand, some Americans wanted to get in on the quick and easy money by buying a home and flipping it in a year or two and pocketing an easy profit. It's hard to know what percentage of these buyers were speculators. Many of us know someone who did it. Other Americans just wanted to get a loan in order to buy a home for themselves and their families. There were plenty of sharks waiting for them at the credit counter.

## CARNIVAL BARKERS LURE THEM IN

There were new mortgage lenders coming at home buyers from every direction offering seductive new home loans for that very purpose. Part of the new culture was revealed in their approach to advertising home mortgages. It was directed at everybody, even those with bad credit. Most Americans have seen the television ads that described that change. They were like the carnival barkers of old, beckoning crowds to come see the bearded lady.

A company called Zoom Credit advertised, "Credit approval is just seconds away. Get on the fast track at Zoom Credit. At the speed of light, Zoom Credit will preapprove you for a car loan, a home loan, refinance, or a credit card. Even if your credit's in the tank. Zoom Credit's like money in the bank. Zoom Credit specializes in credit repair and debt consolidation, too. Bankruptcy, slow credit, no credit. Who cares?"

I am not making this up. Nor this—Millennia Mortgage Corporation teased potential customers with the following: "12 Months No Mortgage Payment. That's right. We will give you the money to make your first 12 payments if you call in the next 7 days. We pay it for you."

Those were just two examples of many. Most Americans, as they watched those television commercials, were puzzled at how companies could advertise that they wanted to grant home loans even to those who had bad credit ratings. The fact is, it doesn't work. That was a business strategy destined to fail and designed by some get-rich-quick shysters.

## THE COUNTRYWIDE EXAMPLE

Let me describe this scandal through the actions of one company—Countrywide Financial, which became the nation's biggest mortgage lender. They were not the only lender involved in this, but they were the largest and they should have known better.

Countrywide Financial was a mortgage banking firm that included a bank, a mortgage-servicing company, a company that offered real estate closing services, an insurance company, and a company that was a broker-dealer to trade in government securities and to sell securities that were backed by home mortgages. In 2007 Countrywide was servicing over two hundred thousand loans a month.

Countrywide not only made the loans; in many cases, it serviced the loan and then packaged and sold it in security instruments to investors.

Led by Angelo Mozilo, earlier in this decade Countrywide became a home mortgage company that created new, riskier loans and targeted both those who could repay the loans and those who could not. Their advertising, like that of many other companies in the industry, became a joke. "Less than perfect credit? Late mortgage payments? Denied by other lenders? Call us!" read one Countrywide advertisement.

So, the company began to attract borrowers through advertising and through telephone solicitations even to those who would not qualify for traditional loans. Countrywide created new loans for these home owners such as "affordability loans," "adjustable rate mortgages (ARMs)," "interest only loans," and "reduced documentation or no-documentation" loans.

These "no-doc loans" really take the cake. That meant if you agreed to pay a higher interest rate, you weren't required to document your financial information, including how much money you made. Of course, how much income you have will largely determine whether you can actually afford the loan. But in this new age of high finance, what did fundamentals really matter?

In the middle of this decade, the mix of Countrywide's housing loans changed dramatically. In one year the percentage of loans written in ARMs went from 18 to 49 percent. That is, they went from conventional, fixed-rate loans to the risky adjustable rate ones, in many cases with provisions that nearly guaranteed that the borrower could not repay the loan.

Among the other new mortgages Countrywide began to offer were "interest only loans." With these, the borrower was required to pay interest charges only and would defer any payment of principal until later years.

Another new type of loan was something called the pay option adjustable rate mortgage, which allowed the borrower to pay only a portion of the interest and none of the principal during the early period of the loan. The portion that the borrower didn't pay was added to the backside of the mortgage.

So think of that for a moment. These mortgage companies were offering borrowers the opportunity to get a mortgage without documenting the borrower's income and without even having to pay the full interest charges, let alone any reduction in principal. Does this sound like a sound business proposition to you? The mortgage companies boasted that they could cut your monthly payment by two-thirds. They didn't emphasize that the interest rate would reset at a much higher rate in two or three years (to a payment that the borrower often would not be able to pay). But when asked about it they said, "Don't worry. Houses are continuing to increase in value. Just sell it and make a profit In the meantime, our loan for the next several years will save you loads of money." At least that was the seductive pitch.

Countrywide pushed these new types of loans because they were more lucrative to the company and also more valuable to roll into mortgage-backed securities because borrowers were paying higher interest rates and higher fees. And many loans had prepayment penalties, which locked in the higher return to the mortgage company and to the investors who purchased the securities that came from bundling the loans.

The key was to offer ridiculously low teaser interest rates in the first two or three years of the loan so that the borrowers thought they were getting an unbelievably good deal with a low, low monthly payment. Then the terms of the mortgage reset the interest rate in two or three years to a much higher one, often one that the borrower couldn't pay. And then the mortgage company added prepayment penalties so that they could lock in the borrower to the bad mortgage. It was a sweet deal for all of those who were earning fat fees for finding suckers. And, as P. T. Barnum said, there's a sucker born every minute!

Meanwhile, the career of Countrywide Financial CEO Mozilo was soaring. In 2005 his company was included in *Fortune* magazine's prestigious company of the year honor roll. He received the Horatio Alger Award, and *Barron's* named him as one of the world's thirty most respected CEOs that year. In 2006 Mr. Mozilo earned $142 million and was celebrated as a growth-oriented executive who was taking this high-flying mortgage lender to new heights.

But according to a *Los Angeles Times* report by Kathy M. Kristof, even as Mozilo was touting his company's success, he was busy unloading $138 million of his company's stock. That took place just prior to the time the rest of the stockholders and investors began to understand how much trouble the firm was in because of its business practices.

As the stock price plummeted from $45 to $15, it so rattled customers that there was a good old-fashioned depression-style run on the bank. On August 17, 2007, E. Scott Reckard and Annette Haddad reported in the *Los Angeles Times*:

> Anxious customers jammed the phone lines and website of Countrywide Bank and crowded its branch offices to pull out their savings because of concerns about the financial problems of the mortgage lender that owns the bank. . . . The rush to withdraw money—by depositors that included a former Los Angeles Kings star hockey player and an executive of a rival home-loan company—came a day after fears arose that Countrywide Financial could file for bankruptcy protection because of a worsening credit crunch stemming from the sub-prime mortgage meltdown.

When the subprime scandal became evident, regulators and others finally began to take a closer look at the mortgage loan practices of Countrywide and many other companies in the industry. What they found was appalling. *Greed!* In every direction!

The brokers were fast-talking people into mortgages they couldn't afford. In many cases brokers were making cold calls to existing home owners, pushing subprime loans to people who, scandalously, *could have gotten into a lower-cost mortgage.* But the brokers made more money by selling subprime loans. We are told of brokers who sold a $1 million jumbo subprime loan, getting a $30,000 commission.

That is powerful motivation to sell loans, no matter the consequence.

And we now know these companies were even making loans to people who had previously filed for bankruptcy or had failed to make payments on their current mortgages. The brokers and the companies both made boatloads of money if they could place a subprime loan with prepayment penalties where the interest rate reset after three years and the home owner was locked into the mortgage with expensive fees and interest rates.

It was almost like a bank heist . . . except it was the bank doing the heisting. Picture Jesse James in a Hickey Freeman suit and a pair of Ferragamo shoes!

## LIKE PACKING SAUSAGES WITH SAWDUST

And on the other side of the transaction, when the subprime mortgage loans were pooled with other loans, bundled into "securities" to be sold to investors, the presence of all these bad loans folded into the new security gave the investors a higher rate of return on paper.

For a while, investors would pay more for a security that contained subprime loans with prepayment penalties and interest rates that were going to reset at higher levels because such securities promised to produce a better cash flow. This technique was akin to the meatpacking plants' using sawdust as filler in sausage in earlier times. In the financial world, they created securities for sale that combined some good loans with some risky loans and then they sliced them up and sold them off with what appeared to be lucrative returns on investments, many of them rated AAA by rating agencies that still haven't been required to answer for their errant behavior.

In short, they all, including the brokers, the mortgage banks, and the security firms, were blinded by profits and greed. Then came the crash.

By the way, as this book was being written, Bank of America bought the assets of Countrywide Financial, which had blown through its line of bank credit. But not to worry! Mr. Mozilo found a safety net. He was left with his hundreds of millions. And it turns out that Bank of America will be able to use the accumulated losses racked up by Countrywide to reduce the tax liability of Bank of America by well over $150 million. So, there is a silver lining. But it is just for the people at the top who find ways to make lemonade for themselves while the rest of America sucks on the bitter lemon rind.

And as further demonstration that the big shots at the top of the heap never quite feel the pain the rest of the employees and stock-holders do, the two top executives of Countrywide got a $22 million bonus package as an incentive for them to stay as their company was collapsing around them and being acquired by the Bank of America.

In addition, to add insult to injury, it was announced in the spring of 2008 that a number of the top executives of Countrywide were forming a new company to buy distressed mortgages and resell them for a profit. That's unbelievable. After what they did, they shouldn't be allowed to get anywhere near a mortgage business again.

Though I long ago taught economics, I don't think you have to be an economist to figure out that this was destined to end badly. All it would have taken to avoid it was common sense and reasonable regulation.

You would think that some federal agency whose job it was to protect the public and to expose the companies that try to take advantage of the consumer would notice these business practices described by the advertisements and take some action to stop it. But the federal regulatory agencies, snuggled in the arms of a new administration that came to office describing itself as "more friendly" to business, apparently decided these practices were not a problem and did their best to imitate a potted plant (a ficus, I think). All the while the investment banks, the brokers, the rating agencies, and the hedge funds were scratching each other's backs with all of this new business and newfound cash. It was almost pornographic. There was nothing to slow this steamroller. It was destined to be a repeat of the final scene in *Thelma & Louise* . . . right off the cliff. It had everything but the handholding.

And the rating organizations (those who are paid to investigate and rate securities) were apparently asleep, brain-dead, or cheerleaders for bad business practices. They were giving toxic assets AAA rating. They let the financial institutions roll up these suspect mortgages into securities and gave them high ratings. At the same time, hedge funds, investment banks, and others were busy rolling in cash from buying and selling securities that contained a built-in future explosion of bad debt and future defaults. Those rating agencies have a lot to answer for.

It shouldn't have been surprising that in a couple of years, when the interest rates on these home mortgages began to reset at much higher rates, many borrowers wouldn't have the money to make their monthly mortgage payments. But it wasn't just a few borrowers. First it was hundreds, then thousands, then hundreds of thousands, and finally millions. As of late 2007, there were 7.2 million subprime mortgages, with 14.4 percent in foreclosure, a 292 percent increase from 2003. Some estimates say 1 in 5 subprime loans taken out in 2005 and 2006 will default.

Add it all up and it spells grand larceny.

## CHICKENS COME HOME TO ROOST—BUT THE COOP IS IN FORECLOSURE!

As the old saying goes, the chickens came home to roost. The failure of some of the country's biggest financial firms began to be a lead weight on the entire economy and threatened to cause a massive collapse.

In late 2007, E. Stanley O'Neal, a celebrated CEO of Merrill Lynch, was fired for losing $8 billion because his company was purchasing securities imbedded with subprime loans that were going bad. The simple announcement said that he "would retire immediately." The CEO of Citigroup, Charles Prince, was fired for losing $11 billion from investments in securities that contained subprime loans. The CEO of H&R Block, Mark Ernst, "was replaced" in the aftermath of losses from the subprime investment collapse. And that was just a sample of the trouble in the boardrooms as they started asking questions about how good companies and smart people could have been so blind.

And the chairman of the Federal Reserve Board played a central role in allowing the excesses and speculation to happen. Joseph Stiglitz, the Nobel Prize winner in economics and former World Bank economist, said, "Alan Greenspan really made a mess of all this. He pushed out too much liquidity at the wrong time. He supported the tax cut in 2001, which is the beginning of these problems. He encouraged people to take out variable-rate mortgages."

Even more than that, Greenspan sat on his hands while these excesses occurred because he believed that "self-regulation" would be sufficient. Yup, and the world is flat, too!

His book was a bestseller, though.


## THE SOLUTION

The solution to all of the issues described in this chapter is no more sophisticated than just using some common sense. No country can go to war and offer tax cuts to its wealthiest citizens while it adds the cost of war to its federal debt. At least it can't do that without catastrophic consequences to its economy.

And we can't allow regulators to deregulate that which they are supposed to oversee. Willful blindness by those the taxpayers are paying to regulate should be a felony offense.

All of us know that we can't have the mortgage industry selling mortgages to those who can't possibly repay them and then selling the bad paper back into the marketplace. That is predatory lending, which should be prosecuted.

With ten years of history with the Financial Services Modernization Act, it should be obvious that we are required to restore the elements of the Glass-Steagall Act to separate the basic banking functions from the speculation in real estate and securities.

And we need to shine a light on dark money by requiring the regulation of hedge funds and derivative trading immediately.

In late 2008 Congress responded to the request of the Treasury Secretary to give him authority to spend $700 billion in bailout money to stabilize the large financial firms. He said he wanted to use it to purchase toxic assets from the big financial firms.

Congress gave him the $700 billion, but it turned out the Treasury Secretary then changed his mind. He said he wouldn't purchase toxic assets after all. Instead he would use it to purchase equity in banks in order to expand lending and unfreeze the credit markets. He shortly purchased $125 billion in nine banks (some of whom didn't want the capital investment) but did it without any requirements that they expand lending. It was a "no strings attached" use of taxpayers' money. No restrictions on bonuses for the top executives of the firms. No restrictions on dividends. No requirements on expansion of lending. Unbelievable!

And while the Treasury Secretary and the Fed were busy taking action to help the largest financial firms, they did nothing to require some help for home owners who were victims of predatory lending practices and found themselves unable to pay their mortgages. And the Treasury Secretary and the Fed did nothing to regulate the very activities that caused the financial crisis to happen.

And they failed to create a federal panel with broad investigative powers to bring to justice those who broke the law while building their fortunes at the expense of the American people.

And Congress should have but did not try to create a safety net for those families who were living in their homes and facing foreclosure. It doesn't mean a giveaway program. It just means a helping hand to try to get these families through some tough times and to try to stabilize home prices at the same time. But Secretary Paulson and others were more intent on making sure the big investment banks had a safety net than they were on helping the families that got caught in financial trouble.

Purists say that a bailout rewards stupidity, and in some cases it does. Sometimes the stakes are so high, you have to look past that and be completely pragmatic. But a government that bails out those at the top who have fleeced the rest of us should be able to provide some help to the other Americans who are facing financial trouble.

The problem is that the economic fallout potential from this debacle stands to drag even prudent borrowers down as the value of their homes and retirement dollars evaporates. In one way or another, it will impact virtually everyone, so solving the issue makes sense for the good of the whole.

It wasn't just big shots who showed poor judgment. I found myself talking to my television at news stories about woe-is-me home owners who had clearly speculated on the real estate market and now were perfectly willing to stick the bank with a bad loan when the market went south. One California woman told the cameras that while she could afford the $5,000 monthly payment on her second home, the plummeting value made it a poor investment, so she was going to walk away. It might make business sense, but it strikes me as unethical. I grew up in a time and place when a handshake was a contract, but today a contract isn't even a contract. It isn't just unscrupulous lenders who are to blame for this greed fest. There are plenty of unscrupulous investors at fault here, too.

But even home owners who used common sense are suffering. The glut of foreclosed homes drives down prices and equity. So, not only is the housing industry reeling, but also consumer spending will slow, because home equity is used to borrow money for personal consumption. According to a study by Greenspan himself and economist Joseph Kennedy, home equity–fueled personal consumption accounted for $310 billion annually from 2004 to 2006. Now, if you don't have the equity, you can't borrow. And if you can't borrow, you can't spend. That hurts an economy. It's common sense.

Bailing out the most audacious and irresponsible borrowers and lenders wouldn't be right. There is going to be some pain involved here, and that's sad, but that is what happens when lenders, borrowers, and regulators shun responsibility. Had any one of the three groups stepped up and challenged this flawed business strategy, much of this could have been averted. Ultimately, it reinforces the notion that in a free market rules and regulations are necessary to make sure the market works in a fair way.

Our free market is very much like a horse race. Even the fastest thoroughbred requires a jockey and reins. Sometimes the whip comes into play. But most of the time, a great horse (or economy) just needs to be reined in and occasionally guided through traffic jams.

Is there a silver lining? It's hard to see it from here. But if somehow we can steer this economy out of this deep ditch, there will be opportunities for home ownership and investment as values drop. Simply by securing jobs, raising wages, and stabilizing household expenses burdened by health-care, energy, and education costs, we can mitigate the long-term effects of the subprime scandal. But the economy as a whole has to work for the middle class as well as for the wealthy investor class if it is to work at all. That's just simple common sense.

The consequences of this orgy of greed will be with us for a number of years. No one yet knows the full effect of this scandal on our economy. But the entire affair begs the question: *Where were the regulators?*

How could an entire industry believe that it was all right to loan money to people who would not be able to repay it—and to aggressively seek them out and fast-talk them into loans, the provisions of which many did not understand? How could an industry believe that it was appropriate to loan money to people with bad credit? And how could people be gullible enough to get in so deep? And if ever again some politicians try to sell you on the notion that "regulation" is a four-letter word, don't you believe it!

When government regulators fail to do their jobs, all of us pay. The recent subprime scandal and the impact it has had on the

economy demonstrate how costly it is when regulators fail to regulate. Regulations are important, and so are the regulators we hire to
stand guard.

We can fix this. It's not hopeless. But we need to learn from
these experiences. Most important, we must remember that just a
little common sense can go a long way.

# CHAPTER 3

. . .

## *Addicted to Debt*

T HE FINANCIAL COLLAPSE in 2008 was headline news around the world. And the news trumpeted the subprime loan scandal, unbridled speculation on Wall Street, and the collapse of some of the biggest financial institutions in our country. It's clear that was the trigger for the current economic crisis, but there was more to it than that. The collapse can also be connected to our government's fiscal and trade policies that have created mountains of public debt.

The combination of some of the most reckless financial behavior in the private sector with the failed fiscal and trade policies in the public sector created a near-perfect financial storm that has badly injured our economy.

Our government has been running big fiscal policy deficits (it borrowed over $2 trillion in 2008, while in 2009 it is expected to be much worse), and at the same time it has been clocking $700 to $800 billion a year in trade deficits. Both government and business leaders should have known this was heading toward a cliff. The rampant borrowing in both the public and private sectors created risks that are bringing our economy close to a collapse.

All of that has to stop!

The current financial crisis now has President Obama proposing large stimulus spending to try to pull the country out of the financial crisis. It's not surprising that none of that spending is paid for. It goes right to the federal debt.

I understand that unusual times require unusual actions and the deep financial crisis requires action by the government to try to boost the economy. But, at some point, the President, Congress, and the American people will have to come to terms with a different economic future. We can't continue to spend money we don't have without serious consequences for our way of life. The same is true in trade. We can't continue importing $700 billion more than we export every year without serious consequences. The resulting large trade deficits we owe to foreign countries must be repaid. And we can't allow speculators and Wall Street tycoons to build dangerous levels of debt believing that that if things go wrong, the government will bail them out. It all has to stop.

Fixing these things is not rocket science. But it requires the will and courage to do it.

## ALL I REALLY NEED TO KNOW . . .

In the book *All I Really Need to Know I Learned in Kindergarten*, author Robert Fulghum describes some simple lessons for living: "Play fair, don't hit people, share everything, clean up your own mess, and don't take things that aren't yours, wash your hands, flush." They are simple lessons that apply in almost every circumstance.

I was thinking about those lessons and wondering what we could have been thinking in recent years when we allowed the administration to sell us a fiscal policy claiming that a nation could go to war, charge the costs to future generations, and enjoy tax cuts and nonstop shopping here at home, even as we sent American troops abroad to fight.

We knew better. We had learned these lessons early in life. No President has ever cut taxes in a time of war . . . until now. How in the world could this nation have accepted this train wreck of an idea that has led to the rapid growth of dangerous federal deficits in this decade?

And how could we have failed to see the danger in companies that were advertising home loans to people who didn't have the income to make the payments or in companies that were sending credit cards to people with no job and no income? How could we have watched passively as the decisions in the corporate boardrooms gave the average CEO more income in a day than the average worker receives in a year? And how could we have thought that even with the rapid growth of hedge funds that were making a mint from wagers on everything from currencies to stocks to commodities, it would be fine if it happened outside of the view of regulators? And how did we get suckered into believing that "regulation" was somehow antibusiness and if we just deregulated nearly everything, things would be much better?

We shouldn't have needed an "All I Really Need to Know . . ." book to avoid the mistakes that have led our country in the wrong direction in recent years. Simple truths that seem so foreign today to some of our political and business leaders should have been obvious.

Instead of admitting that we have problems, our leaders, in both the public and private sectors, started altering the facts to fit the circumstance. Ideas like *deficits don't matter* (former Vice President Dick Cheney) and *outsourcing jobs is good for America* (a top Bush economic advisor). Or, *don't worry about hedge funds, their actions pose little risk to our economy* (Alan Greenspan). Most Americans instinctively knew better.

In 2008 it all came home to roost and our economy melted down from the reckless policies that had allowed our financial foundation to erode. Most of the response was to work feverishly to prevent a complete collapse of our economy. That was the priority. But there is so much more to do to restore our economy to more solid footing.

We need to relearn some simple lessons if we are going to fix a reckless government fiscal policy, clean up the mess of the subprime

loan scandal, curb the excesses of hedge funds and derivative traders, and hold corporations accountable for the scandalous compensation for some CEOs. Moreover, we need to cut government spending
in areas where government programs are no longer working and
where the spending growth in recent years is not justified.

The fix isn't too complicated. It just requires some common
sense. These are lessons all of us would have known when we finished school.

Somewhere along the way, Presidents, government officials (yes,
Senators, too), business executives, and even some of the electorate
have forgotten these simple lessons:

PAY YOUR BILLS. If you are going to spend money, you have to
   pay the bills. That rule also applies to government.
DON'T TAKE ADVANTAGE OF PEOPLE. If you are lending money,
   be honest with the borrower and don't lend money to those
   who you know can't pay it back and then sell these loans to
   banks and investors.
YOUR PRIVATE INTEREST NEEDS TO BE BALANCED WITH THE
   PUBLIC INTEREST. Remember that a hedge fund is not an ac-
   cumulation of money to take care of gardening needs. It is a
   sophisticated form of wagering that when used to excess can
   pose big risks to the economy. The same is true of derivatives
   like credit default swaps and similar exotic financial products.
   Common sense says they should be regulated.
"REGULATION" IS NOT A FOUR-LETTER WORD. Excessive government regulation of private business can, at times, be a
   burden to those who just want to do business and make a fair
   profit. But effective regulation is essential in cases where business has developed enough muscle to interfere with the free
   market and put our economy at risk or where the private interest is in serious conflict with the public interest.
SOME GOVERNMENT SPENDING IS GOOD AND NECESSARY. BUT
   SOME IS EXCESSIVE AND SHOULD BE TRIMMED. The federal
   government is a giant organization that has an insatiable ap-

petite for funding and a natural inclination to grow. But the President and Congress have a responsibility to keep spending in check. It is important to get rid of government programs that are not accomplishing the purposes for which they were established.

## THE FOX GUARDS THE CHICKEN COOP

There is no better metaphor for the green light given corporate greed in the recent past than the invitation offered by Harvey Pitt, the new head of the Securities and Exchange Commission (SEC) in 2001. He announced that it was going to be a new day at the SEC, which was going to be a business-friendly place.

President Bush had appointed this man who as a Wall Street lawyer had once urged "that clients destroy sensitive documents before they could be used against them," according to the story titled "Harvey Pitt: Accounts Angel Who Supped with the Devil," which appeared in the British publication *The Independent* on August 11, 2002.

In short order the Enron, MCI WorldCom, and Tyco scandals hit and the American people began demanding to know what the SEC had been doing. It was supposed to be keeping an eye on the chicken coop, not feeding the fox. The problem wasn't just the SEC but also included a large number of what were supposed to be regulatory agencies looking after the public interest.

The regulators' refusal to regulate was an engraved invitation to those who wanted to do things that had long been denied by the agencies that were created to be the referees. In short, some companies cooked the books, siphoned off cash for themselves, and used the inflated financial health to puff up stock prices. They were able to sell their own overvalued stocks for millions while investors who had been deceived about the solvency of the company were investing in lies.

When Enron tanked, it devastated employees whose retirement plans were invested heavily in worthless Enron stock. It is estimated that top management cheated both their customers and investors out of $60 billion. They inflated the value of the company by hiding losses, and their accounting firm, Arthur Andersen, helped them do it. It is estimated that Enron bilked West Coast electricity customers out of tens of billions of dollars. The Tyco and MCI WorldCom scandals followed suit.

In 2008 the $50 billion hedge fund scandal by a man named Bernard Madoff further undermined whatever remaining confidence some Americans had in the financial marketplace. This scandal combined all of the worst elements of what Americans have come to believe about high finance and the people whose greed seems to have no boundaries.

Madoff was a well-respected money manager who had formerly been the chairman of NASDAQ. His fund consistently made financial returns for the investors of 12 percent a year. And the fund never had a down year. It was almost an automatic exceptional return for the big-money investors. The investors were some of the best-known Americans from Hollywood, New York, and in between, and some large charities as well. According to news reports, Madoff made a personal fortune and lived like it: multiple large homes in various parts of the country, vacations in southern France, ownership shares in two private jets (including a Citation X, the fastest commercial plane in the air).

It appears that Madoff had it all . . . except for the $50 billion of assets that had been entrusted to his care by investors. In December, Bernard Madoff confessed that his $50 billion hedge fund was a giant Ponzi scheme. The money was gone! The investors had been bilked. Most would receive pennies on the dollar.

Madoff was arrested and released on home confinement (a multi-million dollar apartment in New York City) and he will ultimately be tried for his larceny. But the many victims, including the charities that lost billions, are left wondering how it could have happened.

This tale of greed and crime raises once again the issue of where the agencies like the Securities and Exchange Commission were while all of this was happening. In fact, we learned after the scandal broke that some people had previously contacted the SEC and raised serious questions about Madoff's hedge fund, but no one followed up. Where is the accountability for federal agencies that demonstrate that kind of incompetence? And it isn't just about the SEC. The same question can be asked about countless other federal agencies that have regulatory responsibilities.

And what about the accounting firms that had been doing yearly audits and certifying the accounting and financial statements that Madoff was providing to his clients? Was this a reprise of the Enron scandal, where the accounting firms became the enablers?

As this book is being written, the Madoff scandal is still unfolding. But the fact that the scandal exists is testimony to years of willful neglect by authorities who were supposed to be protecting the public interest.

It is a strong answer to the question "Do we really want federal regulators who, like Harvey Pitt when he took over the reins at the SEC, made it known that it was going to be more business friendly?" Mr. Pitt and his successors were supposed to be the referees making sure that investing was safe and fraud-free for investors and not giving free rein to corporate chicanery.

The documentary movie about the Enron scandal was titled *Enron: The Smartest Guys in the Room*. It made me wonder, why does it always seem to be the so-called smartest guys who are at the root of the biggest scandals?

There are some who rise to positions of great power and start to assume their intellect has grown along with their place in the world. Arrogance, avarice, and horse's asses (as they are colorfully known in my hometown) are the problem. Could it be because the smartest guys often don't have what you can't learn? They may be book smart but commonsense stupid.

What else would explain the departure from sanity by some business executives and government officials who should have known better?

## ECHOES OF THE GILDED AGE

This isn't the first time America has experienced an age of excess, but it ranks right up there. The rampant speculation and greed during the Gilded Age in the late 1800s made it a time of polarizing wealth and indulgence. It was a time marked by greed and excess by those who were oblivious to the growing poverty around them even as they amassed a greater share of the nation's wealth. Sound familiar? It should. Each year we see evidence of greater concentration of wealth, with more and more income going to the upper income groups at the expense of the American worker.

Recent data shows the top 1 percent of households own 38 percent of the wealth, according to William Gates and Chuck Collins, authors of *Wealth and Our Commonwealth.* The bottom 60 percent of households own just 4 percent, according to economist Edward N. Wolff's 2007 study, *Recent Trends in Household Wealth in the United States: Rising Debt and the Middle-Class Squeeze.* Wolff writes, "The richest 1 percent received over one-third of the total gain in marketable wealth over the period from 1983 to 2004. In fact the top 20 percent of Americans collectively accounted for 89 percent of the total growth in wealth, while the bottom 80 percent accounted for just 11 percent."

The latest IRS data shows that the top 1 percent of Americans received 21.2 percent of all personal income in 2005. That compared to 19 percent one year earlier. Just like assets, income in the United States is increasingly going to the very wealthy while the bottom 80 percent of the population are losing ground.

On March 29, 2007, David Cay Johnston reported ominously in *The New York Times* that in 2005 the top 1 percent of Americans had received the largest share of national income since 1928. The story quoted Emmanuel Saez, a University of California, Berkeley, economist who said, "If the economy is growing but only a few are enjoying the benefits, it goes to our sense of fairness. It can have important political consequences."

Whenever someone cites these facts and trends, those who are on the receiving end of this growing inequality make accusations of "class warfare." Warren Buffett says it best. He said, "If this is class warfare, my class is winning."

## RECKLESS SPECULATION

All of this is happening at a time when there has been both a reckless fiscal policy in our federal government as well as irresponsible speculation and greed in private-sector finance.

We are on the razor's edge. When you have corporations with larger economies than many countries and unregulated hedge fund managers moving billions of dollars in a keystroke, the potential for a disaster is obvious.

Our U.S. trade deficit of $2 billion a day is financed by borrowing from banks in other countries, but most of it from Japan and China. So they are invested in American dollars. No investor wants to be too heavily invested in one sector or, as in this case, one currency. Therefore, what happens when the dollar starts to fall, as it has precipitously in recent years? Those who hold a large quantity of dollars get nervous and think about selling dollars. That further drives down the value of the dollar.

When currency speculators judge an economy to be unsound, they can move against the currency in unison, causing economic panic and trouble in a wide range of areas. The potential that a central bank of a foreign country or even a hedge fund manager (or several large hedge funds) heavily invested in the dollar could move against the dollar and create a major collapse and panic is very real.

I once knew a drunk who thought he was invisible when he drank. It reminds me a little of those in our government who think that we can continue on our current course and no one will notice. Others who have invested in this country see the very serious trade and fiscal policy problems and expect our country to face them and solve them.

In this new economy, speculation is a fact of life. And excess speculation in currencies, commodities, stocks, and real estate can have a very damaging impact on our economy. Predictions of a wobbly dollar alone caused former Reagan economist Clyde Prestowitz to say in 2005 that the potential for global depression was very real:

> Every day $6 trillion of derivative instruments trade on international markets. If there are four people in the world who understand those trades, I'd be surprised. So the potential for another disaster is not insignificant. This is why Warren Buffett, chairman of investment giant Berkshire Hathaway, is betting $21 billion against the dollar. This is why currency speculator and hedge fund manager George Soros has also made a big bet against the dollar. . . . When markets are going down, all the weaknesses get concentrated, and you need intervention at the right time to stop things from getting out of control. If the dollar started to melt down, the results could be really nasty. A 1930s-style global depression is not out of the question.

That was before the housing bust . . . and before the meltdown of the economy in late 2008. Combine the threats that come with the speculation in the hedge fund/derivative markets with the unprecedented level of foreclosures in the housing market and you have a setup for major economic trouble.


## WHERE HAVE THE REAL FISCAL CONSERVATIVES GONE?

All of this was happening against the backdrop of a Bush administration that seemed determined to ignore the fundamentals of sound fiscal policy.

"You know, Paul, Reagan proved deficits don't matter." That was Vice President Dick Cheney telling Treasury Secretary Paul O'Neill not to worry about federal budget deficits during the first

Bush term. A month later Cheney fired O'Neill because the Treasury Secretary wasn't buying it.

Dick Cheney's comment came to be the hallmark of the new fiscal policy of the Bush administration. It became a decade marked by the borrow-and-spend philosophy of candidates who were self-proclaimed conservatives.

Even as times and circumstances changed, the Bush/Cheney fiscal policy did not. They continued to spend borrowed money to fund the wars in Iraq and Afghanistan, homeland security, and the fight against terrorism. They just flat refused to raise the money for it. They were comfortable adding it to the federal debt. It was a reckless policy that was completely at odds with what most Americans would expect from real conservatives.

It is true that the lack of fiscal discipline should not be laid only at the feet of the one political party. In recent years, neither Republicans nor Democrats have shown a willingness to confront the budget deficits as well as the growing challenge of funding both Social Security and Medicare for the baby boomers who will retire soon and impose a burden that those two programs are not yet prepared to meet.

But for sheer irresponsibility, the Bush administration's fiscal policy is head and shoulders above any other. It began in 2001 and continued for eight long years. And we will bear the consequences for years to come.

In 2001 President Bush and a Republican Congress inherited a budget surplus for that year of $236 billion and projected budget surpluses of $5.6 trillion for the coming ten years. These surpluses in 2001 and the projected continued good economic news came as a result of a fiscal policy pursued by the Clinton administration that finally turned around decades of deficit spending under both Republican and Democrat administrations.

In 1993 President Clinton and Congress (by a margin of one vote in both the U.S. Senate and House) made some tough decisions about spending and taxes, and for the first time in many years they put the country on a path to turn the large budget deficits into budget surpluses.

That action also spawned increased confidence in the future and helped create a vibrant economy.

When President Bush assumed office he looked at the large projected budget surpluses as an opportunity to provide big tax cuts to the wealthy Americans. It framed his philosophy that most of the investment and, therefore, job creation occurred because upper-income Americans took the risks. And he wanted to reduce the tax burden on upper-income investors to stimulate economic growth. He had a willing partner in offering big tax cuts when Federal Reserve Board Chairman Alan Greenspan said he was worried that the budget *surpluses* could become a problem if we accumulated big surpluses and paid down our national debt too rapidly.

*What?* I hope he didn't lose a lot of sleep over that notion.

Greenspan, ever the politician, became an enabler for the new President's fiscal policy. It has been a bad habit of Greenspan's over his long career to cuddle up to his political buddies in the executive branch and deliver the needed cover for their fiscal policy plans even when these plans are at odds with what the economy needs.

Years later, Greenspan wrote a book, *The Age of Turbulence*, in which he made it sound like he was exploring the surface of Mars while all of this was happening. The fact is that he gave the green light to what he should have known was a reckless fiscal policy (it should also be noted that he failed as chairman of the Fed to regulate the reckless practices in the home mortgage industry and he opposed regulating the hedge funds and derivatives trading).

At the very time that our country should have been saving some of that surplus to meet the future needs of the two entitlement programs that were going to need additional funding (Medicare and Social Security), Greenspan and President Bush were anxious to push their tax cut agenda. Added to the historical error in Greenspan's fiscal policy judgment was his belief that self-regulation by financial institutions would protect stockholders, investors, and the American people. We will be paying for that mistaken notion for decades.

Meanwhile, Treasury Secretary Paul O'Neill, a straight shooter and a real conservative (that means a fiscal policy pragmatist), objected to the plan because he felt it didn't add up. He thought it would result in large budget deficits in the years ahead. It also resulted in a pink slip for his candor. *We mustn't tell the Emperor he has no clothes!* So the new Bush administration, with its supporters in Congress, pushed ahead with its plans to cut government revenue by giving the large tax cuts to wealthy Americans, while denying that that was what they were doing.

## HOW THE LITTLE GUY GOT TRICKLED ON

That philosophy of tax cuts for wealthy Americans is not new. Republicans have dubbed it the trickle-down theory, which holds that if you provide tax cuts to those at the top, benefits will trickle down to the folks at the bottom. Thus, everybody benefits, proponents of trickle-down claim. There's not much evidence to support this assertion, but it has been driving much of the Republican Party fiscal policy for decades. There's a saying on the prairie where I come from: "Don't piss on my leg and tell me it's raining." It's pretty obvious that most Americans are being trickled *on* but not trickled *down to*.

So in 2001 as the new President was pushing ahead on a budget plan that would use the next ten years' projected budget surpluses for some very large tax cuts—mostly for wealthy Americans—some of us in Congress were warning that the budget surpluses were just projections. "What if something happened? We should be conservative and not spend surpluses we don't have on tax cuts for the wealthy," we argued. But the President would have none of it. He pressed ahead with support from his political party in control of Congress because he claimed tax cuts were necessary for economic growth.

In the months and years ahead good news turned into bad as we experienced in short order a recession, the terrorist attacks of 9/11, the war in Afghanistan, the war in Iraq, and the continuing war against terrorism. The projected surpluses turned into very large budget deficits.

But that didn't deter the President. He decided to fund the war and the fight against terrorism by borrowing the money. And still, he pushed for even higher levels of spending and *more* tax cuts for the wealthy, all the while adding well over $5 trillion to the national debt. It was a reckless fiscal policy that has left our country in a deep hole.

What was he thinking? How could he imagine that you can *increase spending* and *cut revenue* and things will work out just fine? Did he think he had a magic checkbook?

And looming just over the horizon was the Medicare program funding problem that everyone knew needed to be dealt with. But the administration and its allies were content to pretend that the Medicare funding issue didn't exist. "Be happy," they preached. "These good times will last forever. And we can deal with Medicare funding later." It turned out to be a giant miscalculation that could haunt us for decades.

## REGULATORS AS CHEERLEADERS

At about the same time the Bush fiscal policy was beginning to turn surpluses into massive deficits, the private sector was enjoying a field day with a new administration. They came to office believing that government regulation was harmful to business. So it was Katie, bar the door! Big industries in such fields as energy, health care, financial services, and others found a sympathetic ear and a blind eye in the Bush administration.

The table for some of it was set under the Clinton administration. According to David R. Baker, in an article that appeared in the *San Francisco Chronicle* in 2005, "Bankrupt energy trader Enron Corp. started manipulating California's electricity market a month after it was deregulated in 1998, according to internal documents and phone transcripts."

While there is evidence of market manipulation before Bush took office, it became brazen afterward. Businesses ran wild. The Enron Corporation was bilking electricity ratepayers on the West Coast out of billions of dollars by controlling and manipulating the supply of wholesale electricity. Enron wasn't the only culprit, but it set the standard for illegal and unethical behavior.

The Enron executives concocted schemes called Fat Boy and Get Shorty, which were designed to manipulate supply in a way that would drive up the price and maximize revenue for the energy companies. This is all fact. Yet in early 2008 when I and others suggested that there could be similar manipulation by speculators in the oil markets as the price of oil rocketed to $147 a barrel, the wise men spilled their mint juleps and swooned like Scarlett O'Hara: "Why, I nevuh!" Interestingly, the price collapsed just as quickly as it went up when some of the same interests that made money speculating on the rise in prices turned around and made money by bringing the prices back down.

But back to Enron! With Enron's close association with the new White House, Bush pal Ken Lay believed he had a green light to fully exploit the market. And he did. There was even some talk that he might become Energy Secretary.

It wasn't until four years after the Enron collapse that recordings of some Enron energy traders were made public, showing the brazen criminal activity. Those recordings were in the files of the U.S. Justice Department and were only made public over the Justice Department's objections after the filing of a Freedom of Information (FOI) request. One lawsuit in Washington State alleged that Enron manipulated power to its advantage in one stretch 400 out of 537 days up to June 1, 2001.

Because Ken Lay had, at the invitation of the White House, helped in the selection process of the new chairman of the Federal Energy Regulatory Commission (FERC), I assume he didn't worry much about interference by that regulator. And sure enough, while Enron and others bilked the consumers to the tune of billions, it was the FERC that sat on its hands, acting deceased.

Both President Bush and Vice President Cheney mocked those who wanted an investigation into what we later learned was criminal behavior through supply manipulation. This was simply the free market at work, they claimed. The result was billions of dollars being extorted from citizens on the West Coast who were paying inflated prices for electricity to air-condition their homes in the hot summer and heat them in the winter.

Now, where I come from, it's called stealing. And when you lie to investors about the financial health of your company, that's stealing, too

Ken Lay, who had been one of the largest fund-raisers for President Bush, was called Kenny Boy by the President. After the Enron scandal broke, he became "Kenny who?" at the White House. As Enron collapsed like a house of cards, many employees and investors who held Enron stock and who had been advised by Lay to hold on to the stock even as Lay was selling his lost their life savings.

I chaired the Senate Commerce Committee hearings when we subpoenaed Ken Lay to testify. He walked into the hearing room and asserted his Fifth Amendment rights and refused to answer any questions. But his lawyer publicly insisted that Ken Lay had no knowledge of the financial manipulation that had created the house of cards that was Enron.

Lay was going to be portrayed as either stupid or a criminal. I guess he chose stupid, but it never washed with me. He clearly had to have known what was going on in his corporation. Those profits didn't result from magic . . . some of them were from criminal financial manipulation. Lay died of a heart attack after he was convicted of securities fraud but before he was sent to prison, but a number of his subordinates in the executive suite at Enron are now serving time in prison for bilking investors, customers, and the government.

As is usually the case, Congress and the government regulatory agencies took action (too late) to address the scandal just passed. In my hometown, we call it closing the barn door after the horse is gone.

Even the Bush administration finally grudgingly acknowledged that something needed to be done. Congress passed legislation called the Sarbanes-Oxley Act to try to reduce the chances of this type of financial scandal from happening again. But remember Harvey Pitt. Regulations work only if regulators are seriously willing to enforce them.

Finally, the Madoff case in late 2008 demonstrates how much more work there is to do to really protect the American people. The Securities and Exchange Commission has begun an investigation into how that Ponzi scheme was allowed to happen. The answer isn't very complicated. It was a culture that developed over the years that regulation was bad and less regulation was good.

The early work of the new Obama administration has to be to establish regulatory oversight that is serious and effective. Especially in times of financial crisis, nothing is more important than restoring confidence that the government is doing what is required to safeguard the public interest.

I don't propose that we overregulate or stifle legitimate business. There must be a balance. But what we have learned in recent years is that when government regulation fails, the American economy is injured and the American taxpayers are stuck paying the bill. That is not a lesson we should need to learn more than once.

# CHAPTER 4

· · ·

# *Shining a Light on Dark Money*

THERE'S A SAYING on Wall Street: "If you want to see who is swimming naked, wait until the tide goes out." In late 2007 and early 2008, when the tide started to turn on the American economy, it became apparent who was swimming in the buff. It wasn't a pretty sight.

The list included some of the biggest names at blue-chip investment banks as well as a lot of speculators who had been making money hand over fist while the economy was growing. But they were leveraged to the hilt, and when the economy started to sour we learned how irresponsible many had been.

The reason there is so much peril in our economy at the moment is because in recent years there has been unbelievable growth in fancy new financial products and methods of securitization that made a lot of people wealthy as long as the economy was growing rapidly but created great risk when the economy hit the rocks. These are sophisticated financial instruments that for the most part are created and traded outside of the view of regulators. I call it dark money.

Mysterious terms like "collateralized debt obligations" and

"credit default swaps" are now bringing sleepless nights to those who were using leverage to buy things they didn't fully understand from those who didn't have full knowledge of what they were selling.

Think of it this way. As I referenced earlier, it is said that in the old days when meatpacking plants were not closely watched by inspectors, some plants made sausage using sawdust as filler. I'm tempted to spin a yarn stating that soon people were coming down with Dutch elm disease. Of course *I'm kidding!* The consumer never knew.

That is what has happened in finance. Sawdust packed in security sausage . . . and the consumer doesn't know. Until it all goes bad. Then everybody, even those pushing the filler, begins shouting in mock surprise, "Who the hell put sawdust in there?"

The subprime loan scandal included all of the worst of these new practices. Fancy new mortgages, new complicated mortgage-backed securities, credit default swaps, and much more. In the end it contributed to the most significant economic collapse since the Great Depression.

In American neighborhoods, it put millions of people out of their homes because they had been sold mortgages that far exceeded their ability to pay. While some of the borrowers went in with eyes wide open, hoping to flip a home for a profit, most of the home owners were just plain fooled. If you are one of those who blame the victims, tell me that you have read through your home mortgage paperwork.

The new sophisticated financial engineering, by which the largest financial institutions created products so complicated few people understood them, put those same financial institutions at great risk. But that risk was hidden from public view in unregulated markets.

In this chapter I am going to describe the issue of hedge funds and derivatives called credit default swaps. But any discussion of these forms of investment and of these financial instruments includes the role of the largest banking institutions in their investment in the same. Those banks have been involved in so many ways with all of the new, fancy financial products and they are closely related to all of the issues this chapter will discuss.

## CREDIT DEFAULT WHAT?

Ominously, we have a large number of hedge funds that are unregulated and operating outside the view of any regulation, often with high debt and substantial risk. The total value of hedge funds is estimated at up to or even over $2 trillion. But that really understates their importance. Those hedge funds are responsible for fully *one-half* of the daily trading on the New York Stock Exchange.

The financial collapse in 2008 undoubtedly had a big impact on hedge funds. Some estimate as many as one thousand of them would not survive the downturn. As this book is being written, no one yet knows how extensive the damage was to the hedge fund industry. But we do know how profitable hedge funds were leading up to the financial collapse.

Hedge funds have been deep into something called credit default swaps. *Forbes* magazine's Daniel Fisher explained them this way: "A credit swap is an insurance policy on a bond, often a junk bond. The fellow selling the swap—writing the policy, that is—collects a premium. If nothing goes wrong, he pockets the premium and looks like a financial genius. But if the bond defaults, the swap seller has to make good."

According to the International Swaps and Derivatives Association, there are over $60 trillion of these swaps floating around and no one knows whether in an economic downturn those who provide the guarantee for the swaps will ever be able to pay, because the whole scheme is held together with massive borrowing from all sorts of institutions and possibly some duct tape. The economic collapse in 2008 demonstrated how dangerous it is to have the credit default swaps out in the economy with no regulation and no transparency.

Those who knew all of these facts and were still unconcerned about the future were going to live a life of blissful ignorance. The fact is, it all added up to serious economic trouble and we experienced the full effect of it in 2008.

Now about those hedge funds: All of us have heard the phrase "hedging your bets." In most cases that is our only acquaintance with the financial term "hedge." And hedging against the risk of loss is an important, legitimate business strategy for big and small businesses as well as family farmers. It goes on every day, and the financial markets and institutions that create the opportunities for hedging risk are a necessary business tool. And many hedge funds are responsible and necessary and provide an essential service to the world of finance.

In recent decades, however, we have read about the dramatic growth of hedge funds. It is a way for big investors to pool money, and in most cases the hedge funds operate outside of the traditional regulated financial markets. Hedge funds are generally available only to very wealthy investors, often requiring $1 million minimum investment. And they have grown large and powerful in recent years.

As I said earlier, it is estimated that hedge funds are somewhere near the $2 trillion level. That sounds like a lot of money. But mutual funds totaled about $9.2 trillion in 2008. And the stock and bond markets totaled over $40 trillion during the same period. (Their value is lower now following the collapse in late 2008.) But sheer size is not the only way to measure the impact of hedge funds. Because hedge funds are responsible for half of the daily trading on the New York Stock Exchange, *their influence far exceeds their value.* One expert called it trading on steroids. The important fact about hedge funds is that they are hyperactive in the bond market and the derivative markets.

Many hedge fund managers are looking for anomalies in the market they can exploit and turn into a profit. Some are becoming more aggressive by taking positions in big companies and pushing for business strategies that might serve the hedge fund even if it is not consistent with the public interest.

Hedge funds are deep into derivatives such as credit default swaps. It is estimated that hedge funds account for 58 percent of trading of these derivatives. Derivatives have been around almost forever. Essentially, traders are betting on the rise or fall of markets and commodities that they do not own outright, and they are allowed to bet millions by putting only thousands on the table.

For instance, Party A may agree to sell a million Widgets on a certain date to Party B for $1 each. Keep in mind, he doesn't necessarily have a million Widgets; he's just making a promise to deliver.

If the price of Widgets has fallen to 75 cents when the contract is up, Party B loses because he is paying higher than market price. But in some circumstances, that may be acceptable. Essentially Party B has taken out a sort of insurance to "hedge" against a much greater loss. This higher price may still pencil out for his company. His expenses are just higher and his profits lower. But as long as he's making a profit, all's well.

So you can see why this process can be a useful tool. Now, if the market value of a Widget is $2 when it comes time to deliver, Party A will lose his shirt, assuming he can deliver to a smiling Party B, who, at this point, is convinced he's a financial wizard.

But if Party A cannot deliver, because he has bet more than he can cover, a nasty chain reaction can be set into place.

The Financial Policy Forum's 2002 study on derivatives helps explain the domino effect, when things go wrong with these high-risk bets:

Taking on these greater risks raises the likelihood that an investor, even a major financial institution, suffers large losses. If they suffer large losses, then they are threatened with bankruptcy. If they go bankrupt, then the people, banks and other institutions that invested in them or lent money to them will face losses and in turn might face bankruptcy themselves. This spreading of the losses and failures gives rise to *systemic risk*, and it is an economy-wide problem that is made worse by leverage and leveraging instruments such as derivatives.

When people suffer damages, even though they were not coun-
terparties or did any business with a failed investor or financial
institution, then individual incentives and rules of *caveat emptor*
are not sufficient to protect the public good. In this case, prudent regulation is needed—not to protect fools from themselves, but to protect others from the fools.

Because of the heavy use of leverage, which is essentially a pile of
credit, these hedge funds' influence extends far beyond their estimated $2 trillion size. If the market takes a sudden nasty turn, hedge
funds can lose far more than the value of the funds themselves.

Even in Las Vegas, most gamblers' losses are generally limited to
what they have in their pockets, but on Wall Street, because of the
heavy leveraging that occurs, when someone loses big, the implications can extend deep into our economy.

The Financial Policy Forum study illustrates some recent examples:

Long-Term Capital Management collapsed with $1.4 trillion
in derivatives on their books [and it nearly caused a major collapse in our economy]. Sumitomo Bank in Japan used derivatives in their manipulation of the global copper market for
years prior to 1996. Barings Bank, one of the oldest in Europe, was quickly brought to bankruptcy by over a billion
dollars in losses from derivatives trading. Both the Mexican
financial crisis in 1994 and the East Asian financial crisis of
1997 were exacerbated by the use of derivatives to take large
positions on the exchange rate. Most recently, the collapse of
a major commodity derivatives dealer Enron Corporation has
led to the largest bankruptcy in U.S. history.

Not all hedge funds place large risky bets on stocks, currencies,
bonds, commodities, and gold while using lots of leverage. The
modern version of hedge funds has been around since 1949. Some

employ conservative strategies. Others live on a high wire of high risk and high return.

Warren Buffett once called derivatives "financial weapons of mass destruction" because of the damage they could do to Wall Street in an instant. For nearly a quarter of a century, until 2004, nothing was done by federal authorities against hedge fund fraud or manipulation affecting others. When action was finally taken, it was an Attorney General of New York who moved against a hedge fund that had cheated mutual fund account holders.

In 1998, after the collapse of the hedge fund Long-Term Capital Management, which nearly brought on a global financial collapse, it took the Federal Reserve Board and a coalition of banks working together feverishly to provide a safety net that rescued the financial system. That experience with hedge funds and the risky credit derivatives should have convinced policy makers to move to provide even modest regulations.

President Clinton formed an oversight group, which included the SEC as a member. But efforts were stymied when an SEC rule designed to oversee hedge funds was invalidated by the U.S. Court of Appeals. It limited but did not end SEC oversight. However, the court decision means hedge funds do not have to register or submit to investigations.

You certainly won't see the fund managers themselves putting on the brakes. The reason is that hedge funds have a fee structure (the 2 and 20 formula) that nearly guarantees success for those who are managing them. The managers typically charge a 2 percent management fee. That means that they will earn 2 cents on every dollar they manage, and that has nothing to do with their success or failure in turning a profit for the investors. But there's more. Managers also typically take a large percentage of the profits that exceed their benchmarks—some are around 20 percent, some even higher. So, the way it works is they make staggering amounts of money if they are successful and some have earned a massive income even when they failed.

Some of that changed in 2008 when some hedge funds experienced major losses as the house of cards collapsed. But, up until that point, a good number of the hedge fund managers made massive amounts of income.

## HE'LL EQUAL YOUR SALARY
## IN SIX MINUTES

James Simons ranks in the top three hundred of the world's wealthiest people. He was king of the hill in hedge fund pay in 2006 with a $1.7 billion income in that one year, according to an article by Jenny Anderson and Julie Creswell in *The New York Times*. If you're on a monthly salary and want to compare yours to his, Simons's salary was $141 million a month, or about $4.5 million a day. For a ten-hour day, that's about $450,000 an hour. That means he makes in a matter of minutes the salary an average American worker makes in an entire year. I hope he tips well.

But in 2007 the top hedge fund manager made a much higher income: $3.7 billion. That's over $300 million a month. Neil Weinberg and Bernard Condon noted in a 2004 article titled "The Sleaziest Show on Earth" that hedge fund managers are paid "fees that would be outlandish or even illegal if extracted from a plain old mutual fund."

Simons is a mathematician and former military code breaker, who, according to Alistair Barr, "employs roughly 80 Ph.D.s who develop computer programs to seek out price anomalies in a wide range of markets, including equities, commodities, futures and options." Translated, it means Simons is always looking for an angle. And he's finding them.

Published reports said one of his company's funds—the Medallion Fund—gained 44 percent in 2006, with an average return of 36 percent since 1988. And, after a 5 percent management fee and a 44 percent performance fee, Mr. Simons went home with $1.7 billion for himself in 2006. Such is the rarified air of success.

Of an estimated eighty-eight hundred hedge funds in 2006, only

twenty-five hundred were registered with the SEC, said SEC chairman Christopher Cox. He told the U.S. Senate Committee on
Banking, Housing, and Urban Affairs on July 26, 2006, "Given the
general lack of public disclosure about the way hedge funds operate,
the lack of standards for measuring a fund's valuation and its performance, the possibilities for undisclosed conflicts of interest, the un-
usually high fees, and the higher risk that accompanies a hedge
fund's expected higher returns, these are not investments for Mom
and Pop."

## HOW TO MANIPULATE THE MARKET

Some have called the boom of hedge funds a kind of gold rush, with
the usual mix of honest prospectors and plain cheats. The opportunity for manipulation by the big players stands to bury some investors. Nixon could have learned a few dirty tricks from these guys.

On June 17, 2007, Barbara T. Dreyfuss reported in *The American
Prospect*:

> Jim Cramer, who ran a major hedge fund, Cramer, Berkowitz
> & Co., for more than a dozen years, recently boasted publicly
> that market manipulation is indeed how the system works. . . .
> Cramer detailed how easy it is to manipulate stock prices.
> Suppose, said Cramer, his investments were tied to Apple's
> stock tanking, and suppose that stock began to rise. In such a
> case, he said, he would "pick up the phone and call six trading
> desks" at brokerage houses and tell them people at Verizon
> were panning Apple. "That's a very effective way to keep a
> stock down," he chuckled. "I might also buy January puts"—
> stock options that anticipate a stock going down. This, said
> Cramer, creates an image that bad news is coming. And, he
> added, you then call investors and reinforce that image. "The
> way the market really works is you hit the nexus of the bro-
> kerage houses with a series of orders that can be leaked to the

SHINING A LIGHT ON DARK MONEY     { 81 }

press, and you get it on CNBC, and then you have a vicious
cycle down."

It's disappointing if we turn these kinds of people into heroes. If
this is the way Jim Cramer talks about doing business, why are we
idolizing such behavior? He is the host of CNBC's *Mad Money*, a
show in which he offers financial advice while, at times, sounding
and looking a bit like a lunatic. I guess that sells in some quarters.
He did, however, redeem himself somewhat with me when, during
the late 2008 stock market collapse, he advised people that if they
needed their money within the next five years, they should be taking it out of the stock market. That was sage advice.

In today's instant media, a blip of bad news can snowball into a
panic. Pros can always react faster than casual investors, who can be
financially wounded by the type of shenanigans Cramer describes.
It is market manipulation, and it is wrong.

The answer to lessening the risk of an economic meltdown
driven by hedge funds is obvious. More oversight and regulation!
Instead of putting out the fire, President Bush signed legislation designed to put gas on the fire, making it *easier* for pension funds,
school endowments, and charities to invest in these high-risk ventures.

A Bank of New York study predicts such investments will account for about *one-third* of new money to hedge funds by the end of
this decade. Why does this matter? Because in the beginning the
high ante to play the hedge fund game was limited to those with
enough chips so that if a few high rollers lost a bundle, it wasn't a big
deal, with one exception—if it had a snowball effect on others. Yes,
it sounds exclusionary, but the fat cats could afford the loss. But
when *pensions* are on the line, it affects people who can't afford to
lose.

Iowa Senator Charles E. Grassley, a Republican, has sought more
oversight of hedge funds. "We recently enacted pension reforms to
increase transparency for pension-holders about how their money is
invested," Grassley said in October 2006. "Now we're learning

hedge funds pose huge risks to pension-holders. It's disturbing that we can't even come close to understanding the extent of the risks because hedge funds operate in such a secretive way. We need to get a handle on this situation before more hedge funds go belly-up and leave rank-and-file investors in the ditch."

Laudably, the Connecticut Department of Banking set up a hedge fund oversight department in 2006. (Many hedge funds and corporations are located in the state.) They're on the right track. Hedge funds need to be registered. The evidence of market manipulation by these fast-trading hedge funds is so strong that the idea that the status quo is just fine is laughable. The marketplace should be safe for all investors, not just those in the know or those powerful enough to manipulate markets.

But alas, we discovered in late 2008, the market isn't really safe for anyone as long as the gamblers are out there creating the undertow that pulls innocent people out to sea when things go sour.

## ONE HEDGE FUND TRADER SEIZES CONTROL OF THE NATURAL GAS MARKET

The danger of unregulated hedge fund trading was demonstrated in 2006 when some smart investigation by a congressional committee disclosed that a thirty-two-year-old trader named Brian Hunter had found a way to virtually control the market for natural gas. He did it by conducting an excessive number of trades on unregulated markets from his hedge fund in order to obscure what he was doing. The trader controlled up to 70 percent of the natural gas market on the New York Mercantile Exchange (NYMEX) at one point, and he allegedly manipulated prices in a manner that finally led to the collapse of a hedge fund called Amaranth. Federal regulators say his positions in the natural gas market were so big that he could cause prices to move as he wanted by buying or selling giant holdings in the last thirty minutes of trading on NYMEX (a move known as "smashing the close").

The strategy employed by Hunter allowed him to shift his trading to an unregulated foreign exchange after NYMEX, which is regulated by the Commodity Futures Trading Commission (CFTC), told Amaranth that it had to reduce his holdings. That strategy didn't always work out. He lost $5 billion in one week alone. Eventually, Amaranth collapsed. Hunter later found himself the target of a federal lawsuit for his shenanigans.

His scheme was only discovered by a yearlong investigation by a subcommittee of the U.S. Senate. But the damage was done and millions of investors and home owners lost because of such trading. What this episode illustrates clearly is that the CFTC is not able to effectively regulate trading in energy commodities as long as much of that trading occurs on exchanges that are unregulated. It's like an NYC beat cop being expected to break up crime in London. Even more important, the CFTC, which is supposed to be the referee, has issued a series of "no action" letters that have allowed much of the trading to be done outside of the vision of the regulators. The CFTC is truly a toothless regulator and willfully derelict in its duty.

In recent years there has been an explosive growth of the trading of contracts that look and are structured exactly like futures contracts but are traded on over-the-counter electronic markets outside of the regulatory authorities. Some call them futures look-alikes. The only real difference is that the look-alikes (derivatives) are traded on unregulated exchanges.

The trading of these energy commodities by large firms on the over-the-counter electronic exchanges was exempted from the CFTC oversight by a provision inserted at the urging of Enron and other big companies when the Commodity Futures Modernization Act of 2000 was passed at the end of the 106th Congress.

In 2007 the CFTC itself, in a move akin to shooting itself in both feet, decided to allow the Intercontinental Exchange (ICE), the biggest operator of electronic energy exchanges, to use its trading terminals in the United States for trading U.S. crude oil futures on the ICE futures exchange in London—called ICE Futures. What are the implications? While traders at the New York Mercantile Exchange must keep detailed records and report large trades, the Senate's Permanent Subcommittee on Investigations says traders "now can avoid all U.S. market oversight or reporting requirements by routing their trades through the ICE Futures exchange in London instead of the NYMEX in New York."

It means traders like Brian Hunter have another dark corner to hide in.

## SPECULATION AS PRICES RISE AND FALL

Given the experience in 2007 and 2008 with the run-up of oil prices, we know that another area of "dark money" can have a major impact on consumers and on our country. That is the trading in the futures market of oil futures contracts.

It is important for policy makers, analysts, regulators, investors, and the general public to understand the reason for energy price movements. If price increases are caused by imbalances in supply and demand, economic policies to encourage investment in new exploration or conservation can respond to those increases over time. If prices are increasing because of a natural disaster or unanticipated factors in a producer country, policies can be developed to react to that new reality.

But if prices are a result of market manipulation or excessive speculation, only an effective regulator will be able to do the job. But today, with respect to certain energy futures, the CFTC is like a referee who lacks both glasses and a whistle. And even if the CFTC had impeccable vision and the will to regulate, it has, by its own decisions, given an opportunity to oil futures contract traders to conduct their activities outside the view of the CFTC. That is, the agency that is supposed to regulate decided on a strategy of willful blindness by creating an entire area of dark money.

In late 2007, when oil prices were fluctuating between $90 and $100 a barrel, many experts believed that there was no justification for that price that had any connection to worldwide supply and demand. Fadel Gheit, a widely respected energy analyst for Oppenheimer & Co. in New York, had this to say to a *McClatchy Newspapers* reporter, Jack Smith: "There is no shortage of oil. I'm absolutely convinced that oil prices shouldn't be a dime above $55 a barrel. . . . Oil speculators include the largest financial institutions in the world. I call it the world's largest gambling hall . . . it's open 24/7 . . . unfortunately it's totally unregulated. . . . This is like a highway with no cops and no speed limit, and everybody's going 120 miles per hour."

Gheit was referring to the bubble of speculation in oil futures that had grown rapidly. For the first time, hedge funds and even investment banks were up to their necks in these markets. They were betting that oil prices would increase and if they purchased oil and withheld it from the market for sale later, they would profit. This strategy even had investment banks purchasing oil storage capacity for the purpose of keeping it off the market and selling it later. This, of course, had the effect of continuing to push up oil prices. It was a frenzy of speculation that some oil market analysts believe contributed to an inflated price that had little or nothing to do with the supply and demand of oil.

In the first six months of 2008, the prices spiked even further, to the $147-per-barrel range. That meant that the price of oil had doubled in a year. And yet nothing in the relationship between supply and demand changed during the year that would justify the doubling of the price of oil. It was relentless, excessive speculation in the futures markets.

That strategy likely was very profitable for the big interests, but it was enormously costly to the American people, who were paying a highly inflated price for gasoline as a result of the speculation. The irony of it all was that much of the trading could be done outside of the view of the regulatory agency, because it had created the loophole that allowed the over-the-counter trading to be obscured and out of reach. We now refer to it as the Enron Loophole. And although Enron is gone, the recent speculation in oil prices reminds us of the danger of unregulated, rampant speculation.

In mid-2008 the price began a significant decline. Once again that oil price movement had virtually no connection to supply and demand. By the end of 2008, the price of oil had dropped again to less than $40 a barrel. A part of that can be explained by a worldwide economic slowdown. But there is nothing in the tracking of supply-and-demand relationships of the production and use of oil that justified the roller coaster of oil prices (from $40 to $147 back to $38 a barrel) . . . except rampant speculation by new traders in the energy futures markets who never intended to take possession of the commodity. It was hurtful to our economy and it is an unhealthy trend.

And frankly, the prospect of oil prices going even lower than the $38-a-barrel price as this book is written is not good news for those of us who are pursuing policies that will make us less dependent on foreign oil. The development of renewable energy will be undermined if the price of oil collapses, and the drilling for oil in areas that are promising will also suffer. I don't think that is in our country's interest, either. (More about that in a later chapter.)

The oil marketplace is strange and different. The American people are told to rely on "the free market," but too often it a rigged market.

Consider the structure we put up with. The Organization of the Petroleum Exporting Countries—OPEC—itself is a group that colludes to set prices. Twelve countries (Algeria, Angola, Ecuador, Iran, Iraq, Kuwait, Libya, Nigeria, Qatar, Saudi Arabia, the United Arab Emirates, and Venezuela) hold sway over the rest of the world. When it comes to standing up for our economic and energy interests, this country has had no backbone. Why? Because an influential few stand to benefit greatly from the status quo. Collusion mixed with speculation threatens our economy for the foreseeable future and dramatizes the necessity for energy independence. We need to approach it as if our country's future depends upon it, because it does. Regulation at home is a vital first step.

Excessive speculation and manipulation of energy markets has to stop. We need to use some common sense in standing up for the public interest.

The solution to the speculation of hedge funds and others is effective regulation.

Here are the steps we have to take. It's late but not too late to put all of this back on track:

REGULATE HEDGE FUND TRADING AND THEN REGULATE ALL TRADES IN THE FUTURES MARKETS. With what has happened in our economy, there is no longer any justification for failing to regulate the hedge funds and the sophisticated financial products they trade, including derivatives and especially credit default swaps. And with the volatility of the energy futures markets, it is imperative that the trading on that market be transparent and regulated.

REQUIRE LARGE TRADER REPORTS. Congress should enact legislation to provide that persons trading energy futures "look-alike" contracts on over-the-counter electronic exchanges are subject to the CFTC's large trader reporting requirements.

MONITOR U.S. ENERGY TRADES ON FOREIGN EXCHANGES. Congress should enact legislation to ensure that U.S. persons trading U.S. energy commodities on foreign exchanges are subject to the CFTC's large trader reporting requirements.

INCREASE U.S.-UK COOPERATION. The CFTC should work with the United Kingdom Financial Services Authority to ensure it has information about all large trades in U.S. energy commodities on the ICE Futures exchange in London.

INCREASE MARGIN REQUIREMENTS OR ENACT STRONG POSITION LIMITS FOR SPECULATORS. Congress should require the CFTC to develop the criteria for separating the normal commercial hedge transactions from the speculation going on in the market and then increase the margin requirements on the speculators in order to wring the excess speculation out of the market. The commodities market for oil should be restored to its original purpose: to allow legitimate commercial hedging.

The Bush administration's foot-dragging on effective regulation of the markets that are trading what I call dark money has been a costly mistake. We need rules that bring these financial transactions into the sunshine of public view.

If you're an average middle-class American, you realize that you are disenfranchised by a manipulated market and unbelievable speculation by a bunch of highfliers. That racket didn't end with Ken Lay or Bernard Madoff. We can fix it . . . but we have to do it now.

# CHAPTER 5

* * *

# Tax That Guy Behind the Tree!

Two brothers on National Public Radio, Tom and Ray Magliozzi, who do a program called *Car Talk* answering questions about automobile repair, credit their law firm, "Dewey, Cheetham and Howe," at the end of the show. It's all in fun, but it is the perfect name for a law firm that would handle the tax affairs of big economic interests in the United States who want all that U.S. citizenship offers them without the obligation of paying their share of taxes.

This chapter is about who they are and how they do it. And it's about how we can stop it. Get your Rolaids and check the batteries on your pacemaker, because when you understand the scandal that is our tax system you will be plenty steamed.

## WHO SHOULD PAY?

"Don't tax you. Don't tax me. Tax that guy behind that tree."

That was the way the late Senator Russell Long described how Americans feel about paying taxes.

It is an age-old problem, determining who should pay taxes and how much. And there are deep philosophical differences about that. Some believe there should be a flat tax, with everyone paying the same tax rate. Remember "Joe the Plumber," whom Senator McCain continually referred to in the third presidential debate? When interviewed later on television about the tax system, Joe the Plumber said people who make more money shouldn't pay higher tax rates. He said that would be penalizing success. His was a simple explanation for those who think we should have just one flat tax rate for everybody. (It turned out that Joe didn't really have a plumber's license and he actually owed some back taxes. So much for his expert opinion.) But he was expressing an opinion that some share. They believe that Warren Buffett should pay the same tax rate as the corner barber or the schoolteacher. They don't believe that a tax system should relate to one's ability to pay.

Others do believe the tax system should be based on the ability to pay and the wealthy should pay a higher tax rate. The theory goes that Donald Trump and Bill Gates can afford to pay a higher tax rate than someone working two jobs at the minimum wage.

Our country has chosen that philosophy over the past century to employ a progressive income tax rate requiring those who make more to pay more. Other taxes, including sales taxes and payroll taxes, do not follow that same philosophy.

The evidence strongly suggests, however, that in recent decades there has been a continuing shift of the overall tax burden from the wealthy to the middle class, who pay more of their income, as a percentage, in taxes.

David Cay Johnston, author of *Perfectly Legal: The Covert Campaign to Rig Our Tax System to Benefit the Super Rich and Cheat Everybody Else*, says, "There is an underground economy among the super rich that lets them understate their true income and overstate their tax deductions." (The quote appears in Ralph Nader's *The Good Fight*.)

Taxes have been called the price of civilization. It doesn't make sense for each of us to have a school in our home. So we build a public school system and we pay taxes to support it. We do the same to build roads and bridges. We create fire and police departments for our public safety. We establish a court system to enforce our laws. We create Centers for Disease Control to protect our health. We need a military to defend our freedom, so we create a defense department and form an army. All of that costs money, too. So we pay taxes.

No one *likes* paying taxes. But we know government is necessary. Without the basic infrastructure government is responsible for producing, society would disintegrate.

But who pays, and how much, is hidden in the maze of a scandalously complicated tax system that only the wealthy and powerful seem to be able to navigate, by paying accountants, lawyers, and tax advisors whose sole purpose is to help their employers avoid paying the toll.

For the most part, Americans who work for a salary pay their taxes, on time and in full. They may not particularly like it, but they know if they are going to send their kids to school, drive on good roads, have police and fire protection, they have to pay something to the government to offset the costs of providing these basic services. It's not paying their fair share of taxes that most middle-class Americans resent—it's the idea that some other wealthy Americans and corporations do not. Middle-class Americans know the tax code has become a punchboard of holes and loopholes for a select few. And they don't like it.

## A NOTABLE EXCEPTION:
## THE WORLD'S RICHEST MAN

Last spring, following a meeting in the Capitol, I walked to Constitution Avenue with Warren Buffett, who had come at my invitation to meet with a handful of Senators about trade issues.

Warren Buffett is the wealthiest man in the world, worth an estimated $62 billion as of 2008—slightly more than his bridge partner, Bill Gates. What is striking about Warren Buffett is how unaffected he seems by his wealth. He is a public-spirited man guided by a deep reservoir of common sense.

As he got into a taxicab after the meeting (yes, he took a taxicab) and left for a meeting in downtown Washington, D.C., I was thinking how different he was from most of the high-powered executives who come to the Congress, delivered by a car service and surrounded by aides. As we walked and talked, Warren told me of an informal survey he had taken in his corporate office in Omaha.

He polled the people who work in his Berkshire Hathaway offices in Omaha (he said about twenty or so employees) to do a comparison of how much they were paying in income and payroll taxes.

It turned out he was paying only 17.7 percent of his annual income in payroll and income taxes while the average the others in his office were paying was 32.9 percent. He said that the receptionist in his office was paying a higher tax rate than he was. In fact, his tax rate was the lowest in the office.

He said his low tax rate was not the result of clever tax planning on his part. It was because most of his income comes from earning dividends on his stock holdings, which are considered capital gains and are taxed at a low rate of 15 percent.

Most people given such an advantage would keep quiet and enjoy it. But the way Buffett sees it, the tax system is tilting in favor of the rich and away from the middle class. "It's not right and it needs to be fixed," he said.

As I watched him leave in the taxicab, I thought about how unusual it was to see someone come to tell Congress that his tax burden was too low. He didn't come in a big black limousine, either. He chose a taxi. I guess it's about style and he has a lot of it. It's not tuxedos and mansions but a sense of right and wrong that is in his DNA.

The voice of Warren Buffett is nearly alone amid a chorus of corporate CEOs, hedge fund managers, private equity firm managers, and others who now command astronomical sums of money and, in many cases, pay a miserably low income tax rate.

Over the years the tax code has become a web of complexity with loopholes that defy any reasonable explanation. And that very complexity allows some of the biggest economic interests to hide their income and pay a lower effective rate of tax than an average working person or small business. The push to create big tax loopholes and the eagerness to exploit them by some of the wealthiest individuals and corporations in our country lead me to wonder what ever happened to any sense of economic patriotism.

These days we don't hear much about that in our political debates. Commentators contemplate which candidates are wearing a flag pin or who is slapping the right bumper sticker on their car. The whole notion of patriotism has become implausibly artificial in some quarters. I think there is a patriotic response to our country that we ought to expect from our citizens and corporations as well. Those of us who benefit from that which America offers us should be willing to, in turn, help our country. Remember President Kennedy saying, "Ask not what your country can do for you. Ask what you can do for your country."

THE TAX SYSTEM has in recent times favored the upper-income taxpayers. But it has grown even more unfair in recent years as President Bush and Congress have allowed those who get their income through capital gains to pay a 15 percent income tax rate, which is less than half of what many wage earners pay on their earnings.

Because most of the capital gains income is earned by upper-income Americans, they are the ones given the opportunity to pay the lower tax rates while the wage earners end up paying higher rates. According to Leonard Burman at the Tax Policy Center, "The benefits of low tax rates on capital gains accrue disproportionately to the wealthy. In 2007 an estimated 92 percent of the benefit of those low rates went to taxpayers with incomes over $200,000, and 72 percent to those earning over $1 million."

Even this is not enough for some in Congress. They would like to completely exempt all capital gains from taxation. They believe that capital gains should get special treatment in the tax code because those who receive capital gains are the investors who are risking their money to create jobs and they should be rewarded for that.

And what about those Americans who perform the jobs that keep industry moving? Is work any less valuable than investment? Yes, investment is important. But capital without labor is unproductive capital. So, why should the President and Congress present the keys to the city to investors while ignoring the contribution of workers? The easy answer is: they shouldn't.

When some taxpayers are allowed to pay much lower tax rates on their income than other taxpayers just because it is classified as a different kind of income, that creates opportunities for tax games, hard feelings, and broadening economic inequities that rival those preceding the Great Depression. Ignoring the parallels between then and now is just whistling in the graveyard.

## THE CARRIED-INTEREST CAPER

Most Americans have probably never heard of "carried interest." But it is a sweet term for some of the wealthiest Americans who earn megaincomes and yet are able to pay income tax to the U.S. government at a 15 percent rate.

Carried interest is complicated, but in its simplest form it allows hedge fund managers, private equity fund managers, and some others at the top of the money tree to define the income they earn from investing other people's money as *capital gains*, which is taxed at a 15 percent rate.

As I explained in an earlier chapter, typically hedge fund managers are compensated in two ways, according to the 2 and 20 formula. First they earn a fee (usually 2 percent) applied to the funds they are managing. Then they receive a larger percentage of what the fund earns for the year (usually 20 percent).

For all practical purposes, they are being paid a fee for managing money. That fee in all other circumstances would be considered "ordinary income" and be taxed at the regular income tax rates. But the hedge fund managers and private equity firm managers have managed to find a crack in the tax code and define their income as "carried interest," which wipes out a large part of what they would otherwise owe the federal government in taxes.

So, when a top hedge fund manager reports $3.7 billion (that's right . . . it's *billions*) in 2007 income, he saves hundreds of millions of dollars in taxes he would otherwise pay to the federal government because he defines his income as carried interest eligible for the lower capital gains tax rate of 15 percent.

Warren Buffett weighed in on the controversy, saying, "Hedge fund operators have spent a record amount lobbying in the last few months—they give money to the political campaigns. Who represents the cleaning lady?"

Well, a few of us are still on the case. We need to ask these slackers to pay their fair share. Either that or open the floodgates and let all Americans declare their earnings as "carried interest" and enjoy a 15 percent tax rate, too. Of course, we would come up a fair piece short of the money we would need to run government.

The U.S. Congress should be ashamed for not moving immediately to close this gaping hole of greed. Some of us have been pushing for action. It appeared for a time that Congress would actually plug this loophole that allows the wealthiest to slither through and avoid their taxes. But the big shots had too many friends in the Bush administration and in Congress, and the appetite for doing the right thing waned.

Meanwhile, most Americans who file income tax returns every year are paying tax rates from 10 percent at the lowest levels of income to 35 percent for those with higher incomes. When you add to that the payroll tax of 15.3 percent, the *lowest-paid* Americans who are required to pay taxes are paying a combined tax rate of 25 percent for income and payroll taxes. That is a full 10 percent higher than the tax bill for those earning billions.

The capital gains rate is lower than other income tax rates be-cause it is argued that people who put their capital at risk in an in-vestment should be taxed at a lower rate. Those who make that case maintain that in order to incentivize investment and risk taking, the tax code should allow a lower tax rate on gains from invested capi-tal. I think there is some validity to having a lower rate for capital gains. But lowering it to 15 percent was a step toward injuring any fairness that exists in the tax system. I am willing to support some preference for capital gains, but the current tax rate difference be-tween it and ordinary income is not fair.

In 2007 the fifty highest-paid hedge fund managers made a com-bined income of $29 billion. The lengths to which this select group of Americans goes to avoid taxes could make a crow blush. The cost to the treasury from the absurdly low tax rate paid by these hedge fund managers runs into billions of dollars a year—yet they still want a better deal.

Many hedge fund managers and private equity fund managers have managed to get their income tax ratcheted down to 15 percent, but in many cases they don't even pay that rate. They set up offshore funds in places such as the Cayman Islands in order to defer *any* tax obligation they owe to the U.S. government.

As Lynnley Browning pointed out in a *New York Times* article, the Caymans "once served as a shelter for pirates like Blackbeard" and now serve as a shelter for hedge funds. If you ever run across a hedge fund manager with a wooden leg and a parrot on his shoul-der, you'll know the connection. Cayman authorities say that three out of every four of the world's hedge funds are in a business loca-tion in the Cayman Islands. (As an aside, by the time Enron col-lapsed it had created over four hundred entities in the Caymans to engage in its tax and financial trickery.) With the offshore entities, hedge fund managers can defer paying even the low 15 percent in-come tax on their earnings by moving their money and receiving their income through these Cayman funds.

But it is all a transparent scheme of unbridled greed. The hedge fund managers know their income comes from fees. And it should be taxed at the ordinary income tax rates that the rest of the American people pay. This doesn't require higher math or an advanced course in the theory of taxation.

## CROSS-BORDER LEASING

While the carried-interest tax avoidance scheme I just described is an embarrassment to the tax code, it doesn't hold a candle to some recent corporation tax strategies to reduce or eliminate their tax obligation. The most brazen and outrageous are called SILO and LILO. I know. It sounds like foreign language again. But, in fact, it is sophisticated tax dodging by some big American corporations.

Let me start by defining SILO. In most cases the word "silo" would describe a round building on a family farm that holds grain or animal feed. In this case "SILO" means "Sale In/Lease Out."

What that means is that the abuse of the tax system has become so egregious that we now have American corporations "owning" sewer systems and streetcars in foreign countries so that they can use the depreciation deduction to reduce or eliminate their U.S. tax bill. Go ahead. Read it again. I'll wait. I was as astonished as you are when I discovered this.

The tax scams would rank as low comedy if they hadn't caused such serious damage. My colleague and former Senate Finance Committee Chairman Charles Grassley calls it "good old-fashioned tax fraud."

Here's how it works. I'll use Wachovia Bank (a U.S. bank formerly named First Union and more recently described as needing a savior because of toxic assets it held) as an example. It decided to purchase the underground sewer system of a city in Germany named Bochum. Yes, a sewer. You'll soon see the irony.

The U.S. bank paid $500 million to the German city for the sewer pipes, then immediately leased them back to the city for the city's use. The city used the proceeds from the sale to pay the lease over the years. Wachovia Bank paid a $20 million fee to the German city for the opportunity to buy and take ownership of their sewer system. This left the city "flush" with cash. (Sorry. I couldn't resist.)

I suppose it is hard to grasp the prestige that comes with ownership of such a sewer system, even with German engineering being what it is. And I certainly don't want to discourage those with dreams of owning German sewage systems.

But I'm willing to bet that the Wachovia Bank executives know as much about German sewers as you or I do. Still, they apparently had an insatiable urge to try to avoid paying U.S. taxes, even if the transaction looked and smelled (oops!) bad. The transaction reportedly saved Wachovia about $175 million in U.S. corporate income taxes that they otherwise would have paid to the federal government.

It was a transaction that allows the purchased property to be depreciated as a business asset. You see, in the hands of a German city a sewer system is just a sewer system. It isn't depreciable on some accounting ledger because it is owned by a city rather than a corporation. But when a corporation buys the sewer system, things change. Now it becomes a business asset that can be depreciated and will represent an expense against profits and therefore tax savings for the corporation.

Of course, the entire transaction I have just described is really just a sham. The German city never really sold the sewer system. They still had the sewer pipes. But the city received a $20 million up-front sweetener. Then they signed papers giving ownership of the sewer to a bank, and the bank got the tax breaks from depreciation. This is called Sale In/Lease Out . . . or SILO.

Robert McIntyre, the director of the Institute for Taxation and Finance, demonstrated how valuable this tax avoidance scheme was to Wachovia Bank in an interview with the television program *Frontline*. McIntyre said, "Amazingly, in 2002, even though it reported $4 billion in profits, [Wachovia] reported that it didn't pay any taxes. . . . They worked it by sheltering all of their income. . . . They said they saved $3 billion in taxes over the last three years from leasing . . . huge write-offs." So you can probably see why Wachovia required a bailout in late 2008. Their executives apparently were so busy arranging unseemly schemes to avoid paying income taxes, they forgot to keep their eyes on the basics of real banking . . . taking deposits and making loans. They weren't the only ones.

Now, let's talk about LILO, and I'm not referring to the first half of Disney's *Lilo & Stitch*. In one example of Lease In/Lease Out (LILO), First Union Bank leased the twenty-five-year-old streetcars of Dortmund, Germany. According to a PBS *Frontline* report by Hedrick Smith, the First Union lease generated $10 million for Dortmund and "the $150 million that First Union paid for the front-end lease likely resulted in tens of millions of dollars in U.S. tax savings for the North Carolina bank." For all intents and purposes, these tax dodgers could just as well be leasing thin air. These are paper transactions dreamt up by shady tax lawyers.

It is not just banks buying sewers and streetcars in Germany. FleetBoston Financial and Sumitomo paid about $140 million for the emergency 9-1-1 Call System belonging to the city of Chicago and then leased it back to the city. It is estimated that this produced up to $77 million in tax savings for the corporations and a net benefit of $16 million for the city of Chicago.

You can see how this might look attractive to a city councilman. Chicago gets a front-end fee, never loses the use of the Emergency Call Center as it leases it back, and the bank gets big tax write-offs. All of the lawyers with blue suits sign the papers and the taxpayers get hurt. Just like that! Shame on all of them!

And a fair number of other units of local governments got into the act by selling their transit systems to private corporations and then leasing them back. Again, all these transactions are, in my judgment, a fraud. And yet both corporations and some local governments engaged in it willingly to try to cheat Uncle Sam out of the income taxes they otherwise would have owed. Again, shame on them!

An article in *Tax Notes* by Marc Quaghebeur reported that similar leasing schemes involved the railcars of the Belgian railway, a toll tunnel in Antwerp under the Scheldt River, and the list goes on— one corporation even leased the town hall of Gelsenkirchen, Germany, in a scheme to avoid paying taxes to the United States.

The Germans meanwhile are flabbergasted and bemused that U.S. companies were allowed to enter into such schemes. *Frontline* reported that when the schemes were revealed in German newspapers, they generated headlines such as "Cities Milk U.S. Tax Cow" or "Make Money with U.S. Leasing."

The IRS did challenge the rental and interest deductions generated by LILOs, and this effectively put an end to the use of tax loss–creating LILO transactions. However, this was just a finger in the dike. The industry regrouped and replaced LILOs with SILOs and then asserted that the IRS rulings did not cover these "unique and different" transactions!

In 2004 Congress limited the tax benefit available in these transactions by allowing U.S. taxpayers to take tax breaks only up to the amount of income recognized on a year-by-year basis under the leasing agreement. However, there are some foreign leasing transactions entered into prior to March 12, 2004, in which the lessee is a foreign tax–exempt entity that is not affected by this law change. This means that large U.S. companies that already had completed foreign SILO transactions will siphon from the Treasury General Fund—and therefore the American taxpayers—an estimated $4 billion over the next decade.

And to top it all off, when the financial collapse of late 2008 occurred, some of these schemes with local governments selling their transit systems went sour, and some sympathetic members of Congress tried to bail them out in a federal bailout bill. Fortunately, it didn't happen.

It's hardly worth mentioning that the people who work for a living and pay the taxes they owe, on time, could not and would not engage in this kind of underhanded behavior. And the fact that our government has allowed it to continue is a good reason for average American taxpayers to be upset that they pay what the large corporations avoid.

According to *Forbes* magazine in 2004, the amount corporations paid in federal taxes had fallen to less than 10 percent of total federal tax revenues. That year, according to MSN, President Bush's budget forecast that corporations would pay $169 billion in income taxes while workers would pay $765 billion.

Charles Rossotti, IRS commissioner from 1997 to 2002, told Hedrick Smith of *Frontline*, "The tax shelter business has become basically stealing from the treasury." Furthermore, he said, "You could double everybody's refund if you just collected all the taxes that were due."

Congress has in recent years taken some steps to shut down some of the abusive leasing activity, but not all. Much more needs to be done. It's hard for me to take seriously the claim that American corporations are overtaxed when I discover abuses like this. There are more loopholes than in a knit sweater, and increasingly large numbers of corporations pay no taxes at all.

And a special room of disgust is reserved for some of the large accounting and law firms whose financial engineers have created and sold these abusive tax shelters.

## THE UGLAND HOUSE

In my previous book, I gave credit to David Evans, an enterprising reporter for Bloomberg News who went to the Cayman Islands and discovered the Ugland House. It is a five-story white building on a quiet street called Church Street.

But it isn't just any white building. This building, according to David Evans, packs 12,748 corporations inside like sardines in a can. That's right! Over 12,000 corporations crowd into this rather small building. Okay, they aren't really there. It's just an address concocted for them by some slick lawyers so that the corporations can claim that they are a Cayman Islands corporation for tax purposes.

You see, the Cayman Islands is not only known for its secretive banking operations that allow people and corporations to park money there outside the view of those who might want to know where it is. It is also a tax haven country, which attracts those people and corporations looking to avoid paying their taxes to the United States.

So, lawyers create a "make-believe" world in which corporations that have no employees or even a telephone in the Cayman Islands are able to claim a legal residence to fool the U.S. Internal Revenue Office. Hey, I could claim I live in Buckingham Palace, but it doesn't make it so.

This isn't a minor problem. It is a growing tax dodge that is costing the U.S. government massive amounts of needed tax revenue. A GAO report I requested earlier in this decade found that 59 out of the 100 largest publicly traded corporations that were federal contractors had established hundreds of subsidiaries in offshore tax havens. Exxon-Mobil had numerous tax havens in the Bahamas. Halliburton had seventeen tax havens in the Cayman Islands as well as two in Liechtenstein and two in Panama. The Enron Corporation was the Babe Ruth of foreign entities, including 441 located in the Cayman Islands alone. That may be why a number of their top executives are now in prison.

And, of course, the taxes these corporations avoid are ultimately paid by regular folks who go to work, earn a salary, and have their taxes withheld at the end of each pay period. If ever a building needed to be fumigated, it is the Ugland House on Church Street in the Cayman Islands.

It is my goal to enact legislation in Congress that will empty the mailboxes in that building in a hurry. My legislation says that you can't claim to have a residence in a foreign country for tax purposes when you don't have real and active business activity in that country. If you are there just to avoid taxes, we will treat your company as if it never left the United States. That will shut down the problem of the tax haven subsidiaries created to avoid U.S. taxation.

## LOSING MONEY BY OUTSOURCING TAX DEBT COLLECTION

So far this chapter has given the boot to those who try to game the system on their taxes. But sometimes it is the government itself that deserves to be sanctioned.

Here's a good example. And it describes a level of incompetence in the IRS.

If you saw me selling tomatoes at a stand on the main highway just south of town, is there any way you think I could lose money *if I got all my tomatoes free*? Well, if the Internal Revenue Service were running the tomato stand, it would lose money. Let me explain—the IRS is supposed to collect taxes, not sell tomatoes. But a recent goofy plan by the IRS convinces me that they don't have the ability to do either.

The IRS has some smaller taxpayers who haven't been paying their tax bills. And because the Bush administration had been on a tear to try to privatize many government functions, the IRS decided they would outsource the collection of these delinquent tax accounts.

So the IRS decided to hire a private-sector debt collection agency. Actually, they hired three private companies to collect the back taxes from people who owed them.

The IRS already had some experience hiring private debt collection agencies a decade ago and it was a disaster. But, apparently, experience is overrated. So the White House and the IRS once again pushed the program to outsource tax collections.

And guess what? The IRS spent more money on the program than it brought in. That's right. In the first year of the program, the private debt collection agencies actually cost the government money. Hold on to your tomatoes—here's how that happened.

The plan was to compensate the companies by allowing them to keep 25 percent of the money they collected. In 2007 it was estimated they would collect up to $65 million. But the actual collections were just $32 million. Compounding the problem were significant start-up costs. The IRS ended up with a first-year loss of $50 million to the U.S. Treasury.

According to the Taxpayer Advocate Service, a neutral branch of the Internal Revenue Service, if the IRS had applied the money that it spent on the private debt collectors to hire tax collectors for the IRS, instead of losing $50 million in 2007 it would have collected $1.4 billion.

Fast-forward to 2008 and the latest IRS projections have the private tax collection firms bringing in gross revenues of as little as $23.4 million, down from $32 million the preceding year. After the private companies take their cut and the operational costs are deducted, the IRS projects, the second year of the program it will still be deep in red ink. In fact, after the first two years of this IRS privatization program, the government will have lost $31 million total!

Even more disturbing is that several of us in Congress could see where this was leading and tried to head it off. The U.S. House passed legislation shutting down the privatization program. The Senate Appropriations Committee did the same. But because of some other appropriation difficulties unrelated to this issue, the legislation did not get to President Bush to be signed into law.

The IRS had decided to ignore the clear signals they received from Congress not to begin this program and plowed ahead to privatize. And the taxpayer got hurt by an administration determined to privatize without regard to the result.

How can a tax-collecting agency lose money collecting taxes? Ask the Bush administration and the IRS. And how can they complain about the behavior of other taxpayers if they can't get their own act together? The Obama administration is now reviewing this policy, and I hope they do the right thing!

## BITING THE HAND THAT FEEDS YOU

Another disgusting tax dodge that was uncovered in 2007 was the practice of companies that had received U.S. government contracts for services in Iraq listing their employees as belonging to subsidiaries the companies had created in tax haven countries to avoid paying payroll taxes on the employees' wages.

Kellogg Brown & Root (KBR), then a subsidiary of Halliburton, avoided paying taxes to the U.S. government by listing their U.S. employees in Iraq and Kuwait as employees of a subsidiary they own in the Cayman Islands. It saved the defense contractor hundreds of millions of dollars, according to press stories that disclosed the practice.

Farah Stockman reported in *The Boston Globe*:

> More than 21,000 people working for KBR in Iraq—including about 10,500 Americans—are listed as employees of two companies that exist in a computer file on the fourth floor of a building on a palm-studded boulevard here in the Caribbean. Neither company has an office or phone number in the Cayman Islands. . . .
>
> The Defense Department has known since at least 2004 that KBR was avoiding taxes by declaring its American workers as employees of Cayman Islands shell companies.

According to the *Globe*, "Heather Browne, a spokeswoman for KBR, acknowledged via e-mail that the two Cayman Islands companies were set up 'in order to allow us to reduce certain tax obligations of the company and its employees.' "

It is interesting that in another court case, Halliburton is contending that these same employees whom they employ through the Cayman Islands subsidiary in order to avoid paying their payroll taxes to the United States are really U.S. employees for the purpose of shielding the corporation from the lawsuits by the employees. I guess that is one corporation that doesn't experience the emotion of "embarrassment."

In another chapter I discuss the controversial defense contracts with Halliburton Corporation and its subsidiary Kellogg Brown & Root (KBR). They have been the beneficiaries of the largest no-bid contracts offered by the Defense Department for the war in Iraq.

You would think that of all the companies that would want to give back to the government that has been so generous to them, the Halliburton Corporation would be the first in line. But that's not the case. In fact, it is just the opposite. After this story broke, Halliburton spun off KBR as a separate company.

The minions in the Defense Department who were the enablers

for this sorry spectacle deserve some blame as well. This story begs the question of who in the Defense Department knew this was happening. And why did they allow it to happen? Has this kind of disgusting behavior become an accepted way of doing business?

In May of 2008, Stockman reported in *The Boston Globe* that "one of the Pentagon's most trusted contractors—Virginia-based MPRI, founded by retired senior military leaders—won a $400 million contract to train police in Iraq and other hotspots. Two months later, MPRI set up a company in Bermuda to which it subcontracted much of the work."

The article also pointed to a previous $1.6 billion contract the company had won, after which they established a company in the Cayman Islands to do the work.

Although the company isn't talking, it appears that it, too, is basking in the success of winning U.S. defense contracts while scheming to find ways to avoid paying its taxes to the same government that awarded it the contract.

While the company keeps mum about what it has been doing, its former employees are talking. The *Globe* article refers to a former MPRI employee in Iraq who said he made $154,000 for the year in Iraq while he and his employer paid no payroll taxes on the salary.

There are some troubling messages from this type of behavior. First, the very companies that are benefiting from wartime contracts are busy trying to avoid paying U.S. taxes by setting up sham corporations in foreign tax havens.

Second, and just as disturbing, is that the Pentagon has apparently been aware of it and some in the armed services even think it is just fine because it ends up costing the Pentagon less money. But this isn't about just the Pentagon. This practice ends up costing the American taxpayers lost tax revenue, and it cheats the employees.

There's some good news here. Congress, responding to my outrage and the outrage of others, has just recently taken some (but not all the necessary) steps to close this loophole. I think we should do more. I believe that if a contractor tries to run their employment through tax haven countries to avoid paying U.S. taxes, that contractor should be ineligible to continue contracting with the federal government.

## FREE ACCESS TO THE AMERICAN MARKET

In my book *Take This Job and Ship It*, I document in great detail the way the tax code rewards companies for taking jobs overseas. That loophole still exists, but finally there is hope that it will be closed. During his presidential campaign Senator Obama said over and over he would work to close this nutty loophole. So I think there is help on the way.

What is the attraction of moving a company offshore? Of course, there is the cheap labor, which insidiously pits American workers against third-world workers forced to work in often-dangerous conditions. But there is also an attraction in our tax code that tells a company that if you move your company and your jobs overseas and ship your product back to be sold in the United States, you will pay less in taxes to the United States. Said another way, "we will give you a tax break if you move overseas." I think that is nuts. I've tried four times to abolish that perverse tax break and lost the vote four times in the Senate. Those companies that ship their jobs overseas must be forgetting that unemployed workers don't shop and they can't pay taxes. Progress, these companies call it. I don't think so. This is a tax break that has to be abolished.

We have to make domestic tax policies with one eye on the rest of the globe.

There is a worldwide trend to lower corporate taxes to attract business. That is the reality in which we live. I don't want taxes to be any higher than they have to be for corporations or citizens, but almost a *third* of our biggest, most profitable corporations paid no federal income tax between 2001 and 2003. And according to one 2004 study by Citizens for Tax Justice, these companies still received billions of dollars in tax rebates!

## A VALUE-ADDED TAX

I'm not ready to give up on the income tax, but I am finally ready to consider something that most other industrial companies now use as a substitute for a portion of both the corporate and the individual income tax. I think it is time to consider some form of a value-added tax.

If so many corporations (and some creative individuals) are now able to avoid paying the income tax, it's time to consider an alternative.

And there is another compelling reason as well. When other countries use a value-added tax and we don't, we are put at a disadvantage in international trade.

The value-added tax has some advantages. It can be eliminated as the product is exported, thereby making a country's products more competitive in international trade. Other countries have been successfully using a value-added tax system for many years. They impose the tax on the various stages of value added during the production of a product. So, the tax is passed along in the product price. But when the product is exported, the tax is removed. When products are imported from countries that impose a value-added tax, a tax equivalent to the value-added tax is imposed as the products are imported into our country.

I understand the value-added tax can be complicated, but other countries have used it for years and found it to be a successful way to raise revenue for the government while eliminating loopholes.

The case is made by some that the United States has one of the highest corporate tax rates in the world. It is true that what is called the statutory rate (the rate spelled out in law) is high. But that ignores the reality. Corporations don't pay the statutory rate. They use loopholes and special tax breaks to reduce their tax burden. As a result, the "effective tax rate" (the rate that the companies actually pay) is near the lowest of all of the OECD (Organisation for Economic Co-operation and Development) countries.

But, as I pointed out earlier, the corporate tax system has become such a punchboard of gimmicks that it allows some to make billions and completely escape any tax obligation. I think it's time to admit this isn't working and that we need to find a better way.

It's time for our country to think seriously about reforming the entire tax system, and I am ready to consider an alternative to the corporate income tax system, which is broken beyond repair.

## WHAT ABOUT THE REST OF US?

As we put our economy back on track, it's a good time to consider overhauling our tax system. People have lost confidence in it . . . and for good reason.

If we can eliminate the loopholes and simplify the rules, we may find that we can have a lower tax rate as well as a simpler and fairer tax system.

So, let's start over and create a tax system that requires everyone and every profit-making enterprise to support the country that has allowed them to prosper in the greatest marketplace in the world. It has been twenty years since the last major reform of our tax system. It is time now to tip it upside down, shake it, and make it fair and make it work for all Americans.

# CHAPTER 6

• • •

## Incomes from Outer Space

As a new President and Congress try to evaluate what went wrong with the economy and how to fix it, one of the pieces of the puzzle is finding a way to deal with what I call incomes from outer space.

It used to be that in our country and in our economy there was some sort of relationship between effort and reward that was reflected in income. Increasingly that isn't always true anymore. An example of that is CEO pay in America's publicly traded corporations. In 1980 the average CEO earned about forty times the salary of the average worker. Today CEO pay has grown to over four hundred times the salary of the average worker. But even at that, the CEO salary looks small compared to money earned by those running a hedge fund or a private equity firm, for example.

If you're having trouble making ends meet or maybe you don't have the money to pay your monthly bills, then you need to consider going to work for a hedge fund.

With all of the eye-popping incomes we hear about in the stratosphere of the wealthy, none has competed with the hedge fund managers. (The financial crisis that will bring down a lot of hedge funds will probably mean the end of the income party for some, but it is useful to review the splendor of their earnings leading up to the financial trouble.)

According to Institutional Investor's *Alpha* magazine, which prints the compensation of the top hedge fund managers, there were some whoppers in 2007.

Take John Paulson, for example. You might not know him, but he was the champ of the hedge fund group in 2007. He made an income of $3.7 billion—about the gross domestic product (GDP) of Tibet. It works out to just a bit more than $300 million a month. Can you imagine his wife inquiring about how he's doing? "About ten million dollars a day, sweetie."

To put it in terms we can understand, he made about $100,000 every six minutes in the workday (I'm figuring a ten-hour day, because he's probably no slacker). That means he makes more money in *four minutes* than the average American worker does in a year.

Gregory Zuckerman, in reporting on John Paulson's income for *The Wall Street Journal*, said he "bet big on [the] drop in housing values" and ran up $15 billion in profits for his hedge funds for 2007. So, betting on the drop in housing values makes him the five-hundred-pound gorilla of the hedge fund income earners. When I view this in the context of the unprecedented carnage wrought by the housing crash in 2008, it's hard for me to see Paulson as any kind of hero or visionary.

For an economy to thrive, everyone has to thrive. It is incredibly simple, but given the opportunity—through lack of oversight and regulation—greed grows like dandelions in the spring. Greed means someone at the table is getting a much bigger slice of the pie without justification. That's just asking for trouble.

Beyond the hedge fund managers, how did other Americans fare in the mortgage meltdown of 2008? What about the investors who unknowingly held overrated bundled mortgages? How about the families who lost homes and the many others who watched their home's equity and their net worth shrink as the market collapsed? They found trouble in every direction, and they were the very same taxpayers who were called upon to provide the money for the bailout to shore up the market.

For the economy to function well, there has to be a free flow of capital. Loans are taken out against equity, but when home owners no longer have equity they cannot borrow and they cannot spend. The economy grinds to a screeching halt. A lack of transparency in the market causes uncertainty, because no one knows how much bad debt is out there. It is the dark money I described in the previous chapter. Unknowns shake the confidence of lenders and borrowers alike.

So the earthquake shake-up of the mortgage market in 2008 and the aftershocks serve as a cautionary tale. Oversight is necessary. Regulation is necessary. Capitalism in its purest form, completely unregulated, is like a race car with no brakes. When you come to a curve in the road there is going to be a crash. It's all well and good to have a fast car. A steering wheel is a good idea, too. Unfortunately, history will record that in recent years no one was steering the U.S. economy.

In a touch of irony, the *Journal* reported that John Paulson has hired former Federal Reserve Board Chairman Alan Greenspan as an advisor. Yes, the same Greenspan whose policies helped provide the helium for the housing bubble and was at first content to be a spectator as the subprime scam was occurring. And later he was just plain derelict in his duty to police the schemes that were developing in the subprime industry. So now he's an advisor to the guy who made money betting on bad news. Somehow, nothing seems surprising these days in the wacky world of high finance.

Don't get me wrong, there are some creative and valuable people who live and work in high finance and who run America's corporations. And many of them are worth their weight in gold. They deserve substantial compensation when they create wealth, run successful businesses, and expand our economy.

But what is happening today in the world of executive compensation, in many instances, is way out of line. Some of the incomes are farcical.

But back to the top of the list of oversized incomes.

George Soros and James Simons each made about $3 billion in

2007. If you're still calculating with me, that's about $250 million a month. Simons, who owns 40 percent of Renaissance Technologies corporation, is slipping a bit. He increased his yearly income from 2006 to 2007 by $1.4 billion and yet dropped from first on the earnings list. He increased his monthly take from $140 million to $250 million and *dropped* to third place on the income ladder. It's a dog-eat-dog world.

In 2006 Kenneth Griffin of Citadel Investment came in at the runner-up position with a paltry income of $1.4 billion. Don't expect any bake sales or lemonade stands in his yard anytime soon. He gained ground in 2007 with compensation of $1.5 billion—a meager $125 million a month. No living paycheck to paycheck for him. As of 2007 his estimated wealth was $3 billion, according to *Forbes*. In 2006 the top twenty-five hedge fund managers "earned" $14 billion—that means that those twenty-five people earned more than any of the ninety countries at the bottom of the World Bank list of countries by GDP.

One of the consistent top earners is George Soros, well known for being a supporter of Democratic Party causes and raising the ire of the right-wing talk-show crowd. But he is obviously paying attention to things other than politics if he is making $3 billion a year.

There is a lot we don't know about these things called hedge funds, because they are unregulated and shrouded in secrecy. But what we do know is that many of the people who run them were making obscene amounts of money before the collapse. Is any one person really worth several billion dollars a year?

At a time when there are startling disclosures about the people at the top of the economic ladder running away with most of the money, the amount of money grabbed by some of the hedge fund managers is setting a new low bar for greed.

In 2007 the median American family income was $60,500 a year. John Paulson makes more than that in just over four minutes. The *New York Times* story on this issue, by Jenny Anderson (April 16, 2008), quoted William H. Gross, the chief investment officer of the

PIMCO bond fund, as saying, "There's nothing wrong with it. . . . It's not illegal. But it's ugly."

I second that last part. Invariably, massive concentrations of power and wealth subvert the economy and, ultimately, democracy itself.

The same *Times* story reported that the top twenty-five hedge fund managers had to make $360 million in order to make the list last year. That is eighteen times higher than the amount that was required to make the list just five years before. Not double, triple, or even quadruple. Eighteen times! That's what I call moving the bar in a hurry.

The *Alpha* magazine survey reported that the top twenty-five hedge fund managers each earned an average of over $800 million in 2007. That compares to $570 million each in 2006 and only $362 million in 2005. All of this at a time when the average working family was losing ground each year.

While hedge funds have been around for a good many years, they have taken on new life in recent years and have been central to the creation and trading of sophisticated new securities and derivatives. The trading in derivatives has become big business with new and complex trades of securities that derive their value from other prices of products. The private equity firms have also been having an income field day. The hedge funds, derivative trading, and private equity firms have created a type of worldwide economic casino with more and more wealthy participants interested in placing their bets.

Most of the activity in hedge funds, derivatives, and private equity firms involves increasingly complicated financial transactions that are out of public view and largely unregulated. Many of these transactions are so complicated, even the participants have difficulty explaining them. The players in this speculation are limited to a relative few who have built massive wealth. And as the data shows, the income being collected at the top of these mountains of speculative investment is piling on top of already large fortunes for those who participate.

Private equity firms are also a relatively new entry in the financial sweepstakes. The people involved in this business accumulate their wealth by buying public companies, taking them private, and making bundles of money by breaking them up and reselling. In some cases, the private equity firms are doing investors a service. Big corporations can become large, bloated organizations that are inefficient and waste money. And the threat of being bought by a private equity firm and taken private has forced companies to shape up.

But there are many other cases where the motive of the private equity firm has to do only with their own self-interest, which sometimes runs opposite to the interest of a business investing for the long term or opposite to the public interest. But, whatever the motives, it is creating another class of the superwealthy in America.

## BIG INCOME, SMALL TAX BILL

Notable among the new wealthy investors is Steve Schwartzman, the man who, with another billionaire, Pete Peterson, founded the Blackstone private equity firm. Schwartzman drew some attention a while back by throwing himself a sixtieth birthday party.

Schwartzman, with an estimated net worth of $7.3 billion, was reported by *The New York Times* to have spent over $5 million on his birthday party. It was held in his large Park Avenue apartment (reported to be a thirty-five-room, $40 million dwelling) and included performances by Rod Stewart and Patti LaBelle.

The interesting thing about all of this wealth is that Mr. Schwartzman's income (and the income of many others doing what he does for a living) is taxed at only a 15 percent income tax rate. The reason for that is our old friend "carried income," which gives him the ability to pay the same tax rate as the capital gains rate. But it is not just Mr. Schwartzman who enjoys paying a low, 15 percent income tax rate. Many of his colleagues in both hedge funds and private equity firms are privileged to pay some of the lowest tax rates in the country. I've described that in greater detail in the chapter about the tax system and how the big interests avoid paying their share.

Henry Kravis is one of the most successful at buying companies and taking them apart. Kravis once said, "Once you buy a company, you are married. You are married to that company." If that is the case, why does he always end up with most of the assets when the marriage is over? Apparently there is no community property in that industry.

Let me be quick to make the obligatory disclaimer that there are many people in the hedge fund industry and the private equity firms who earn salaries that are not huge and whose work contributes in a positive way to our economy. But still, the money at the top gets and deserves attention in describing what is happening in this economy to the people at the top and the people at the bottom.

It's worth noting while describing the stratospheric incomes for some in 2007, that according to Jared Bernstein at the Economic Policy Institute, "Since 1913, the United States witnessed only one other year of such unequal wealth distribution—1928, the year before the stock market crashed" (as quoted by Jenny Anderson in *The New York Times*).

It's no coincidence that we have experienced the economic trials we have. When incomes get so out of balance, it is a sign that ambition has been sublimated by greed. In our capitalistic free-market system, we encourage and want each person to be able to do what is in his own best interest. We celebrate success, and we should. But we also should want to see that a fair reward for work goes to the working families, the small businesses, and others who make up the middle class. Expanding opportunities for the middle class is what has distinguished our country from many others. It has made us stronger and more prosperous.

## CORPORATE GENEROSITY

Salaries at the top of major corporations in America are also turning heads. I know some outstanding CEOs who are worth every penny. But in recent years the staggering amount of money paid to some CEOs seems almost completely disconnected with performance. In the past, in our market system, there was always expected to be a

relationship between performance and reward with corporate executives. The harder you work, the better you perform and the
more income you make. It is a pretty simple calculation.

But that is changing.

CEO pay in the past five years has grown at an unprecedented
rate. In 1980 the average CEO was making about forty times the
earnings of the average worker. CEO income has grown tenfold in
the past several decades. Read this slowly: *the CEOs are now making
over four hundred times the income of the average worker in the corporation.*
That's unbelievable. Had the minimum wage advanced at the same
rate, it would be somewhere north of $22 an hour. The average
CEO is making in one day what the average worker earns in an entire year.

According to *Forbes* magazine's annual report on CEO compensation, in 2006 the CEOs of the five hundred biggest corporations
averaged $15.2 million in total annual earnings. That was up nearly
10 percent from the year before. Again according to *Forbes*, the top
eight CEOs each received more than $100 million.

The CEOs were not only being paid well, but their severance
packages when they left their jobs were skyrocketing, too. According to the Executive PayWatch Database, the average severance pay
for CEOs with employment contracts was 170 weeks of severance
pay for each year on the job. Compare that with two weeks of pay for
each year worked, which is the average severance pay received by
workers—if they are lucky enough to get severance pay at all. Sometimes it's just a pink slip and a boot out the door.

Growing up, we are taught that there is, or at least there should
be, a logical connection between effort and reward. Work hard in
school and get good grades. Work hard on your job and earn a promotion and a pay raise. But in recent years, we've seen that the rule
of thumb about effort and reward might not apply to people in corporate executive suites.

Even as most folks are now trying to make ends meet and stretch
their paychecks from month to month, the CEOs of some of America's major corporations are padding theirs. And as workers are

learning that their pension programs are being reduced or eliminated, they read about nearly unbelievable pension arrangements for
the people at the top of the corporate pyramid.

In 2005 Exxon gave Lee Raymond one of the shiniest golden para-
chutes ever—nearly $400 million, including pension, stock options,
a consulting deal, and other perks such as use of a corporate jet.

Consider the disclosure of the executive perks given Jack Welch,
the former CEO of General Electric. It's true that he led what had
been an appliance company to become a worldwide corporate power-
house. But when he retired he was more than handsomely rewarded
for those accomplishments. When his lavish retirement perks were
disclosed in a divorce proceeding, it caused him so much embarrassment that he would surrender most of the perks because they could
be "misportrayed."

You think? How could one "misportray" a life of free flowers,
free use of an $11 million Manhattan apartment, a wine budget, a
cook, sports and opera tickets, free dry cleaning, twenty-four-hour
jet airplane and helicopter service, and a car and driver? What? No
masseuse?

So Welch and GE negotiated a new deal. And according to published reports, he will end up with a $9 million annual pension and
he will pay to clean his own suits and pay for his own flowers and he
will still have the use of the corporate jet and the apartment, but he
will have to pay for it out of his $9 million pension.

The real owners of General Electric (the stockholders) were un-
aware of how their money was being spent. If it hadn't been for his
divorce proceeding in which Mr. Welch's ex-wife disclosed these
lavish perks, we would never have known. Nor would the Securities
and Exchange Commission. But it was an instructive window into
the retirement packages offered to some of those who run major
American corporations.

The SEC took some action against GE for failing to disclose the
perks, but even the SEC likely wouldn't have known except by
chance. According to an article written for the Minneapolis Fed
by Ronald Wirtz, "such pay is 'stealth compensation,' because it is

rarely disclosed, or obscurely so when required, and so flies under the radar of investors, the public, even boards themselves."

## IF IT'S ALL LEGIT, WHY ARE THEY TRYING TO HIDE THEIR ACTIONS?

So don't misunderstand my position, here. What I am saying is simply that all of this needs to be aboveboard. The fact that some of these companies are trying to hide ostentatious compensation packages tells you it's wrong and they know it's wrong.

When executives succeed and the business grows and the stockholders benefit, I understand the need and justification for generous compensation. I know some CEOs who do an outstanding job and deserve substantial compensation. But even those CEOs will tell you in private that executive compensation has gotten out of hand.

To its credit, the SEC finally took some steps in 2006 to keep stockholders better informed. According to Equilar, an independent provider of executive and board compensation information, "The SEC indicated that its new disclosure requirements would significantly alter the format of executive and director compensation disclosure in annual proxy filings, and that the goal of the new regulations will be improved and comprehensive disclosure of executive compensation, related party transactions, director independence and corporate governance information in 'plain-English.'" The SEC also promised improved disclosure of severance packages.

That's all well and good. I hope it translates into more than lip service.

## BEING PAID WELL FOR FAILING

These days you don't have to be a successful or a retired CEO to rake in the big bucks. You can actually be paid some big money for failing. Take the case of Richard Grasso. He was fired by the New

York Stock Exchange. It turns out he had a pay package that allowed him to earn $193 million for eight years of work. When he was fired he claimed another $140 million in contract severance pay. You have to admit, America is the land of opportunity. Where else other than Wall Street can a man make millions by getting fired? As it turns out, it happens all the time.

Hewlett-Packard decided to get rid of CEO Carly Fiorina and it was reported that she walked out with $46 million. You may remember Fiorina—she provided some comic relief during the 2008 presidential campaign when, speaking as a supporter of John McCain, she declared he wasn't competent to run Hewlett-Packard. Then, stuffing her Manolo Blahniks deeper down her throat, she added that neither was Sarah Palin, Barack Obama, or Joe Biden—her premise being that it's tougher leading Hewlett-Packard than being the leader of the free world. This from a fired CEO! Well, never mind.

Home Depot's Robert Nardelli was booted out of that company and left with a parting compensation of $210 million. Despite the fact that he was pushed out by the Board of Directors, Nardelli was to receive a reported settlement of cash and stock worth $210 million, coupled with a $20 million severance payment and retirement benefits of $32 million. All of that for *not* doing the job that the Board of Directors evidently expected of him.

After Pfizer dumped Hank McKinnell, he got a send-off worth a reported $200 million. In his and Nardelli's case, they were fired because the Boards of Directors were concerned about the companies' poor performances but the CEOs still were handsomely rewarded. Let's hope that the business school students in college aren't looking at these rewards and aspiring to become failed CEOs.

Ford Motor Company lost $12.6 billion in 2006 and then hired a new CEO, Alan Mulally, for a pay package of $39 million. But, so that there were no hard feelings, Ford paid $10.5 million to the former CEO, Bill Ford. That will soothe the hurt in the executive suite. But should the stockholders really be pleased with that?

In 2006, according to an analysis performed by the Associated

Press after culling through annual reports of publicly traded companies, compensation for CEOs was continuing to skyrocket, with some 386 of the 500 CEOs of the Standard & Poor's 500 receiving a combined $4.16 billion and more than half of the executives earning more than $8.3 million for the year. Some of them had incomes that rang the bell for excess according to the study.

Terry Semel, Yahoo CEO: $71 million
Bob Simpson, XTO Energy: $59 million
Ray R. Irani, Occidental Petroleum: $52 million
E. Stanley O'Neal, Merrill Lynch: $46 million
H. Lawrence Culp, Danaher Corporation: $46 million
Angelo Mozilo, Countrywide Financial: $43 million
Alan Mulally, Ford Motor: $39 million
Edward Whitacre, AT&T: $31 million

"About half of American industry has grossly unfair compensation systems where the top executives are paid too much," said Charlie Munger, Warren Buffett's partner at Berkshire Hathaway, according to Rik Kirkland writing for *Fortune* magazine.

I'm sure you could make a case that some of those salaries are justified. But there will be other cases where there seems to be no relationship between actual performance and pay. In the case of our well-heeled friend from the oil business, Lee Raymond, his supporters justified his golden parachute because Exxon had done extraordinarily well. But then, all oil companies did when oil prices started their run-up.

According to the previously quoted *Fedgazette* article, Harvard economist Lucian Bebchuk suggests an alternate reality when measuring performance—"that performance benchmarks use indexed options that compare a company's stock price appreciation to a basket of competitors, and offer compensation to the degree that the company beats the competition in stock price appreciation and is the result of firm-specific performance. . . . The idea has reportedly been slowly winning some board converts."

The lowest-paid major CEO was Costco's James Sinegal, who earned $411,000. But he owns an estimated 2.4 million shares of Costco, which would be worth over a billion dollars, so don't pass the hat just yet; he's doing just fine. Unlike some other corporate leaders, however, Sinegal spends a lot of his time working on ways to make sure his employees benefit from the company's success. He's a leader.

While there are rising concerns in Europe about CEO pay, European CEOs still lag behind American captains of industry. According to Jeanne Sahadi's 2007 CNNMoney.com story, "The top 20 CEOs of U.S. companies made an average of $36.4 million in 2006. That's 204 times that of the 20 highest-paid U.S. military generals, and 38 times that of the 20 highest-paid nonprofit leaders. They also made three times more than the top 20 CEOs of European companies who had booked higher sales numbers than their U.S. counterparts."

## HOW SHOULD CEOS BE PAID?

I know some outstanding corporate CEOs. They commit themselves to their company, work hard, long hours, and are worth a great deal to the corporations that employ them. I don't suggest that these CEOs shouldn't be compensated very well. They are integral to the success of some very large corporations, and they are worth a great deal to the companies they lead. But when we hear of these stratospheric salaries, it is reasonable to expect that there would be some connection to performance. Unfortunately, that is not always the case these days.

Common sense and old-fashioned business ethics tell us a CEO salary should reflect performance not only for stockholders but for employees, too.

Stockholders have a hard time reconciling a CEO pay raise while the stock is in the toilet. In a perfect world, company boards would begin reining in these salaries based on a formula with some semblance to reality. Failing to do so, because these are publicly traded companies, they run the real risk of intervention from Washington.

Certainly, outrageous salaries adversely affect stockholders and employees, so new rules governing salaries should not be off the table. I am specifically speaking about publicly traded entities and not private companies. If corporations want the advantages of being publicly traded, responsible, commonsense behavior shouldn't be too much to ask. Honesty and ethics are not too high a price to pay to be granted admittance to the greatest market on earth. Any company with government contracts should also have to abide by fair rules of compensation.

A rather remarkable result of the recent financial crisis was watching governments buy stock in financial institutions to increase liquidity. The logic was that it was the quickest way to stabilize these institutions and buck up confidence and get them lending to one another. However, governments also became stockholders in these businesses with a voice that could have been capable of addressing things like CEO compensation. But it turns out the proposal was for nonvoting preferred stock. So no dice!

It is ironic that lack of oversight in the interest of less regulation has led to actual government *intervention*. No one wants that. The best option is honest oversight and regulation.

So, what's the magic number for a CEO in a given company? There's no one-size-fits-all answer. But I believe it should be performance based. There should be some reasonable multiple of the salaries of the average worker in the corporation as a starting point for a base salary. (And four hundred times is not a starting point. . . . It is absurd.) And beyond that base salary, there should be some form of performance-based pay.

There is significant concern about stock or stock options being offered as part of the compensation package. As it relates to the company's success, I don't have a problem with that, but when stocks become the dominant financial factor in CEO compensation, it can lead to trouble. The CEO becomes an insider trader, and too much stock equals too much power and too much temptation. A reasonable base salary combined with stocks ought to motivate a CEO to perform.

And when a CEO starts dumping shares, it should be reported immediately—within the hour. The SEC now allows a two-day lag. Great. That's just what the pros need, a two-day head start on the average investor. If a CEO has lost confidence in his company or thinks the stock has peaked, everyone ought to know immediately.

If the private sector won't take action to correct this area, Congress should.

The Institute for Policy Studies (*Executive Excess 2007* report by Sarah Anderson et al.) suggests the following remedies should be considered:

ELIMINATE THE TAX REPORTING LOOPHOLE ON CEO STOCK OPTIONS. Corporations are currently allowed to report one set of executive stock option compensation figures as expenses on their financial statements and a completely different set of figures—often a much larger amount—on their tax returns. Proposed legislation in Congress would require corporations to disclose the same information about executive stock options to the IRS as they do to their shareholders.

LINK GOVERNMENT PROCUREMENT TO EXECUTIVE PAY. Federal law already limits the amount of pay that a company with a government contract can bill the government for executive compensation. But corporations whose stock soars after gaining a federal contract can pay executives whatever they please. The federal government could limit these windfalls.

MAKE SURE HEDGE FUND AND INVESTMENT FUND EXECUTIVES PAY THEIR FAIR SHARE OF TAXES. Top partners in America's private equity and hedge fund industry currently pay taxes on most of their multi-million-dollar incomes at less than half the 35 percent tax rate in effect on ordinary income. President Obama has now proposed eliminating the carried-interest loophole, and I think chances of finally getting this done are much improved.

Any economy depends greatly on emotion—confidence. If average American investors do not have confidence in the companies on Wall Street, their CEOs, and the fairness of the system, they will pull out.

As Rik Kirkland wrote in a probusiness *Fortune* article, "What's at stake, in short, is nothing less than the public trust essential to a thriving free-market economy."

When people of power yield to the temptation of greed and abuse their positions to consolidate and accumulate more wealth, the result is an economic aristocracy. Remember, we are a young country. One need only look across the pond to Great Britain to see that social stratification is very real even today, having had centuries to grab a foothold.

I am not against generously rewarding performance. But I firmly believe that when it comes to publicly traded companies and those funds that invest in them, it is entirely fitting to have oversight over executive compensation, because what goes into their pockets comes out of the pockets of shareholders. If a company wants to take advantage of the capitalization and opportunity for growth that come with being publicly traded, we should not be shy about making sure the owners of the company (the investors) are treated honestly. And making sure that fund managers don't have their hand too deep in the cookie jar is just common sense. Our economy will do much better if there is a sense of trust that the game isn't rigged.

The reason so many people want to come to America is because they see our country as the best opportunity for a fair shot at success. That tells us that despite our flaws, we remain the best hope for individual and economic fairness and freedom. People still see America as a meritocracy, where advancement though merit is still possible.

Expanding inequality eats at the foundation of what our country is about. Our country has been seen as the place where everyone has an opportunity to do well. It is supposed to be a place where effort is connected to reward.

This means an eternal struggle for the proper balance. So the pendulum will probably always be swinging in one direction or another. It is clear that the pendulum has swung too far to the right and the rush to privatization and deregulation and oversized salaries and compensation with no oversight stands to create such great inequities that it will, if left unchecked, change our country in a manner that undermines much of what we have aspired to achieve.

It's akin to the credo of the old wagon trains that crossed the Plains on their journey westward. These pioneers believed that you can't move ahead by leaving some behind. It's a reasonable credo for our country as well.

It is also understood that we live in an ever more competitive world and as our corporations compete internationally, we would be well advised to put the fundamentals in order. And yes, that includes dealing with the issues of compensation at the top, which has become disconnected from reality.

As a final note, I prefer that the private sector deal with this issue. But if it will not, the public sector has a role in setting fair rules for publicly traded companies.

And one more thing! I admire success and salute those at the top of our large institutions. Most of them sacrifice much and work hard, long hours. But even most of them will admit the compensation programs are out of balance and need to be brought back to some reality.

It is likely that the economic crisis of 2008 will increase the pressure for these changes to occur.

# CHAPTER 7

. . .

# *The Price of War*

THE QUESTION OF whether the Iraq war was a major blunder or a necessary step in the fight against terrorism will be debated for decades. That debate will be about the issues of sacrifice, morality, and security.

But another major issue of the Iraq war is what it has done to the American economy. How long will we suffer the effects of fighting a war without paying for it? How much did the President's decision to fight the war without paying for it contribute to the current economic crisis? And when will we learn the full story of the waste, fraud, and abuse that attended the fighting of that war?

More about that in chapter 8, but first some straight talk about how our country marched into the Iraq war.

## THE ATTACK ON SEPTEMBER 11, 2001

On September 11, 2001, at 9:00 A.M. I was in the U.S. Capitol Building attending the usual Tuesday morning Democratic leadership meeting with Senator Tom Daschle and about eight other

Senators. As we started the meeting, the television in the room was showing images of a fire at one of the World Trade Center buildings. The live news reports were describing it as the result of a possible collision by a small plane that had gone off course.

Within minutes we saw the horrifying image of a large commercial airline jet flying into the second World Trade Center building. Later, as we were absorbing the shock of what we were seeing and what it meant, we saw from the window of our meeting room on the west front of the Capitol billowing clouds of smoke coming from the Pentagon, which we later learned was caused by a commercial airliner crashing into it.

We were trying to comprehend the full dimension of what was happening when the door burst open and several security personnel rushed into the room shouting that there was an incoming airplane targeting the Capitol Building and we had to leave immediately.

As we quickly evacuated the Capitol, we gathered on the east front lawn in the bright morning sunshine. Up in the blue sky overhead we saw and heard F-16 Air National Guard fighter jets from Langley Air Force Base scrambling to provide air cover over our nation's capital during what we then knew was some kind of an attack against our country. It was a surreal moment. (I learned later that the Air National Guard F-16s flying air cover over the Capitol that morning from Langley Air Force Base were planes attached to the Happy Hooligans, the Air National Guard unit from Fargo, North Dakota, and piloted by North Dakota pilots.)

During the following hours and days we learned that the attack, which killed nearly three thousand innocent people, was engineered by an international terrorist organization called Al Qaeda, headed by a man named Osama bin Laden.

I knew immediately, even as we began to understand the shock of that day, and even as we mourned the deaths of innocent Americans, our country would not allow this to stand. We would hunt down those responsible and bring them to justice. There would be no place on earth for them to hide.

In an address to a joint session of Congress, President Bush pledged that we would bring to justice those who had done this despicable act. Later, in a bit of Texas talk, he referred to getting them "dead or alive."

I couldn't have known how wrong I was to think that this was going to be our top priority.

We now know as a result of subsequent investigations that President Bush had different plans. Despite his address to Congress and the American people stating that we would bring to justice those who had attacked our country, the President was asking his staff to connect the 9/11 attack to Iraq and asking the military to prepare plans for an invasion of that country.

President Bush was determined to go to war with Iraq. And nearly eight years later, many of those who boasted of killing the Americans on 9/11 are still free and, according to our intelligence services, planning additional terrorist attacks.

Years later the American people wait and wonder why: Why is the man who masterminded the attack against our country still out there planning more attacks? And why did President Bush take us to war with Iraq instead of finishing the job of destroying the terrorist group that attacked our country?

We may never fully know all of the answers to those questions, but the actions of our government over the past years have unfortunately led to an unhealthy distrust and cynicism about our government that may take decades to dispel. Much of it can be traced to the events leading up to and during the conduct of the war in Iraq.

Underlining the distrust is the fact that Americans now know much of the justification for the preemptive war itself was based on false information.

History will decide whether the misinformation given Congress and the American people prior to the invasion of Iraq was the result of a deliberate effort to manipulate intelligence information or just the result of staggering incompetence. Whatever the case, I believe it has led to one of the great intelligence failures in our country's history.

In addition to the tragic loss of lives of our soldiers and the deaths of so many citizens in Iraq, the Iraq war further undermined the confidence people had in their government as they read about the incompetence in the planning for the war and scandal after scandal in the contracting and profiteering that accompanied the war.

The American people have been witness to an almost unbelievable orgy of greed and fraud in the contracting in the Iraq war. I believe it represents the greatest waste and fraud and abuse in our country's history.

The war in Iraq has resulted in the deaths of over four thousand American soldiers and the injury of tens of thousands more who were doing their jobs because their country asked them to. They are truly heroes who, in the tradition of our country over two centuries, left their families when called and traveled across the world to face danger.

It wasn't the soldiers who let our country down. It was our leaders who developed a failed strategy.

In addition to the tragic loss of lives and large number of war injuries, the war has drained the treasury. A new book by Nobel Prize winner Joseph Stiglitz estimates that when it is totaled up, the conflict will have cost our country $3 trillion—it's right in the title, *The Three Trillion Dollar War.* The $10 billion a month spent in Iraq has had a crippling effect on our country. As history has taught time and time again—most recently with the Soviet Union and Afghanistan—the economy of a country is its lifeblood. Suck the money out of a country and you sap its power domestically and globally.

Finally, the war in Iraq caused very serious breaches in our relationships with other countries around the world. Most of the goodwill and support that other nations had for our country after the attack on 9/11 was squandered. People from around the world grew puzzled and then angry by our inexplicable foray into Iraq.

Meanwhile in America, as we have aggressively debated the war in recent years, there has been something very troubling about the debate. It's been a type of almost sanitary, white-glove discussion with a real disconnect from the horrors of war. Except for the soldiers and the families whose loved ones are a part of the volunteer army and have been deployed in a war halfway around the world, most of the American people have not been disadvantaged or inconvenienced. For most the war has been a television event.

## THE BUSINESS OF WAR

War is big business. Early in 2008, according to the Congressional Budget Office, the number of people employed by private contractors in the Iraq theater was about 190,000, compared to 146,000 American soldiers—an astonishing ratio. In addition to the deaths of our soldiers, by April 2008 more than one thousand civilian contractors had also been killed in Iraq.

By contracting with corporations to do what the U.S. military used to do in a much more cost-effective manner, the government can make the war appear to be much smaller than it is. So, thanks to this contracting, combined with stop-loss programs that entrap soldiers in an extended cycle of service, the administration was able to avoid confronting the American people with a military draft.

Some patriotic Americans in an uncertain job market saw a way to provide for their struggling families while (they believed) helping to rebuild Iraq. So they signed up with Halliburton and KBR and other war contractors. But back home no one except the soldiers and their families has been much disadvantaged by the war.

The Bush administration didn't have the courage to ask the American people to sacrifice financially for this war of choice, so they placed the load on the military and forwarded the bill to the next generation of Americans. We are borrowing much of the money to fight this war from China and Japan (the countries that hold massive amounts of U.S. debt securities). The American people were not asked to pay for the war, and the President insisted that all of the money for the war be "emergency funding," which means that it

was added right to the federal debt. And he threatened to veto legislation that would raise taxes to pay for the war.

It is unheard of to push for tax breaks during wartime. Yet that is
exactly what the Bush/Cheney administration did. They not only
decided to fight the war by putting the bills on a charge card; they
also pushed tax breaks for the wealthiest Americans at the same
time. And they fought hard against efforts to roll back those tax cuts
and use the money to pay for the war. The war cost the U.S. nearly
three-fourths of a trillion dollars in the first five years, and *all* of it
was borrowed.

And it wasn't just the money. Our factories were not put on a
war footing to produce the equipment the soldiers needed when
they needed it, and many soldiers were sent to fight without the
proper equipment. There wasn't enough body armor. The vehicles
many of the soldiers were using were not armored to protect them
from the low-tech improvised explosive devises (IEDs) used by the
enemy in Iraq.

I received e-mails from National Guard soldiers serving in Iraq in
the early years of the war with pictures of the Humvees and trucks
that, they complained, were not armored to protect them against the
IEDs. They told me about having to scavenge from junk piles to find
scraps of metal that they could attach to their vehicles to try to give
them some armor that would protect them while on patrol.

I, along with many others in Congress, continually told the Defense Department of the troops complaining about the lack of both
body armor and armored vehicles, but the Pentagon officials were slow
to respond because they had gone to war without proper planning.

The administration had made a calculation that the war would
be over in a flash and that our soldiers would be welcomed as "lib-
erators," as Vice President Cheney put it. The result was that virtually no planning was done to provide security or order following
the invasion. And no evident planning was done on how to deal
with an insurgency. That lack of foresight was staggering.

Meanwhile our soldiers told me that many of those employed by

Blackwater and other contractors had the best gear available. Soldiers fearing the next IED said they watched in envy as some Blackwater employees motored by in state-of-the-art armored vehicles unavailable for our GIs. How is it that we could pay contractors enough to properly outfit their employees but did not do the same for Uncle Sam's finest?

It was different in World War II, when our entire country went to war. Everyone was called upon to pitch in. There was rationing of gasoline and tires and more. Our manufacturing plants were working three shifts a day, aided by Rosie the Riveter, who left home to go to the factory and do her part for the war. There was unity and a sense of purpose. It was a different time, with different leadership.

Contrast the words of President Bush, who told Americans they would be supporting the war by going shopping (thereby strengthening the economy), with those of FDR, who said in one of his fireside chats:

> Not all of us can have the privilege of fighting our enemies in distant parts of the world. Not all of us can have the privilege of working in a munitions factory or a shipyard, or on the farms or in the oil fields or mines, producing the weapons or raw materials that are needed by our armed forces. But there is one front and one battle where everyone in the United States—every man, woman and child—is in action. . . . That front is right here at home, in our daily lives, and in our daily tasks. Here at home, everyone will have the privilege of making whatever self-denial is necessary, not only to supply our fighting men, but to keep the economic structure of our country fortified and secure.

I know this is a tough assessment of the last administration, but facts are stubborn things. To me this isn't about politics. It's about protecting our country, and I think this administration let us down. Congress did, too. More about that later in this chapter.

# COLIN POWELL'S UN SPEECH

The American people and Congress initially supported the war in Iraq. In the shadow of the 9/11 attacks and armed with the information given them by the Bush administration, the overwhelming majority of the American people thought going to war was the right thing to do.

When Secretary of State Colin Powell went to the United Nations and lent his credibility to the Bush administration's case for attacking Iraq, the American public was convinced and so was Congress.

Colin Powell had a unique credibility. He was a soldier who knew war. A former four-star general who had been chairman of the Joint Chiefs of Staff, he was well known to be skeptical of a preemptive attack on Iraq.

When he finally spoke to the United Nations and the world, citing specific and persuasive evidence about the ominous threat Saddam Hussein posed to the United States, Powell gave a seal of approval to the evidence of the threat that virtually no one else in the administration could have given. It was the support that President Bush and Vice President Cheney had been requesting from him. And the details he provided of that threat convinced Congress and the American people that this war was a course that was necessary to protect the United States.

Here are some excerpts from Secretary Powell's address.

### BIOLOGICAL WEAPONS

- "We have firsthand descriptions of biological weapons factories on wheels and on rails."
- "Confirmation [of Iraq's mobile production program] . . . came . . . [from a source who] was an eye witness, an Iraqi chemical engineer who supervised one of these facilities. . . .

    "This defector is currently hiding in another country. . . . His eye-witness account of these mobile chemical weapons programs has been corroborated by other sources. . . .

    "We know that Iraq has at least seven of these mobile biological agent factories."

### NUCLEAR WEAPONS

- "Saddam Hussein is determined to get his hands on a nuclear bomb."
- "He is so determined that he has made repeated covert attempts to acquire high-specification aluminum tubes from 11 different countries. . . ."
- "These tubes are controlled by the Nuclear Suppliers Group precisely because they can be used as centrifuges for enriching uranium."
- "Most U.S. experts think . . . [these tubes] are intended to serve as rotors in centrifuges used to enrich uranium."

### TIES TO AL QAEDA

- "I want to bring to your attention today . . . the potentially much more sinister nexus between Iraq and the al Qaeda terrorist network, a nexus that combines classic terrorist organizations and modern methods of murder."
- "Iraq today harbors a deadly terrorist network headed by Abu Musab Zarqawi, an associate and collaborator of Osama bin Laden and his al Qaeda lieutenants."
- "Iraq officials deny accusations of ties with al Qaeda. These denials are simply not credible."

The Powell speech included the same type of details (with a few more specifics) that the Bush administration officials had been providing in top-secret briefings to members of Congress over a number of months.

It was easy for Powell's presentation to be believable. It was specific and detailed. And given Saddam Hussein's track record as a brutal dictator capable of using weapons of mass destruction, it was easy to paint him as a menace. He *was* a menace. He ruled with terror and an iron hand. He had even ordered the massacre of several thousand of his own people with poison gas.

But, of course, there are a number of despots on this planet who rule countries with repression, torture, and worse. And we don't invade those countries. Most of us understood that we should only take military action when we feel our national interest is involved (with the exception of the need to stop genocide, as was the case in Bosnia, for example). And Colin Powell made the case that our national interest was at stake. His speech offered the credibility needed to convince Congress and the American people to give the President the authority and support to launch a military attack on Iraq.

It turns out there was one elephant-sized problem. Much of the information in Secretary Powell's speech turned out to be false. It wasn't just wrong; in many cases it was wrong by a country mile.

Was sloppy intelligence the cause? Yes, that was part of it. We know enough now from some sketchy investigations that the intelligence was slipshod and incoherent. But there was more. The CIA Director, who is supposed to have a measure of independence, turned out to be an enabler for the White House. George Tenet called the case against Iraq a "slam dunk." He had become an enabler for what we now know the Bush administration had already decided to do.

The lingering and more ominous question is whether the American people and Congress were intentionally deceived by this administration. And there is some compelling evidence that such was the case.

The type of congressional investigative hearings that would have uncovered all of the facts was never held because the Republican majorities in both the U.S. House and U.S. Senate refused to hold them. It was a disservice to the American people, who deserved to know the truth.

In retrospect, Colin Powell calls his presentation to the United Nations "a blot on my career." It's more than that. It is a swimming pool–sized ink stain.

Powell's longtime Chief of Staff, Colonel Larry Wilkerson, called the selling of the war and the representations made by Colin Powell in the UN speech "the perpetration of a hoax on the American people."

Wilkerson doesn't lay it all on Powell. He suggests Powell was duped by being provided bogus intelligence information. However, I believe Colin Powell is far too smart not to have at least suspected what he was reporting was in some part an exaggeration, if not downright untrue. I believe this former four-star general chose an allegiance to his Commander in Chief over a careful search for the truth. And the consequences for our country have been enormous.

## THE SECRET PLAN TO ATTACK IRAQ

Even without Powell's performance at the United Nations, it is clear President Bush was determined to take the country to war. Former Secretary of the Treasury Paul O'Neill says the decision had already been made to attack Iraq long before Powell's speech. It was discussed in a national security meeting shortly after the President took office, O'Neill maintains.

If there wasn't a connection between Iraq and 9/11, the President was determined to create one. Former Bush advisor Richard Clarke told *60 Minutes* that after 9/11 "the president dragged me into a room with a couple of other people, shut the door, and said, 'I want you to find whether Iraq did this.' Now he never said, 'Make it up.' But the entire conversation left me in absolutely no doubt that George Bush wanted me to come back with a report that said Iraq did this. . . ." When he balked, Clarke said, "he came back at me and said, 'Iraq! Saddam! Find out if there's a connection.' And in a very intimidating way. I mean that we should come back with that answer."

There is plenty of evidence that key members of the Bush administration, including Bush, Cheney, National Security Advisor Condoleezza Rice, George Tenet, Stephen Hadley, and many more, either knew or should have known that inaccurate information was being used to support the invasion of Iraq.

It turns out that the information we got from Colin Powell about the mobile chemical weapons laboratories came from a single intelligence source nicknamed Curveball, who was, among other things, a former taxicab driver in Baghdad. He was considered a drunk and a fabricator by the German intelligence authorities. Given the deception we now have uncovered, the Curveball name could just as well apply to some in the administration who were selling a war strategy with Iraq while Osama bin Laden was escaping from Tora Bora (that's another tale of incompetence for a later time).

The mobile chemical weapons laboratories were a major part of the Powell speech. The trouble was, they didn't exist. It was a hoax.

Vice President Cheney's citing aluminum tubes as "irrefutable evidence" that Saddam Hussein was developing a nuclear program also turned out to be dead wrong. Then National Security Advisor Condoleezza Rice, who was another enabler for the President, chimed in that the tubes were "only really suited for nuclear weapons programs" and said on CNN on September 8, 2002, "We don't want the smoking gun to be a mushroom cloud." Unbelievable! It turns out she knew better. Her statements were undermined by information we now know she had already received in her office from other agencies under the administration's control expressing the opposite opinion.

At the time, the consensus of scientists in the government was that the aluminum tubes were likely for the production of rockets, not a nuclear weapons program. That information was given to the National Security Council run by Rice. So she had the information that the case for the aluminum tubes being acquired for a nuclear weapons program was probably not accurate. It is a fact that other experts in the administration had provided that information to her office. But she and her deputy withheld that information from both Congress and the American people. It appears to me that they all knew that the President was determined to go to war with Iraq and they didn't want to let inconvenient facts get in the way!

The President, in his 2003 State of the Union address, declared that Iraq was trying to purchase "yellowcake" uranium from Niger for the purpose of advancing its nuclear weapons program. It was proved later that the documents the Bush administration relied on were forgeries. More damning is the fact that they had reason to know these documents were forgeries even as the administration used them as evidence to support invading Iraq.

I have a basic observation about merchandising. If you need a big sales job to sell a product, a service—or a war—it means the product and the price are suspect. It appears to me that all of these statements were calculated to develop public support for a war, even though their "truth" was, to be generous, suspect.

In the immediate aftermath of the devastating attack on our country, the American people and Congress were ready to believe what they were being told about Saddam Hussein's intentions by the top intelligence officials and the top elected and appointed officials in the White House.

For their salesmanship, Condoleezza Rice got a promotion to become Secretary of State and her deputy, Stephen Hadley, was promoted to National Security Advisor. When George Tenet, the head of the CIA, retired, he was awarded the Medal of Freedom by President Bush. And Colin Powell quit the government after he had damaged his place in history with his one speech to the United Nations that gave President Bush what he wanted.

## THE "TOP-SECRET" DECEPTION

The prelude to the military invasion of Iraq ordered by President Bush included many top-secret briefings for members of Congress prior to the vote authorizing the President to use force in Iraq. The classified briefings were conducted not only by the head of the CIA, George Tenet, but also by National Security Advisor Condoleezza Rice, Vice President Dick Cheney, and many others from the CIA, the State Department, the Pentagon, and other federal agencies.

The top-secret briefings for members of Congress are held in a special room designed and protected for meetings and briefings that are classified as top secret. The sessions are always serious and somber when members of Congress are being briefed about such classified information.

It is clear to me now, based on information that has been made public through investigative reporting in recent years, that some of the most important information given members of Congress in these top-secret sessions leading up to the invasion of Iraq was wildly inaccurate. Some was just flat-out untrue. Even more seriously, I now believe that a number of the top administration officials who briefed us about so-called top-secret information would have had reason to know that some of the information they were describing about the threat to the United States was exaggerated and probably not accurate. I know that is a very serious charge, but it is what happened. I believe some of them were there only for the purpose of supporting a decision that had been made to go to war with Iraq.

In October of 2002, I along with seventy-seven other Senators voted for a resolution that did several things. First, it urged the President to continue the diplomatic efforts at the United Nations to force Iraq to comply with UN resolutions and to target those responsible for the 9/11 attack. But the most important clause in the legislation gave the President the authority to use military force against the country of Iraq if diplomatic efforts failed.

The President said he needed that resolution as leverage to pressure Iraq to come clean on the weapons of mass destruction. But we now know he was looking for political support for a war he had already decided to wage based on his and Dick Cheney's assertion that Iraq was involved in 9/11.

The resolution required the President to report to Congress "his determination that . . . acting pursuant to this joint resolution is consistent with the United States and other countries continuing to take necessary actions against international terrorists and terrorist organizations, including those nations, organizations, or persons *who planned, authorized, committed or aided the terrorist attacks that occurred on September 11, 2001* [emphasis added]."

In March of 2003, President Bush sent a letter to Congress, complying with the resolution, stating that the use of armed force was necessary and "was consistent" with acting against those responsible for the 9/11 attacks. It was a continuation of the President's previous statements that Saddam Hussein had ties with Al Qaeda, the terrorist group responsible for attacking the United States.

That certification turns out to have been flat-out untrue!

In fact, months later, after the invasion of Iraq, President Bush was asked directly by a journalist whether Saddam Hussein was connected to the 9/11 attacks and the President replied that "there was no evidence that Saddam Hussein was involved" in the September 11, 2001, attacks.

In the immediate shadow of the 9/11 attack against our country, the American people and most members of Congress trusted the President and his team of advisors to steer a responsible course to meet the threats against our country.

It was a misplaced trust. This is a reminder of how important it is for all of us to always question and challenge our leaders when presented with choices that could lead to war. I now believe the long, dangerous excursion into Iraq, based on bad intelligence and a determined sales pitch by a President and his team, will be remembered as one of our major foreign policy mistakes.

## WHAT ABOUT BIN LADEN?

Afghanistan was a different story. There were good reasons for sending our soldiers there. It was bin Laden's sanctuary. After 9/11, Americans were united in our willingness to hunt down this evil man.

The opportunity existed to capture Osama bin Laden at the battle of Tora Bora in Afghanistan, but the unwillingness of the administration to respond to an immediate request to commit the Army Rangers to capture him there meant the Afghanistan fighters from the Northern Alliance were counted on to do the job. Predictably, bin Laden escaped. Seven years later he is still organizing terrorist attacks.

At a press conference on March 13, 2002, President Bush was asked about bin Laden. The President said, "I truly am not that concerned about him."

Hold on! He wasn't "concerned" about the man who masterminded the attack against our country that killed thousands of American citizens? What could the President have been thinking?

If there is anything that makes my blood pressure rise, it is the idea that we let bin Laden off the hook and that he and his followers who boasted of murdering innocent Americans were not brought to justice. Six years after he orchestrated the attack against America he was living in a "secure hideaway" in northern Pakistan, according to the "unclassified" portion of the National Intelligence Estimate.

I don't think there should be even one acre on earth that is "secure" for Osama bin Laden. The American people have a right to be disappointed that the Bush administration failed to bring him to justice. Because of the focus on Iraq and the enormous drain of resources, American soldiers today face a resurgent Taliban in Afghanistan.

In 2007 and 2008, our National Intelligence Estimate and the chairman of the Joint Chiefs of Staff said that the greatest terrorist threat to our homeland was from a reconstituted Al Qaeda. Those who attacked us on 9/11 were described as building new training camps, recruiting more terrorists, and rebuilding their strength. Imagine that. The world's greatest military power was bogged down in a war in Iraq while Osama bin Laden was rebuilding his terrorist network.

It shouldn't have been a surprise that our war in Iraq allowed

Osama bin Laden and the leadership of Al Qaeda to escape justice, because all of the President's attention was on Saddam Hussein. And they got him. Saddam is dead. And the world is better off for it.

But as of the writing of this book, Osama bin Laden is alive and still targeting America. In my hometown they call that failure.

Even as the President focused his attention on Iraq early after the 9/11 attacks, some in his administration who were now hawks on the invasion had counseled a different course years before. Here's what Dick Cheney said about an Iraq invasion when he spoke of the prospect in 1994:

> Once you got to Iraq and took it over, took down Saddam Hussein's government, then what are you going to put in its place? That's a very volatile part of the world, and if you take down the central government of Iraq, you could very easily end up seeing pieces of Iraq fly off: part of it . . . uh . . . the Syrians would like to have to the west, part of it—eastern Iraq—the Iranians would like to claim, they fought over it for eight years. In the north you've got the Kurds, and if the Kurds spin loose and join with the Kurds in Turkey, then you threaten the territorial integrity of Turkey.
>
> It's a . . . it's a quagmire, if you go that far and try to take over Iraq.

Clearly, sometime between 1994 and 2001 Cheney forgot what he knew.

But whatever the reason for Cheney's change of opinion, it turns out his view in 1994 of what might happen was much more accurate than his epiphany in 2002.

The full cost of the war in Iraq will become much clearer in the years ahead as we measure the damage it has done to our economy and in our foreign policy as well as the inattention it caused to other important matters around the world.

Financially, we have a leash around our necks. While we have been busy borrowing hundreds of billions to fund the war in Iraq, China's growing economic muscle has increased its considerable leverage on our economy. Meanwhile, the buying power of the dollar has fallen precipitously globally. Russia has reemerged as a major international player. In 2007 Russian President Vladimir Putin continued to support Iran's nuclear rights, which was his way of "stirring the pot."

You see, turmoil in the Middle East means instability in oil prices, which gives a major producer like Russia much more economic power. So by invading Iraq and saber rattling elsewhere, the Bush administration has had the unsettling effect of also restoring some of Russia's international influence. As America's international standing has suffered, other countries seek to fill the power vacuum.

## FOOTPRINT IN ISLAMIC COUNTRIES

In consideration of these realities, I am more convinced than ever that lightening our footprint in Islamic countries, beginning with Iraq, is one of the keys to peace in the region.

So what's holding us back? First of all, without energy self-sufficiency in America we remain vulnerable to the whims of other nations. So, a real energy policy based on increased production here at home, extensive energy conservation programs, and a national commitment to the development of alternative fuels is an urgent matter of our national security.

Sure, it's expensive! But it is no more expensive than continuing to subsidize foreign oil with our military as we are doing now. That is another "hidden tax" placed upon Americans that no one really wants to talk about. It has been estimated that if the full cost of our military security were included in the price of a gallon of gas, its cost would be about $10 a gallon.

Second, U.S. corporations have billions invested in these countries, so even if one removes the military footprint, economic interests will still complicate the picture. We should encourage these companies to migrate to alternative fuels with the goal of self-sufficiency in a decade. And those who stay involved in volatile regions . . . well, that's all part of the risk and reward of investment, isn't it?

It's long past time for us to disengage in Iraq. Saddam Hussein is dead. The Iraqis have voted for a new constitution and a new government. The United States has spent $20 billion training over five hundred thousand Iraqi police and soldiers. If the Iraqis who have been trained for the security mission still don't have the will to provide security for their country, the United States cannot and should not be expected to do it for them. It is their country, not ours. The job of providing security in Iraq is theirs. They have the resources and the training; now they must have the will.

As of late 2008, the Iraq war was still bleeding the American treasury of $10 to $12 billion a month even as the Iraqi government hoarded a nearly $80 billion budget surplus. Am I missing something or is there something wrong with that? Nor were those Iraqi oil fields bettering life in America. Prices topped $4 a gallon in many parts of the country in early to mid-2008 (before it went back down at the end of the year). The fact that the price of oil actually went up precipitously after the invasion astonished comedian Chris Rock, who said, "If I invaded KFC, wings are gonna be cheap at my house!"

If boots on the ground are necessary to maintain order in a transformation into a peaceful society, an international force is the answer. It would be less polarizing. It can be done. I think our allies are waiting to see if the recent years have been an aberration. They will be taking measure of what we do and what we say. It's important that we look for common ground. President Obama's most difficult task will to be to restore a measure of trust in that office both at home and abroad.

It's time to take the training wheels off in Iraq, and with UN peacekeepers we can. Then we must refocus on the job of bringing bin Laden to justice and destroying the ability of terrorists to threaten our future.

I take no joy in talking about the incompetence and the deception that I believe were part of the Bush administration's policies
dealing with terrorism and Iraq. But to make sure we don't make
that type of mistake again, we need to fully understand what has
happened and how it happened.

Our country will recover from all of this, but it is imperative that
we also learn from it.

# CHAPTER 8

• • •

# The Profits of War

THOUGH THE IRAQ war has receded into the background behind issues like the economy, we would do well to consider the enormous *financial* wreckage this conflict has and continues to cause. The war and the economy are intertwined. We are spending $10 to $12 billion a month picking up the pieces. The legitimate cost of war is one thing. The theft and corruption that has taken place during the conduct of this war is nothing less than a national scandal.

Do you want to get steamed? Get your blood pressure way up? Just listen to the sordid stories about how Uncle Sam wasted your tax dollars as he hired contractors to help prosecute the Iraq war. During the conflict, there were more contractors than U.S. soldiers in Iraq. And the stories about contractor fraud and waste abound. Some of it includes blatant war profiteering.

## NO EXPERIENCE? APPLY HERE!

Efraim Diveroli was a twenty-two-year-old Florida college student with virtually no business experience when he submitted bids to the

U.S. Defense Department for contracts to provide weapons to the Afghan army in support of its war against Al Qaeda and the Taliban. The bids came from a fledgling company called AEY, which was a corporate shell that had been established in Florida by Efraim's father some years before.

Efraim was listed as the president of the company while a twenty-five-year-old masseur (that's right, a massage therapist) was listed as the company's vice president. The firm operated behind an unmarked office door in a building in Miami Beach.

*The New York Times*, in an excellent piece of investigative reporting by C. J. Chivers, disclosed that the Pentagon had awarded over $300 million in defense contracts to this company between 2004 and the spring of 2008. As best as can be determined, it had only the two employees.

AEY was supposed to be shipping weapons and ammunition purchased by our Pentagon to Afghan fighters to assist them in their fight against the Taliban. But at least some of what the Afghan fighters received were antiquated weapons and bullets that the Afghans called junk. Some of the ammunition that was spilling out of unsecured boxes was more than forty years old and of Chinese origin.

When *The New York Times* broke the story, the U.S. Army suspended the company from any future federal contracting and claimed that Mr. Diveroli had misled the Army. But the Army brass wasn't exactly marching straight, either. The *Times* reported that U.S. military officers in the field had previously complained about the activities of this company and the shoddy quality of the weapons they were sending. But the warnings went unheeded by the higher-ups.

Some months after the embarrassing *New York Times* investigative report and after the Army had suspended the contracts awarded to the company, Mr. Diveroli was arrested and charged with fraud.

In other developments, it turned out that the U.S. State Department had suspended contracts for the same company and then given it even more business after the contracts had been suspended. Moreover, when the Army was checking out AEY they failed to check with the State Department, where they would have found that the firm was trouble. This looks to me like gross incompetence of two government agencies.

But just how in the world did a twenty-two-year-old CEO with a twenty-five-year-old massage therapist as a sidekick manage to get just over a third of a billion dollars in contracts from the Pentagon? This was a company with very little experience and with no apparent staff. I know America is the land of opportunity, but this redefines the term "striking it rich."

How did the army general in charge of the Army Sustainment Command in Illinois manage to allow over $300 million to be awarded to these two? The Army is not talking. Neither is the CEO, now that he has been arrested. But I'll bet if the money had been dyed purple, one young man carousing the clubs in Miami Beach would have been recognizable by his purple pockets, rewarded by the incompetence of both the Pentagon and the State Department.

And this little scandal is just one rather small example of the seedy underside of war contracting.

## WAR AS A BUSINESS OPPORTUNITY

Quite simply, I believe the contracting to supply the war and the contracting for the reconstruction of Iraq represent the greatest waste, fraud, and abuse in the long history of our country. It is a sordid story of graft, corruption, incompetence, and neglect.

In Iraq more than in any other war, the United States used contractors to provide many of the supplies and services. In most cases, these were supplies and services that the military had provided for uniformed soldiers in years past. These necessities included fuel, food, water, private security services, and so much more.

The private sector has played a role in past wars, and even in the noblest of causes there have been profiteers. But never before in our history has war become such a blatant business opportunity.

## FAILING TO PLAN FOR THE WORST-CASE SCENARIO

We now know that when the war in Iraq began it was launched with very little preparation, fueled by overconfidence and arrogance. The administration prepared for one thing—a quick victory. With so much riding on the outcome, they failed to consider the worst possible scenario, which even the most novice tactician understands. Colin Powell's plea to wait went unheeded. His warning that "if you break it, you own it" fell on deaf ears. The President and the neocons had already decided that they were going to invade Iraq. Then Powell finally joined them in selling the war.

The Bush administration had developed no plans for Iraq after the military invasion was successful. The result was the complete breakdown in civil order and slide toward a civil war. Tragically, we didn't even have the manpower to keep order or to secure the caches of weapons that were eventually turned against our soldiers.

## A MAKESHIFT U.S. GOVERNMENT IN IRAQ

The administration hurriedly put together an entity called the Coalition Provisional Authority (CPA) to run the country until another government could be created. The story of the incompetence by the CPA is an unbelievable scandal. Both Iraqi oil money as well as American taxpayer money was wasted in unparalleled incompetence and abuse.

Nearly all of the participants in Iraq contracting say there was very little oversight and even less concern by those who were supposed to be making sure that money was spent wisely.

When the CPA set up offices in Saddam Hussein's former palaces, they took control of the entire country. That included Iraqi oil money. When the dust finally settled, investigators said that there was $8.9 billion of Iraqi oil money that was "missing" and could not be accounted for. That's not petty crime. It looks to me like grand larceny.

The CPA was headed by a man named Paul Bremer, who had been picked by President Bush and Defense Secretary Donald Rumsfeld to become the interim government in Iraq until a new government was created. *Like most others affiliated with the CPA, Bremer had no particular experience that would qualify him for the job.*

The CPA had massive quantities of money, both Iraq oil currency as well as U.S. reconstruction money. It issued contracts for all manner of projects in Iraq. And there was almost no accountability as to how the money was spent.

One participant described it by telling me about contracts to install air-conditioning units in some buildings in Iraq. By the time the contractor had hired several levels of subcontractors and paid the necessary bribes and money under the table, the products installed turned out to be ceiling fans. The American taxpayers paid for air conditioners and got fans. And nobody seemed to care.


## EVEN JESSE JAMES
## WOULD HAVE BLUSHED

The CPA also distributed *cash*. The payroll for the Iraqi ministries that were set up and operating under the supervision of the CPA was paid in cash. It seems just about anyone could walk up and get paid. Jesse James robbed a lot of banks. But he never had it as easy as those who robbed the American taxpayers in Iraq.

"This deplorable system created an opportunity for unscrupulous officials and contractors," Frank Willis, a senior employee of the CPA, said. "In one case 8,206 security guards were listed on one of the Iraqi Ministry payrolls, but only 602 individuals could be verified. At another Ministry the payrolls listed 1,471 security guards when only 642 were working." This is the way American taxpayers were fleeced.

We know what that means. That money can likely be traced to Swiss bank accounts in the names of corrupt Iraqi officials.

In 2008, long after the waste and fraud had taken root, I asked that a man named Judge Radhi Hamza al-Radhi be allowed to testify before the Senate Appropriations Committee. Judge Radhi had been appointed to head a Commission on Public Integrity in Iraq. He was appointed by the head of the CPA, Paul Bremer.

The judge told our committee of the substantial fraud and stealing that had occurred while he served in that position. The commission he headed uncovered an estimated $18 billion of *fraud* in the ministries of the Iraqi government. Most of these funds, he said, were American dollars being paid to the Iraqi ministries.

Judge Radhi Hamza al-Radhi reported that the Prime Minister of Iraq refused to recognize the independence of the Commission on Public Integrity and did all that he could to undermine the investigations of corruption in the Iraqi government. And Judge Radhi said $18 billion does not include the full extent of "oil corruption," including metering fraud, theft, and smuggling, that is occurring in Iraq and funding many of the insurgent activities.

Judge Radhi survived several assassination attempts before he got out of Iraq. But he told us that 20 percent of his employees who worked in his anticorruption commission were assassinated, along with twelve family members of his staff as well. They paid a high price for trying to do the right thing. And they did this even as the U.S. Embassy and the Iraqi government were trying to derail the corruption investigations, according to some ex–State Department officials who worked there.

Judge Radhi said of the 3,000 corruption cases they successfully investigated and forwarded to the courts, only 241 were adjudicated with guilty sentences. In a 2007 interview with Corey Flintoff on NPR's *All Things Considered*, he said, "Most ministries are involved. Some officials, such as the minister of defense, have been dismissed,⎯

but we have about $4 billion in corruption cases there [and] $2 billion in cases involving the Interior Ministry."

It is clear from the testimony of the one person in Iraq who was responsible for public integrity that the stain of corruption corrodes nearly everything in the country. Those living in Iraq who yearn to return to some semblance of normalcy are living in a cesspool of greed and violence. But investigations there—just as they have been here in America—are blocked at the highest level. According to that same *All Things Considered* episode, "A secret order from the Iraqi prime minister's office bans the Commission on Public Integrity (CPI) from investigating top Iraqi officials unless they have the consent of Prime Minister Nouri al-Maliki."

In the summer of 2008 Judge Radhi, after having been abandoned by the U.S. State Department, was living in poverty in a Washington, D.C., suburb while applying for asylum in the United States. Despite the fact that his life was in danger because of the corruption investigations he did in Iraq, Secretary of State Condoleezza Rice had turned her back on him by insisting that no one from the State Department could write anything in support of the judge's asylum request.

But I and others supported Judge Radhi, and in the midsummer of 2008 this brave Iraqi was finally granted asylum.

In April 2008 two courageous former State Department officials testified before a hearing of my Democratic Policy Committee. The two had been assigned to the Office of Accountability and Transparency (OAT) at the U.S. Embassy in Baghdad.

Judge Arthur Brennan, a self-described Republican and former New Hampshire Superior Court justice, had been sent to Iraq to serve as the director of the office of OAT, which was directed to reduce the "devastating level of corruption that was destroying Iraq and lengthening the crisis," according to Brennan. He told us a tale that describes a level of complicity by the U.S. State Department that protects and coddles the very corruption in Iraq it is supposed to be fighting.

Here are the words of Judge Brennan about his experience and the experience of other professionals who served at the OAT in Iraq:

> The OAT . . . soon discovered that the Department of State's actual policies not only contradicted the anticorruption mission but indirectly contributed to and has [sic] allowed corruption to fester at the highest levels of the Iraqi Government. The Embassy effort against corruption . . . was little more than "window dressing." . . .
>
> The Department of State has negligently, recklessly and sometimes intentionally misled the U.S. Congress, the American people, and the people of Iraq. In a sense, the Department of State has contributed to the killing and maiming of U.S. soldiers; the deaths of thousands of Iraqi civilians; the bolstering of illegal militias, insurgents and al Qaeda—and the enrichment and empowerment of the thieves controlling some of the Iraqi ministries. . . . Billions of U.S. and Iraqi dollars have been lost, stolen and wasted. It is likely that some of the money is financing outlaws and insurgents such as the Mehdi Army.

Judge Brennan also told of reports giving an accurate account of the corruption that were pulled back and sanitized by the State Department to tell Congress and the American people a distorted story about the real corruption in Iraq. He testified that the U.S. Ambassador in Iraq was either complicit or negligent and probably both in covering up the corruption and protecting some in the Iraqi government who were corrupt.

In the end, it was our own State Department that was complicit in getting Judge al-Radhi removed from Iraq, because he was causing waves with his investigation of corruption.

Aside from wasting U.S. taxpayer dollars that are stolen by corrupt Iraq politicians, it is this very corruption that prevents the Iraqi government from working and prevents our American soldiers from coming home. And from the testimony of Judge Brennan we know that Secretary of State Rice has a lot to answer for.

But there was another pot of money to be plundered even larger than Iraqi oil money and American taxpayer dollars sent to Iraq for reconstruction. It was the Pentagon funds for contracts that were given to mostly large (and some small) companies to support the American troops in Iraq.

During the invasion, the U.S. soldiers made quick work of Saddam's army. It is estimated that as they watched their side losing badly, many units abandoned their posts, took off their uniforms, and, along with their weapons, dissolved back into the civilian population.

Much to our dismay in Congress, it soon became evident after the invasion that there had been little or no preparation to deal with the war's aftermath and the needs of a large American army that would stay in Iraq for years. The administration had to move quickly to write contracts for some big companies to provide the many services an army on the move would need. In addition, the Pentagon began to do the planning that should have gone on long before the invasion to determine what to do with the country after the military invasion was successful. As a result the Department of Defense moved to provide large, mostly no-bid contracts to some very large U.S. corporations. These included a big contract known as the LOGCAP (Logistics Civil Augmentation Program) contract to provide services to the military and the RIO (Restore Iraqi Oil) contract.

The Bush administration belatedly realized that billions of dollars were going to be needed to try to keep the country running, to begin the process of rebuilding the country's infrastructure, and to do the other things necessary to put the country of Iraq back together again.

It would take money . . . lots and lots of money. The administration, afraid to ask the American taxpayers to pay for it, decided to borrow the necessary money in the American people's name. Two words describe the economic theory behind that decision. "Borrow" and "spend."

The President decided he would not put the cost of the Iraq war in the annual budget he sent to Congress. Instead, each year he asked for emergency supplemental appropriations for the war.

Even when Congress enacted legislation that required the President to include spending for the Iraq war in the budget, he refused to do it. That meant the President could add the cost of the war directly to the federal debt. Some will argue that Congress was complicit in that. But Congress did not have the votes to override a presidential veto, so the President had the upper hand and got what he wanted.

For all its bravado, the administration didn't have the courage to tell the truth about the financial cost of the war. It created a monstrous debt and shuffled it off like a lead balloon payment to the next administration and next generation of Americans, who have already endured an economic "rough patch," as the President described it, in part because of this reckless fiscal policy.

## CASH AND CARRY ON C-130S

The stories about the movement of large pallets of cash from the vaults of the Federal Reserve to Iraq paint quite a picture. One-hundred-dollar bills wrapped in plastic and stacked on pallets were flown on C-130s to Baghdad.

One can literally measure the wealth being sucked into Iraq by the ton as reported by Jeremy Pelofsky for Reuters in February 2007:

"Bills weighing a total of 363 tons were loaded onto military aircraft in the largest cash shipments ever made by the Federal Reserve," said Rep. Henry Waxman, chairman of the House of Representatives Committee on Oversight and Government Reform.

"Who in their right mind would send 363 tons of cash into a war zone?" . . . the California Democrat said.

According to Pelofsky, "The money, which had been held by the United States, came from Iraqi oil exports, surplus dollars from the U.N.-run oil-for-food program and frozen assets belonging to the ousted Saddam Hussein regime."

Stories about distributing cash out of the backs of pickup trucks in Iraq made the rounds. And the grand theft began. It was inevitable that some of this money, which was supposed to shore up the emerging government, would end up in the hands of insurgents who may have simply signed a false name on the government payroll list.

Meanwhile, in the bowels of the Pentagon, the brass was busy negotiating different large, mostly no-bid contracts with some of their favorite companies.

The administration was operating in secret, spending money like sailors on shore leave, and Congress, controlled by the party of the President, was uninterested in any form of oversight. The result was that year after year the taxpayers got robbed blind.

At one point, U.S. auditors testifying before a U.S. House Committee said that they reviewed $57 billion in Iraq contracts and found that one in six dollars charged by the U.S. contractors could not be supported or was questionable. *One in six.*

Of the $10 billion in overpriced contracts or contracts where the costs could not be justified, more than $2.7 billion was charged by (cue the ominous music) the Halliburton Corporation.

David Walker, the head of the Government Accountability Office, offered this dismal observation: "There is no accountability. Organizations charged with overseeing contracts are not held accountable. Contractors are not held accountable. The individuals responsible are not held accountable." Here's just a small illustration of what David Walker was talking about:

- The Halliburton Corporation ordered fifty thousand pounds of nails to be delivered to Iraq. But they were too short, so they were discarded, lying in the sands of Iraq. The taxpayers pay the cost when the contract is cost plus.

- Halliburton was charging the government for serving forty-two thousand meals a day to soldiers, but auditors said they were serving only fourteen thousand.

- The Parsons Corporation was paid $200 million for a reconstruction contract for building 142 primary health centers across Iraq. Two years later, the money was gone and there were no more than twenty clinics . . . and those that were completed were done with shoddy construction methods.

- The Parsons Corporation was given a contract to build the Khan Bani Sa'ad prison—a prison that the Iraqis said they didn't want and wouldn't use. Our American officials insisted that it be built even over the objections of the Iraqis. After $39 million went to the Parsons Corporation, they were removed from the contract and another $9 million was spent. Now the prison sits unused, uncompleted, and in terrible disrepair. Local people call it the Whale. The U.S. Inspector General has harsh words for this complete waste of the taxpayers' money.

- The Special Inspector General investigation in mid-2008 reported that the Parsons Corporation also received $140 million to build a number of facilities in Iraq, including prisons and police and fire stations, but they only completed one-third of the projects. Of the fifty-three construction projects, the report said, only eighteen were completed. But the Parsons Corporation got the money.

- Brand-new $85,000 trucks were left on the side of the road to be torched because they had flat tires and no wrench to fix them, or a plugged fuel pump and no tools to fix it. Employees were told it was okay because it was a cost-plus contract. The taxpayers would pay. *You* would pay.

- There were two bids to build an ice plant in Iraq. One was for $450,000 and the other was for $3.4 million. The bidding companies were equally qualified. Halliburton selected the company that bid the $3.4 million. After all, the taxpayers were paying through the nose in cost-plus contracts. (A cost-plus contract is basically one in which a company cannot lose. It will be paid for the cost of services *plus a guaranteed profit* on the contract. That provides a built-in incentive to spend more money.)

- Kellogg Brown & Root was awarded the contract to provide the electrical wiring for the military bases in Iraq. According to employees who worked for KBR in Iraq, the company hired unqualified third-country nationals to do electrical work. Subsequently we learned that eleven soldiers had been electrocuted because of faulty electrical work. I held the Senate hearings where the mothers of soldiers who had been electrocuted testified. They described being informed by the Army that their sons were electrocuted while showering or while power-washing army vehicles.

The response by the Pentagon was to ask the company that allegedly contributed to the problem, Kellogg Brown & Root, to investigate the problem. It was typical of the Pentagon response to the relentless stories about contractor incompetence or abuse. In this case it put the lives of soldiers at risk.

These are just a *few* of *many* contract abuses, most of them reported by former employees who were disgusted by what they saw.

## A PROFILE IN COURAGE: BUNNATINE GREENHOUSE

Because the Republican-controlled Congress would not hold oversight hearings to make sure there was accountability for the billions of dollars that were being spent in Iraq, in 2006 I decided to hold a series of hearings in the Democratic Policy Committee, which I chaired.

I invited Republicans to join in the hearings, but only one did—a courageous U.S. Congressman from North Carolina named Walter Jones. The rest of the Republican Congress did not want to do oversight hearings because the administration didn't want to be embarrassed. To me it wasn't about embarrassing anybody. It was a search for the truth.

So, I plowed ahead and held seventeen hearings in a period of three years exposing the waste, fraud, and abuse in Iraq contracting by our federal government. I was determined to uncover the waste and try to put a stop to it. And I was convinced the Bush administration had not only mismanaged the war but also presided over sweetheart contracts with friends and was willing to look the other way even as our treasury was being looted by some fast-buck artists.

At one of the first hearings I chaired, a witness named Bunnatine Greenhouse came forward to testify.

Ms. Greenhouse, the top civilian contracting agent with the Army Corps of Engineers, was appearing at my request to tell us about the actions of the Pentagon in regard to granting large contracts to Halliburton. The story she related was a disgusting harbinger of hearings to come. Billions of dollars in contracts had been awarded by the Pentagon to Halliburton and its subsidiary Kellogg Brown & Root. Many of them were no-bid, sole-source cost-plus contracts.

The life story of Bunnatine Greenhouse is compelling. According to a story in *The Washington Post* by Neely Tucker, Greenhouse was the daughter of sharecropper parents from the poorest area of the Louisiana delta. They were not able to get an education, but they sacrificed so that their kids could go to college.

Greenhouse's older sister earned a doctorate and was a professor at LSU. Her older brother got his doctorate and was also a college professor. Her younger brother, Elvin Hayes, played professional basketball, won a national championship, and was named one of the fifty best professional basketball players of the century. Greenhouse was the valedictorian of her high school class. She graduated magna cum laude from college in three years and earned three master's degrees in the following years.

She is a tall woman imbued with a commanding presence.

On the day we met, she had decided to accept my invitation to testify before the Senate Democratic Policy Committee on the subject of waste, fraud, and abuse in defense contracting for the Iraq war. Her superiors at the Pentagon told her that it wouldn't "be in her best interests to do so." But she came to the hearing anyway, willing and determined to testify.

"I can unequivocally state that the abuse related to contracts awarded to KBR [the subsidiary of Halliburton] represents the most blatant and improper contract abuse I have witnessed during the course of my professional career," she told my committee.

Neely Tucker called the testimony "stunning in its confrontational nature, its moral conviction, its assurance—and, one might observe, in its full-blown career suicide."

Bunnatine Greenhouse explained that the process by which the contracts were awarded violated the Army Corps' own procedures. In one example, she described a Pentagon meeting to discuss the content of a contract and how they invited the Halliburton Corporation employees to be in the room while they discussed what the contract would contain. To discuss the type of contract and its conditions with company representatives present before it was decided which company would be awarded the contract is a violation of the proper procedure. When Greenhouse complained, the Halliburton employees were finally asked to leave. But it was all a charade, she said. Clearly, the uniformed officers of the Corps fully intended to award the no-bid contract to the single company they had invited to participate in the discussion.

When you consider that Vice President Cheney was the former CEO of Halliburton, you would expect that the administration would go out of its way to avoid any conflicts of interest. Every conceivable effort should have been made to assure the public that decisions were based on merit instead of cronyism. Instead, they fired up the steamroller and flattened Bunny Greenhouse.

You see, she was the highest civilian contract official and had to approve the contracts. She objected to them because she felt that in a number of ways procedures had been violated. The uniformed officers at the U.S. Army Corps of Engineers decided to simply write and award the contracts without the required signature of Greenhouse, once again in violation of procedures.

For having the courage to stand up to the uniformed officers who ran the Corps in the face of what she felt were blatant and deliberate violations of contracting procedures she was summarily demoted by General Strock, the lieutenant general who headed the Army Corps. She lost her job for doing her job—for being honest and blowing the whistle on behavior she believed violated the rules of contracting.

From Donald Rumsfeld on down, the Pentagon officials refused to address the issues this courageous woman raised with Congress. The Corps of Engineers refused to comment. Meanwhile, the favorite contractors got away with the money and the taxpayers got fleeced.

One evening some months later, I called the former head of the Corps, Gen. Joe N. Ballard, who had hired Greenhouse and had always given her the highest performance appraisals. Ballard, who was one of General Strock's predecessors, had retired and was willing to talk about what he knew of the situation at his old command. "Bunnatine was given a raw deal," he told me. "She was an outstanding employee who knew her job and did an excellent job."

In the list of wrongdoings connected to the Iraq war, the manner in which the Bush administration and the Corps of Engineers destroyed this good and honest civil servant's career ranks near the top.

Since then, Bunnatine Greenhouse has become a public speaker on the very topic that ended her career. Her whistle has not stopped blowing.

## DICK CHENEY AND HALLIBURTON CONTRACTS

Because there has been so much discussion about it, the moment anyone criticized the Halliburton contracts the administration immediately tried to say the criticism was merely a political attack on Dick Cheney and the Bush administration.

But, like a hole in a wet bog, when it comes to Dick Cheney and Halliburton the deeper you dig, the darker it gets. And I don't think it passes the smell test. Much but not all of the controversy about contracting in Iraq revolves around the many contracts awarded to the Halliburton Corporation, Cheney's former employer.

The administration insisted that Dick Cheney had nothing to do with awarding contracts to Halliburton and it was unfair to link him to a company he had left years before. They used that strategy for several years while the stories about waste, fraud, and abuse in Iraq contracting continued to emerge. Still, there were persistent allegations that the Vice President was involved in the awarding of a large multi-billion-dollar contract dealing with Iraqi oil (Restore Iraqi Oil) to Halliburton. Cheney vigorously denied it.

However, there appears to be a smoking gun. A March 5, 2003, e-mail from Douglas Feith, the Undersecretary of Defense for Policy, approved the contract going to Halliburton. The e-mail excerpt said the RIO contract "was contingent on informing the WH [White House] tomorrow. We anticipate no issues since action has been coordinated with the VP's office." Three days later the Corps of Engineers gave Halliburton the contract, and no other bids were sought.

Predictably, the Republican Congress ignored the call to investigate the connection between billions of dollars in no-bid contracts awarded to Cheney's former employer and the memo stating that the "action has been coordinated with the VP's office." If there are those who say we don't have all of the facts, then give us more. In the meantime, it appears to me that the e-mail from Mr. Feith demonstrates the important facts with which to judge a serious conflict of interest.

## HENRY BUNTING'S STORY OF BUYING ON COST-PLUS CONTRACTS

Henry Bunting was another witness at one of my hearings. He had been working in Kuwait as a purchaser for the Halliburton subsidiary Kellogg Brown & Root. A middle-aged, pleasant-looking fellow, he took his job seriously and he was upset about what he experienced in Kuwait. He was anxious to come forward and describe the waste he had seen in the contracting.

Henry said, "I'm fed up. I've seen too many abuses, and I had to speak out." He told us what it was like being a purchasing agent for a company that was intent on milking a cost-plus contract with the Pentagon.

Henry said that as a purchasing agent he spent most of his time as a buyer of supplies that the contracts called for. As he sat at the committee witness table he held up a white hand towel. He said one of his required purchases was thousands of hand towels for the American troops. He had written out an order to purchase the ordinary white hand towels, but when his supervisor saw what he was about to do, Henry was told that he had to change the order.

The supervisor told him to order towels with the KBR (Kellogg Brown & Root) logo embroidered on them. Henry protested, saying that this would drive up the cost and mean the towels would be up to three or four times more expensive. Adding the logo to the towels would increase the cost from $1.50 to over $5 per towel. He said his superior told him it didn't matter. It was a cost-plus contract. "Don't question it. Just do it. The taxpayers will pick up the tab," he said.

Henry's supervisors continued to remind him that cost wasn't a problem. The higher the price, the more the company got paid. He finally quit in disgust.

Auditors discovered in one case, reported by Matt Kelley for *USA Today* in 2007, "the contractor proposed charging $110 million for housing, food, water, laundry and other services on bases that had been *shut down* [emphasis added]."

It was reported that from 2003 through 2006 KBR received nearly $20 billion in war contracts. Auditors challenged $2.2 billion in expenditures. KBR was split off from Halliburton in 2006, and Halliburton announced in 2007 that it would move its corporate

THE PROFITS OF WAR { 165 }

headquarters from Houston to Dubai, an Arab corporate tax haven that is closer to the action.

*The Washington Post* and *60 Minutes* have reported that Halliburton used an offshore subsidiary named Halliburton Products and Services, registered in the Cayman Islands to circumvent U.S. laws, to do oil business with Iran—you know, part of the Axis of Evil. According to Jefferson Morley, in an article that appeared in *The Washington Post*, on February 3, 2005, "Halliburton spokeswoman Wendy Hall said the company had not broken the law because all of the work in the South Pars gas field would be done by non-Americans employed by a subsidiary registered in the Cayman Islands." She said, "We are in the service business, not the foreign-policy business."

In March 2008, in *The Boston Globe*, Farah Stockman exposed yet another layer of greed and a lack of patriotism by reporting:

Kellogg Brown & Root, the nation's top Iraq war contractor and until last year a subsidiary of Halliburton Corp., has avoided paying hundreds of millions of dollars in federal Medicare and Social Security taxes by hiring workers through shell companies based in this tropical tax haven. . . .

More than 21,000 people working for KBR in Iraq—including about 10,500 Americans—are listed as employees of two companies that exist in a computer file on the fourth floor of a building on a palm-studded boulevard here in the Caribbean. Neither company has an office or phone number in the Cayman Islands.

The Defense Department has known since at least 2004 that KBR was avoiding taxes by declaring its American workers as employees of Cayman Islands shell companies, and officials said the move allowed KBR to perform the work more cheaply, saving Defense dollars.

But the use of the loophole results in a significantly greater loss of revenue to the government as a whole, particularly to the Social Security and Medicare trust funds.

American taxpayers are footing the bill for $16 billion in KBR contracts, yet KBR chose to dodge American taxes. According to the *Globe*, "The largest of the Cayman Islands shell companies—called Service Employees International Inc., which is now listed as having more than 20,000 workers in Iraq, according to KBR—was created two years before Cheney became Halliburton's chief executive. But a second Cayman Islands company called Overseas Administrative Services, which now is listed as the employer of 1,020 mostly managerial workers in Iraq, was established two months after Cheney's appointment."

There is some good news to end this saga. At my urging and the urging of other members of Congress we passed legislation that put an end to this type of underhanded tax avoidance.

## ALI FADHIL . . . AND THE PHANTOM CLINICS

Ali Fadhil is an Iraqi doctor and journalist who came to the U.S. Senate to tell us about his investigation of the U.S. money that was supposed to be spent to build health clinics in Iraq. The U.S. Army Corps of Engineers contracted with the Parsons Corporation for $243 million to build the clinics, and Parsons received another $70 million contract to repair other health clinics and hospitals.

Dr. Fadhil was excited to know that the United States was going to improve the health of the Iraqi people by providing clinics across the country. But he was troubled when he sensed that most of the promised health facilities were not being built and those that were constructed were thrown up with such shoddy construction they were unable to serve as clinics.

He decided to take matters into his own hands. Calling on the office of the Minister of Health in the Iraqi government, Dr. Fadhil told the Iraqi officials that he wanted to visit and inspect the clinics the Parsons Corporation had been paid by the U.S. government to construct. They told him, "There are no clinics. They are imaginary clinics."

Dr. Fadhil wasn't surprised. He had felt that the promises weren't being kept. The money was gone. The U.S. government had paid the contractor, but the health clinics didn't get built. Some work was done, but it turned out to be of inexplicably poor quality.

How about a description of Dr. Fadhil's visit to the maternity and pediatric hospital in Diwaniya, Iraq, one hundred miles south of Bagdad? This was a clinic that was supposed to be rebuilt in satisfaction of the contract. The account, posted by the Democratic Policy Committee, is here:

> As we walked around, the problems are obvious. Outside we can see an open manhole and sewage in the garden. And in the kitchen, more blocked sewage. Everywhere the standard of work is terrible. Things have melted. Pipes have not been connected. And in the operating room you can smell raw sewage. . . . The flooring has been done so badly it is now a potential killer. I can even see ants crawling under the flooring. And this is in an operating theatre that is going to be used in a week's time.

Shortly thereafter the Parsons Corporation was suspended from contracting work. Too late, it appears, to save the American taxpayers from the waste. And too late to have assured that Iraqis would receive the health clinics the United States paid for.

# CONTAMINATED WATER
# FOR THE TROOPS

The stories about the sole-source contracting in the Iraq war with the subsidiary of the Halliburton Corporation describe a system of government contracting that was out of control. Here are just a few headlines from two months in 2004:

- *Houston Chronicle:* "Uncle Sam Looks into Meal Bills: Halliburton Refunds $27 Million as a Result"
- *Houston Chronicle:* "Halliburton Faces Criminal Investigation: Pentagon Proving Alleged Overcharges for Iraq Fuel"
- *Los Angeles Times:* "Ex-Halliburton Workers Allege Rampant Waste: They Say the Firm Makes No Effort to Control Costs"
- *Los Angeles Times:* "Halliburton Unable to Prove $1.8 Billion in Work, Pentagon Says"
- *Houston Chronicle*: "Millions in U.S. Property Lost in Iraq, Report Says; Halliburton Claims Figures Only Projections"

But of all the outrageous stories about the way the American taxpayers were fleeced and American soldiers cheated, few rival the one about how Halliburton was paid to deliver treated water to the U.S. military bases in Iraq and that its failure to do so threatened the health of American soldiers. Furthermore, Halliburton and the Pentagon did all they could to cover this failure up when it was discovered.

I heard the story at a January 23, 2006, hearing that I held. Ben Carter, a water purification specialist who worked for KBR in Iraq in 2005, testified about the Halliburton water contract at Camp Ar Ramadi in Iraq. It was a base that was home to five to seven thousand U.S. troops.

Carter was in charge of something called the Reverse Osmosis Water Purification Unit (ROWPU) at the camp. At Camp Ar Ramadi the ROWPU was used to decontaminate the polluted water from the Euphrates River that was pumped to the military base for use by the soldiers.

The potable water was used for drinking and cooking and it requires the highest level of purification. The non-potable water was used for things such as bathing, showering, shaving, and laundry.

Even though the non-potable water was not intended for drinking or cooking, it, too, had to meet safety standards because of the likelihood of the occasional use of non-potable water for brushing teeth or making coffee, as occurred at some of the military bases from time to time. The standards for non-potable water in the purification industry were adopted by the Army in its manual.

One day at Camp Ar Ramadi, one of the Halliburton employees reported to management that he had discovered some type of organism in his toilet bowl. Ben Carter told us that he did an inspection and discovered what he said was a larva swimming in the toilet.

The following is Ben Carter's testimony before the Senate Committee hearing:

> I had been told . . . that the water was chlorinated, and knew that such an organism could not survive in chlorinated water. I decided at that point to test the water in the employee's bathroom for chlorination. The test results indicated zero presence of chlorine. I then tested at several other locations in the KBR section of the base, and discovered no chlorine at those sites either. I then tested the non-potable water storage tank and, to my shock, realized that the water in the tank tested negative for chlorine; that the access lid of the tank was not in place, let alone secure; and that the air vents to the tank were turned upward and left unscreened, leaving the water supply vulnerable to contamination from dust, insects, rodents, or even enemy attack. I was stunned. No trained water-treatment specialist could claim that the water was fit for human use.

Carter reports that he rushed out to the ROWPU site at the Euphrates River and found they had *never* chlorinated the water there. He said he learned it was the responsibility of KBR to test the water three times a day to confirm the presence of chlorine, but to his knowledge such testing never occurred. He also learned that they were not using submicron cartridge filters in the ROWPU process.

"That meant water from the Euphrates River—collected less than a mile downstream from a raw sewage outlet—was passing through only a multi-media filter before being pumped into our KBR non-potable water storage tank," Carter said disgustedly. "The same water was being pumped into the Army's non-potable water storage tank."

The reaction by KBR management: they told Ben Carter not to tell anyone.

That was when Ben Carter quit KBR and left Iraq. But he didn't keep his mouth shut. He testified before my committee in January 2006 that he had been affected by the issue he sought to solve. "I have been diagnosed with an unidentified organism in my digestive tract, and that I sometimes suffer from gastrointestinal problems that I did not experience before going to Iraq," he said. "I believe that supporting the troops has to be more than a slogan. Our men and women overseas deserve the best our taxpayer dollars can buy, and it saddens me to report that we're falling short on something as simple and essential as providing them clean, safe water."

The documents that he received from other KBR employees after he quit his job show the measures that KBR took to cover up the water problem. In one, Will Granger, the KBR water quality manager for all of Iraq and Kuwait, wrote that KBR had exposed the entire camp to water *twice as contaminated* as raw water from the Euphrates River. Granger, who detailed the problems to his bosses in a twenty-one-page report, told his superiors in a memo that "I have yet to find an installation that does the required testing, let alone has such documents to support the testing activities."

Several months after the January 2006 hearing broke the story of unsafe water for the troops, I held another hearing after I had acquired a copy of Granger's twenty-one-page internal report that he had submitted to Halliburton headquarters in Houston.

Granger said the lack of good water "caused an unknown population to be exposed to potential harmful water for an undetermined amount of time. This event should be considered a near miss as the consequences of these actions could have been very severe resulting in mass sickness or death."

Not surprisingly, Halliburton issued a statement alleging that they had found neither contaminated water nor medical evidence to substantiate reports of illness at the base. And the Pentagon, continuing its chummy relationship with Halliburton, said, "The allegations appear to have no merit."

The Halliburton denials directly contradicted confidential internal Halliburton memos that I have read. In my opinion, the company was unwilling to tell the truth. The Pentagon, in a stunning demonstration of incompetence, was seemingly unconcerned with an issue that threatened the health of its soldiers.

Even as Halliburton was in denial, further confirmation of Halliburton's malfeasance came in an e-mail to me from a U.S. Army surgeon who was serving in Iraq. Capt. A. Michelle Callahan described water contamination at the Iraqi military base where she was a physician. She said in an e-mail to me:

In January I noticed the water in our showering facility was cloudy and had a foul odor. At the same time . . . I had a sudden increase in soldiers with bacterial infections presenting themselves to me for treatment. All of these soldiers live in the same area . . . and use the same water to shower. I had 4 cases of skin abscesses, 1 case of cellulitis, and 1 case of bacterial conjunctivitis.

. . . I asked [the] . . . officer to test the water . . . [The] results . . . showed no chlorine residual and was positive for coliform bacteria.

She went on to detail her investigation and confrontation with a KBR manager:

Mr. Wallace argued that since the raw water from the Tigris is first filtered through the carbon prior to going into the ROWPU that it is acceptable for hygiene. This argument is

wrong. Charcoal filtration only removes the particulate matter and binds some chemicals. All the bacteria and chemicals
that make it through the charcoal are concentrated to *twice the
level* [emphasis added] as in the raw water. This is the water
with which the soldiers . . . have been showering, shaving,
and brushing their teeth.

Even in the face of facts that proved the opposite, an army general came to the Senate Armed Services Committee hearing to specifically deny the charges that had been leveled at Halliburton for
providing contaminated water to military bases in Iraq. That general denied the entire incident, even though the Pentagon Inspector
General had informed the Pentagon prior to the general's testimony
that the allegations were true. But the soldiers knew better, even if
the general continued to deny it. (The accuracy of that testimony is
being investigated by the Defense Department.) A *Washington Post*
story reported, "At Camp Ar Ramadi in Anbar province, auditors
found that of 251 soldiers interviewed, 44 percent reported water
provided for personal hygiene that was discolored or had an unusual
odor. Four percent of the soldiers said they got sick from the water."
(Dana Hedgpeth, reporting on March 11, 2008.)

So, the Halliburton employees and an army surgeon all testified
to the failure of Halliburton and the threat it posed to American
soldiers. But the Halliburton Corporation and its good friends in
the army hierarchy denied everything.

The biggest disappointment was that the generals at the Pentagon exhibited no interest in the issue except to deny it happened.
However, in March of 2008 the Inspector General of the Pentagon
completed the investigation that I had requested, and finally, from
this thorough investigative report, we know that statements by Halliburton and testimony by the Pentagon officials deceived Congress
and the American people about this matter. As of this publication,
that matter was under investigation as a result of my request to the
Secretary of Defense.

But that is what happened.

## RORY MAYBERRY'S STORY

The contract called LOGCAP was a logistical contract for the purpose of providing services that the military itself used to provide.
We've all heard of soldiers being put on KP (kitchen patrol) and
peeling potatoes or washing dishes. These days in Iraq it is a new
military. No more KP. The Pentagon has contracted many of the
services they used to provide themselves, including food services.

Early on in the war, there were allegations about overcharges for
food services. As I referenced earlier, at one point the Pentagon was
alleging that KBR was charging the government for forty-two
thousand meals a day while serving only fourteen thousand meals
a day.

I can see missing a cheeseburger or two, but to call overcharging
by twenty-eight thousand meals a day a mistake is a real whopper.
Where I come from, if those types of allegations were true and
someone overcharged by twenty-eight thousand meals it would be
called cheating.

While we were conducting the oversight hearings on Iraq contracting, we were contacted by Rory Mayberry, a man who had
been in Iraq working for KBR as a supervisor in food service.

Rory worked for the Halliburton Corporation at Camp Anaconda in Iraq in 2004 as a food production manager. That meant he
was a supervisor in a dining hall that fed American troops. His experience as he related it to our Democratic Policy Committee hearing confirmed other accounts of widespread problems with the
Halliburton LOGCAP contract to provide various services for the
American soldiers.

He said that the Anaconda camp was a transition site for army personnel. Originally there were a large number of troops passing through
every day, so KBR would charge for a surge capacity of five thousand
troops per meal. But KBR continued to charge for the extra meals
even after Anaconda was no longer a transition base. That meant the
taxpayers were paying for meals that were never served.

When Rory confronted the KBR managers about the over-charges, they told him they were adjusting the numbers to make up for money they lost when the Pentagon suspended some dining hall payment.

Because they were charging for meals never served, Rory testi-fied, the KBR managers would triple his food orders every week. They wanted the food orders to compare to their charges for the number of troops being fed. He said most of the food went to waste. In summary, he reported that while he was there the company was charging for twenty thousand meals a day, but they were only serv-ing ten thousand. Another problem he described was that food items were being brought into the base that were marked outdated or ex-pired on the packages, some by as much as a year.

"We were told by the KBR food service managers to use these items anyway," he testified. "This food was fed to the troops." He said that when trucks arrived that had been hit by small-arms fire during transit, the KBR workers were "told to go into the trucks and remove the food items and use them after removing any bullets and any shrapnel from the bad food. . . . We were told to turn the removed bullets over to the managers for souvenirs."

Rory said that government auditors would or could have caught and fixed many of the problems, but KBR managers told the work-ers not to talk to the auditors. He recounted that the managers' way of keeping the workers quiet was to threaten to send them to a base with more hostile action if they talked to an auditor. Rory said he was transferred to Fallujah for three weeks: "The manager told me I was being sent away until the auditors were gone because I had opened my mouth to the auditors."

## CUSTER BATTLES: THE POSTER CHILD

When the Bush administration created the organization called the Coalition Provisional Authority and sent Paul Bremer to run it, they also sent young, inexperienced people to work in the CPA. It has been reported that the administration even chose many of those who were sent to work in Iraq by employing political loyalty tests during interviews, asking things like their views on abortion, before they could be hired.

One example of this is evidenced by the hiring of an inexperienced twenty-four-year-old named Jay Hallen, who was sent to Iraq to set up a stock exchange. It appears that his only qualifications were his Republican credentials. In his book *Imperial Life in the Emerald City: Inside Iraq's Green Zone*, author Rajiv Chandrasekaran documents evidence that the plan was to build a neoconservative-style government in lockstep with right-wing principles—neoconservative political indoctrination.

In the midst of this chaos Frank Willis, an experienced executive, took a leave of absence from the Lynn Institute in mid-2003 to serve in the CPA as a senior advisor to the Iraqi Minister of Transportation and Communications.

Mr. Willis told my committee that in June of 2003 the U.S. government decided to reopen the Baghdad airport for civilian aircraft service. A decision was made to contract with a company to provide security for the airport. They put out a Request For Proposal, allowing three or four days for a response, and mandated that the security team would have to be in place by July 15.

A company named Custer Battles said it could do the job and was ready. In a matter of several days, this new company was awarded the $16 million contract. They were paid $2 million in cash immediately and $2 million more at the end of July.

But just weeks after the contract was signed, the decision to reopen the Baghdad airport was rescinded. Despite the fact that the reason for the contract had disappeared, Custer Battles continued to be paid under the $16 million contract. No one bothered to definitize the contract, so Custer Battles got millions for doing a job that didn't need doing.

According to a July 2006 *60 Minutes* investigation, "Col. Richard Ballard, the top inspector general for the Army in Iraq, was assigned to see if the company was living up to its contract, such as it was.

'And the contract looked to me like something that you and I would write over a bottle of vodka,' Ballard says. 'Complete with all the spelling and syntax errors and annexes, to be filled in later.'"

But because they controlled civilian access to the airport, Frank Willis discovered, Custer Battles apparently began using the airport for a couple of other businesses they had created in Iraq. They had 150 Filipinos located in a few offices to work for a catering business that they had started. They also used an area to build dog kennels, another of their businesses.

According to attorney Alan Grayson, who also testified before Congress, founders Mike Battles and Scott Custer had little experience in the theater of war, but they had formed a company hoping to cash in on the contracting opportunities in Iraq. Their hope was rewarded. In thirteen months the Bush administration lavished over $100 million in contracts on this start-up.

While at the airport on their security job, Custer Battles Company employees reportedly found some Iraqi Airways forklifts. They apparently took the forklifts to a warehouse, painted them blue, and then sold them to the government as "materials" under a different contract.

In a memo to the CPA, the Director of Security for the Baghdad airport described the work of Custer Battles under the security contract. He wrote, "Custer Battles have shown themselves to be unresponsive, uncooperative, incompetent, deceitful, manipulative and war profiteers. Other than that they are swell fellows." Despite the assessment that the company was doing a lousy job, they continued to get new, lucrative contracts for work in Iraq.

The second contract Custer Battles received was to provide security and support for the distribution of the new money (Iraqi dinars) in the country. It was what is called a time and materials contract— which means that the company could bill the government for more than just labor costs. At about the same time, Custer Battles set up subsidiaries in Grand Cayman.

Mr. Grayson told our committee that Custer Battles backdated and forged signatures on invoices from sham companies in the Cayman Islands and then directed employees to sign the fabricated invoices without looking at them prior to submitting them to the government for payment. A former FBI agent working for the firm was recruited to sign the fabricated documents. He refused and said, "You all are going to prison." The second time he refused, according to Grayson, he was held at gunpoint in Baghdad, stripped of his weapons and security identification, and released on the streets of Baghdad.

Custer Battles was paid the first $4 million in new U.S. currency in hundred-dollar denominations. According to Frank Willis, the bills were bundled in plastic-wrapped bricks of one-hundred-dollar bills and they occasionally played football with the bundles. This occurred in a building where there was an estimated $3 billion downstairs in a vault being distributed for contracts that the CPA was letting in Iraq. "It was like the Wild West," Willis said. "We told the contractors, we pay in cash, so bring a bag." Accounting procedures, said Willis, were nonexistent.

When documentation was found, it reeked of profiteering.

One day in October 2003, Custer and Battles attended a meeting with some U.S. military about their currency contract and one of their employees left a company spreadsheet on the table. It showed what Custer Battles had spent for materials on the contract—$3.5 million. And then it listed what Custer Battles Company had billed the government for these same materials—almost $10 million.

Finally, the U.S. Air Force suspended Custer Battles from one of these contracts. But the Pentagon has never really reported to the American people the results of its investigations of Custer Battles and the many other contractors who were accused of fleecing the American taxpayers. We're still waiting.

Three companies named in this chapter, Halliburton/KBR, Parsons, and Custer Battles, have predictably denied the various charges about contract abuses. But they offered no compelling evidence at all, in my judgment, to refute the serious charges that have been leveled.

## THE TRUMAN COMMITTEE SOLUTION

There is a solution to all of the fleecing that was done to the American taxpayers. It's not complicated, and the blueprint for it already exists.

When so much money is spent in wartime for reconstruction as well as contracting for the supplies to equip an army, there is a clear obligation for Congress to do aggressive oversight. I introduced a plan in Congress called the Honest Leadership and Accountability in Contracting Act. It is tough, but it would crack down on fraud and tell those who commit fraud and war profiteering they will be dealt with severely.

*First*, my bill will punish war profiteers. It calls for up to twenty years in prison and at least $1 million in fines for war profiteering.

*Second*, the bill cracks down on corporate cheaters. It calls for a new rule on suspension and debarment to prohibit awarding contracts to companies that exhibit a pattern of overcharging government.

*Third*, it forces real contract competition. No more umbrella contracts on sole-source bids. Bids should be submitted only by companies that have a clean record and can win the contract in a competitive bid.

*Fourth*, it strengthens whistleblower protection by making it more difficult for federal agencies to retaliate against whistleblowers.

A group of us are pushing Congress to enact meaningful reforms that will put an end to the sorry behavior of war profiteering. Until now, we haven't had enough votes to overcome the filibusters by those in Congress who want to protect the contractors, but we aren't going to quit until we have completed the job.

Ultimately, the major reform that Congress must embrace is my proposal based upon the Truman Committee. There are valuable lessons for today to be learned from this experience.

In 1941 then-Senator Harry Truman introduced a bill in the

U.S. Senate to create a special committee to "investigate the types and terms of defense contracts, the methods by which such contracts were awarded, the performance of contracts and the accountings required of contractors."

Truman was concerned about wasteful defense spending following the appropriation of $10 billion for defense needs in 1940. The money was appropriated by Congress in anticipation of the expected involvement in the war in Europe. Soon after the money was appropriated, Truman began hearing about the wasteful contracting, so he took a ten-thousand-mile trip to visit military bases to investigate. What he saw convinced him that there needed to be a special committee formed in the Senate to investigate the waste of defense funding.

Naturally, the generals in the War Department opposed the creation of a special committee. The Roosevelt administration wasn't excited about having such a committee created, either. But President Roosevelt became convinced that if it was going to happen, it would be better done in the hands of someone friendly to the administration, and he thought Truman fit that description. In addition, the Roosevelt administration was told that with a $15,000 budget the committee couldn't do much harm, so the Senate passed the legislation calling for the Truman Committee by unanimous consent.

Thus was born a bipartisan committee that has become known as one of the most effective panels ever created in the Senate. Over the next seven years (from 1941 to 1948) the committee held 432 hearings, called 1,798 witnesses, and released fifty-two reports. That adds up to over sixty hearings a year and it illustrates why and how the Truman Committee is known in history as the gold standard for effective, bipartisan oversight during wartime.

The committee learned that not everything was as it appeared. As the United States began to rearm prior to entering World War II, many business executives began to offer their services to the federal government and, citing patriotic duty, offered to work for just $1 a year. But the Truman Committee found that some of these executives were still being paid by the corporations they had left and, in fact, not only were their old companies working to get massive war contracts from the federal government, but the evidence suggested that most of their efforts were successful.

This raised serious questions about the propriety of the government contracting and whether the government was getting what it was paying for as it prepared for war. The Truman Committee found that in nine months beginning in June 1940 the Army and Navy awarded contracts of nearly $3 billion to sixty-six companies whose officials served the government for just $1 a year.

Although the committee was created with an appropriation of $15,000, over the seven years it was estimated to save the American taxpayers as much as $15 billion. In my mind, Truman's efforts were every bit as patriotic as any during that great struggle. And it tells us something about human nature. Even in a worthy cause, greed often elbows out patriotism.

Congress has created similar committees during nearly every American conflict, including the Civil War, both world wars, the Korean War, and the Vietnam War.

The fact that our military now relies so heavily on private contractors makes it even more important that we, the Congress, create a special committee to investigate the waste, fraud, and abuse in contracting.

In the 109th Congress I offered the proposal to establish a modern-day Truman Committee *three separate times*. Each time it was defeated with all Democrats voting for and all Republicans, with one exception (Senator Lincoln Chafee of Rhode Island), voting against.

The Republicans in Congress were still playing defense for the Bush administration. But they never understood that this wasn't about embarrassing or protecting the President. It was about getting at the truth, making people accountable, and protecting taxpayers.

The American taxpayers deserve to know that Congress will take the actions necessary to put an end to war profiteering and con-

tract cheating. It not only steals from the taxpayers, but it also undermines our soldiers. So stay tuned. I am determined to see my
proposal to create a modern-day Truman Committee to investigate
waste, fraud, and abuse become law.

# CHAPTER 9

• • •

## *Drill, Baby, Drill?*

DRIVING DOWN A highway one day, I saw a man in a beat-up old car in front of me with a bumper sticker that read, "I fought the gas war, and gas won!" I smiled wanly because I understood what he meant. Gas and oil almost always win. It's been going on for a century. And it's not a fair fight. It never has been.

We need oil. And there are some good people and companies out there looking for it. But the money around the oil issues has always been a magnet for speculation, market manipulation, war, and foreign policy blackmail.

If one was going to try to stir up a batch of real trouble for the United States, the first step would be to create an addiction to foreign oil in our economy. Then you would organize a cartel of the countries that hold and produce most of the world's oil so they could fix prices. Finally, you would create an oil futures market for liquidity and juice it up with unbelievable speculation so that with just a little money speculators can amass large profits, as oil prices climb and collapse through oil speculation, by controlling large contracts of oil for future delivery. These aren't people who ever expect to get or want to possess any actual petroleum. They just want to speculate about price through the buying and selling of oil contracts.

All of the conditions I mentioned here now exist. And they are having, and will continue to have, dramatic consequences.

The problem is the United States is addicted to oil. We are the largest consumer of oil in the world, by far, and now import nearly 70 percent of our oil (headed higher), much of it from very troubled parts of the world. In short, the health of the American economy depends on our ability to get the oil we need from places such as Saudi Arabia, Kuwait, Iraq, and other countries in the Middle East.

The countries known as OPEC formed a cartel several decades ago and they now control nearly *50 percent* of the known oil reserves in the world and about *one-third* of the world's production. After decades of trying, the OPEC ministers have finally welded themselves into a real monopoly that affects price through their production decisions.

The OPEC countries' motives are clear: maximize profits from the oil they control. Many of those who control the oil in these countries live in unfathomable opulence and they want still more. It's called greed.

In addition to the control over oil prices by OPEC, there is another trough of greed here at home that is affecting price. What used to be a regulated energy futures market in the United States called NYMEX has morphed into international markets with offshore and over-the-counter unregulated trading. It has become a casino of speculation open twenty-four hours a day, with oil prices bouncing to new highs and then crashing back down, not based on supply-and-demand relationships but rather on sheer speculation.

When this chapter was originally written, the price of a barrel of oil was bouncing up and down around $140 a barrel. However, with the Wall Street crash of 2008, oil prices fell below $40 a barrel, a stunning reflection of the rampant speculation that has both pushed prices up and pulled them down. Some of the price movement was attributable to the influence on price by the production decisions

made by the OPEC countries. And some was a result of the economic slowdown and reduction in demand. But much of it is at-
tributed to the perversion of the futures markets by an orgy of
speculation.

The oil futures market has been on a binge of speculation. It has
gotten more complicated and more volatile because hedge funds,
investment banks, and others are now up to their necks in futures
speculation. In fact, in October 2007 it was reported in *The Wall
Street Journal* by Ann Davis that investment banks such as Morgan
Stanley were even buying oil storage facilities to allow them to buy
oil and then hold it off the market until the price rose. Just as OPEC
regulates the amount of oil on the market, so were some of our own
American corporations desiring to hold oil off the market and benefit from the rising prices.

There is a good reason to have a futures market for the normal
hedging of risk that needs to be done by producers and consumers
of a physical product. But by 2008 in the case of oil futures, the bulk
of the trades had nothing to do with a barrel of oil.

Each day twenty times more oil was being traded than was used.
The world consumes about 85 million barrels of oil a day, but nearly
1.5 *billion* barrels are traded every day on the global exchanges.

Fadel Gheit, the managing director and senior energy analyst at
Oppenheimer & Co., has twenty-five years of experience in energy
trading on Wall Street. He agrees that the futures market for oil "has
become a casino, open twenty-four hours a day, with no cop on the
beat." He believes that the margin requirements for trading should be
raised from the now 5 to 7 percent range to 50 percent. And he proposed setting limits on the number of oil contracts by each account
trader and establishing a minimum holding period for inventory
that is purchased. It's a controversial strategy that sure would punc-
ture the balloon of the speculators.

The problem is these speculators are making wagers on the price
and value of something we all rely on for our standard of living. All
the while the government has been content to be the observer rather
than a regulator willing to take action to right a wrong. When spec-

ulators brought the price of oil back down in late 2008, it was con-
clusive evidence that the regulators who had been saying that the oil
price movements related to supply and demand were all wet. The
wild oil price movements were a result of excess speculation.

## OUR OIL ADDICTION

The consequences of the "oil problem" are dramatic. The price and
availability of oil and the products made from it have a deep impact
on much of our U.S. economy. Because we import so much of our
oil, escalating oil prices increase our trade deficit, which drives
down the value of the dollar, making the oil we import even more
expensive—a vicious cycle indeed that slows our economic growth,
retards job creation, and increases the federal deficit.

But the problem is more complex than we first imagined when
Jimmy Carter talked more than thirty years ago about the crisis to
come. In past years when America discussed the "energy problem"
it usually meant the problem of becoming dangerously dependent
on oil from foreign countries. That is still the case, and it has grown
worse.

But now we also have to understand the ramifications of climate
change. How is our energy consumption affecting our planet and
what can we do to address it? In short, any discussions about oil or
energy now must include the subject of global climate change.

## IT'S SIMPLE! WE NEED IT, THEY HAVE IT

The United States has 5 percent of the world's population and 3 percent of the known oil reserves, but it uses 25 percent of the world's
energy. Meanwhile, the United States produces less than 10 percent
of the world's oil. That is a big problem.

Meanwhile billions of people living in third-world conditions
both see and want the kind of life that we are living here in the

United States and are beginning to make bigger demands for a share of the Earth's natural resources.

For example, people living in China are driving more. Every month there are tens of thousands of new vehicles on the roads, and it is projected that China will add 100 to 150 million more cars in the next fifteen or twenty years. It is also estimated that there will be at least 150 million more vehicles on the roads in India in the next twenty years.

Fast-forward a couple of decades and contemplate a world with hundreds of millions of new vehicles around the planet, all in search of a gas station every few days. Ergo, the energy problem becomes obvious, and acute. Unless we can conserve and manage the market, the economic pain consumers are feeling now will make these times seem like the good old days in a few short years.

It's important to understand the problem. Here in the United States, nearly 70 percent of the oil we consume is used for vehicle transportation. Most of the oil we use comes from outside of our country, including areas where war and terrorism could threaten to shut down the supply at some point in the future. How confident can we be that we will always have oil supplies available from countries such as Saudi Arabia, Kuwait, Iraq, and Venezuela?

It is a curious fact (maybe a cruel irony) that the Creator put most of the oil under the sands of the Middle East and most of the demand here in the United States. With drilling rigs serving as gigantic straws, producers suck about 85 million barrels of oil out of the earth each day. The 300 million of us who live in the United States use about 21 million barrels of that production every day—about one-fourth of the oil produced in the world, which has a population of 6.7 billion. Ever-increasing competition for this resource from India and China alone has the potential to impact us in the future in a very dramatic way unless things change.

We have a choice. We can ignore this issue and sink deeper into all of the danger and risks that it includes. Or, after a century of automobile use in our country, we can decide to use less gasoline and find other means to power our vehicles. We have the ability to use technology and invention to turn a weakness into a strength. We can use the danger of the excessive reliance on foreign oil to motivate us to change our destiny and escape the tyranny of monopolies of OPEC countries abroad and speculators here at home. Wouldn't it be great to be able to tell the OPEC countries, "We don't need your oil"?

But let's be clear. Even as we set ambitious goals to make us less dependent on OPEC oil, at least a part of the solution is to explore more and drill more here at home. I fully support an aggressive push for more renewable energy and new technology that will make our transportation fleet less dependent on foreign oil. But that goal won't be met without understanding our need to produce more of all kinds of energy here at home, and that includes exploring for oil and gas.

## THE SHORT TERM—IT'S RIGHT IN FRONT OF US

The solutions really aren't too complicated. We need to conserve more. And we need to produce more energy. That means producing more oil and natural gas but also producing renewable fuels here at home.

It is imperative that lower prices in the short term not lull us into a false sense of complacency. Even if it requires more subsidies or other means of stabilization in the short run to keep alternative forms of energy competitive, we simply must do it.

Even as we construct a strategy for finding more oil here and converting vehicles to run on a different form of energy, we must consider our impact on the environment.

The overwhelming consensus of scientists is that something dangerous is happening to our climate and that humans are contributing to that change. Most scientists believe that the Earth is warming because of greenhouse gases. The burning of fossil fuels produces a significant portion of those greenhouse gases. Furthermore, they believe that we must take action now or face escalating consequences in the future.

So, if we continue to use large quantities of oil and gasoline to fuel our automobiles and if we are using large quantities of coal to create electricity (50 percent of electricity comes from the use of coal), unless we find a way to capture the $CO_2$ (carbon dioxide), both fossil fuels will be pumping it into the atmosphere and contributing to global warming.

The question looms large—how do we deal with the challenge of solving our energy problem even as we address global warming to protect our environment?

Some make the case that we need to wean ourselves off all fossil fuels. They say we need to find ways to completely stop using both coal and oil. But that is just not going to happen. Over a period of time we can do the things that will make us less dependent on fossil fuels. But even a bold energy plan will not project a future our children will see that includes no coal or oil.

There can be no absolutism. We will need to rely on energy from a variety of sources to solve this crisis. And we need big, bold plans to develop renewable energy. That includes wind, solar, biomass, biofuels, hydrogen, and more. Then we need bold conservation programs, efficiency standards, and innovative ways to combine energy sources and recycling opportunities. And we must settle on alternative energy sources for our vehicles if we are going to really reduce our dependence on foreign oil.

These days there is plenty of bold talk but far less action on these issues.

So let's take them one at a time.

## IMPORTED OIL: THE ULTIMATE ADDICTION

Some object to focusing on the problem of imported oil. But I disagree. First of all, it speaks to the very notion of independence. If we are heavily dependent on Saudi Arabia, Kuwait, and other Middle East countries to fuel our economy, we can never control our fate as a country. Trading for oil in a global economy is fine, but it should be an option, not a necessity. These days it is an addiction and we have to treat it.

The fact that we run up our massive trade deficit to buy foreign oil is hurting our economy. I've outlined the serious economic threat of our trade deficit in my previous book, *Take This Job and Ship It*, so I won't elaborate here other than to say that the net effect of a trade deficit is that it devalues our currency at the same time it enables our trading partners to use the money to buy American companies and real estate and, ultimately, a great deal of *influence*. And that is especially true of the oil cartel countries.

It is a sorry spectacle to see an American President show up in the palace of the Saudi King to ask them to pump more oil. That is what happened in January 2008 and again in May 2008. President Bush visited our "allies" in Saudi Arabia with hat in hand, begging them to pump more oil to lower the price. Even then, as the United States was experiencing the beginning of a recession, the so-called jawboning was met with a cold shoulder by the Saudis. This came in the same week that the newspapers announced that the Bush administration was proposing another record arms deal with Saudi Arabia. It's not as if we don't have the potential leverage to bring production up and prices down; we just have not used it. But it isn't just the Saudis. It is the entire OPEC cartel. When it comes to trade, we are cream puffs, and they know it.

Our dependence on oil is weakening both our economy and our independence, and the rest of the world knows it. In Jack London's harrowing tale *Call of the Wild*, Buck watches as an injured dog, Curly, is surrounded by the rest of the sled dog team and killed. Once Curly is down, the others pounce, leaving behind only a bloody corpse.

I needn't explain the parallel.

I previously pointed out that we use about 25 percent of the oil produced on the Earth every day. Without that oil, America's economy would stop dead in its tracks. To understand how significant our addiction to oil imports has become, consider this: our oil imports equal the imports of the next five top consumers—China, Japan, Germany, Russia, and India—*combined*.

As of October 2007, here are the suppliers of our imported oil ranked from the most to the least. These are the countries from whom we import oil and to whom we export American dollars.

1. Canada
2. Saudi Arabia
3. Mexico
4. Venezuela
5. Nigeria
6. Iraq
7. Angola
8. Ecuador
9. Algeria

It's easy to see the problem of dependency. Of the estimated 85 million barrels of oil that are pumped out of the earth each day, 30 million is pumped by OPEC nations.

According to the U.S. government's Energy Information Administration, if nothing changes, global oil consumption is projected to increase to 118 million barrels in 2030. That will be some trick, to consume 118 million barrels when a fair number of experts believe world oil production may have already peaked. Two-thirds of these projected 118 million barrels will be used for transportation.

Of course, there are as many predictions about the future of oil as there are experts. Some say that even though it is a finite resource, new technology and drilling techniques will continue to allow us to discover and produce larger quantities of oil well into the future. An example of that is a new U.S. Geological Survey Assessment of the oil reserves in what is called the Bakken Shale oil field in eastern Montana, western North Dakota, and central Canada. The USGS estimates that there are up to 4.3 billion barrels of oil recoverable with today's technology. That is the largest assessment they have ever made in the lower forty-eight states. Drilling and producing in that area is going full speed ahead and many new wells are already adding to our U.S. domestic oil supplies every day.

Others paint a bleak picture of the future. In an October 16, 2005, article in *USA Today*, David Lynch writes, "As global demand rises, American consumers will find themselves in a bidding war with others around the world for scarce oil supplies. That will send prices of gasoline, heating oil and all petroleum-related products soaring." He then quotes Kenneth Deffeyes, a Princeton University professor emeritus of geosciences: "The least-bad scenario is a hard landing. Another is a global recession worse than the 1930s; and the worst case borrows from the Four Horsemen of the Apocalypse: war, famine, pestilence and death."

The truth probably lies somewhere among those three views of the future.

But we would be fools to ignore the problem. A future without petroleum would impact us in ways most people don't understand. Pesticides and fertilizers are key ingredients to feeding the world. The fact is, none of us really knows what is ahead. But we can be certain that if we don't make some changes, there is a prospect of real trouble ahead.

## THE FIRST STEP TOWARD ENERGY INDEPENDENCE

How can our nation regain control of our independence in energy?

We need to set a goal for the next decade, an ambitious goal, and then meet it.

When President Kennedy described the mission to put a man on the moon he didn't say "We're going to try," or "We'd like to do it," or "We'll give it our best shot." No. He said we were going to put a man on the moon by the end of the decade. That's what we need to dedicate ourselves to doing with energy independence.

If we don't decide to do that, every ten years we will be debating once again where we are going to get more oil. It makes no sense to me to make our economic future dependent on the willingness of someone else to sell us more oil.

The first step is to set a goal of being able to tell OPEC, "We don't need your oil."

We need to reduce our necessity of oil imports from all sources. But the first place to start is to free ourselves from the cartel that has us over a barrel. To do that we have to find ways to make up that 5.5 million barrels a day we buy from OPEC.

There is good reason to start with OPEC. Extricating ourselves from dependence on those strife-ridden countries in a hostile neighborhood means we will be less compelled to intervene militarily as we have in the Middle East in the past. Does anybody think that the first Gulf War wasn't about oil? If Kuwait had merely consisted of sand dunes rather than oil covered by sand, do you really think Washington would have cared who governed it? And with better vision through the rearview mirror, it's clear that oil policy and the desire to provide security for future oil supplies played at least some role in the decision by President Bush and Vice President Cheney to invade Iraq.

Perversely, by doing business with OPEC we have also been filling up not only our gas tanks but also the coffers of some of the terrorist organizations that want to harm America. Unless you were completely hypnotized by the Bush administration's misdirection after 9/11, you now know that there were no Iraqi hijackers. There were fifteen Saudis, one Egyptian, one Lebanese, and two from the United Arab Emirates. In short, enough oil is spilling from the barrel in the Middle East to fund a substantial amount of terrorist activity, much of it concentrated on us.

I'm not making the case that the terrorist attack of 9/11 was state-sponsored terrorism, but it's a fact that some countries have created a climate that spawns such radical thinking. There is a distinct connection between terrorism and the willing ignorance of the dictatorship of Saudi Arabia.

David Kaplan of *U.S. News & World Report* sums it up when he writes:

Starting in the late 1980s—after the dual shocks of the Iranian revolution and the Soviet war in Afghanistan—Saudi Arabia's quasi-official charities became the primary source of funds for the fast-growing jihad movement. In some 20 countries, the money was used to run paramilitary training camps, purchase weapons, and recruit new members. The charities were part of an extraordinary $70 billion Saudi campaign to spread their fundamentalist Wahhabi sect worldwide. The money helped lay the foundation for hundreds of radical mosques, schools, and Islamic centers that have acted as support networks for the jihad movement.

American oil dollars have been funding extremist textbooks for children in Saudi Arabia. The Center for Religious Freedom has examined textbooks that taught that Jews and Christians are enemies of Islam and that "the hour [of Judgment] will not come until the Muslims fight the Jews and kill them."

So, as we fuel our gas-guzzlers, we fuel Islamic extremism.

The Institute for the Analysis of Global Security adds on its Web site:

The Saudi regime has been complicit in its people's actions and has turned a blind eye to the phenomenon of wealthy citizens sending money to charities that in turn route it to terror organizations. Furthermore, Saudi government money funneled into madrassas where radical anti-Americanism is propagated has been instrumental in creating an ideological climate, which generates terrorism.

Former CIA director James Woolsey describes the Saudi-sponsored Wahhabism and Islamist extremism as "the soil in which Al-Qaeda and its sister terrorist organizations are flourishing."

Do we need more evidence of the urgent need to extricate ourselves from the addiction to oil in the Persian Gulf? I believe it is an issue of patriotism and national defense.

## HOW CAN WE SAVE 5.5 MILLION BARRELS A DAY?

If we want to start by weaning ourselves off the Middle East oil, we have to find a way to replace 5.5 million barrels of oil or their energy equivalent.

But first, it's helpful to know just what we get from a barrel (or 42 gallons) of oil. We produce:

- 19.6 gallons of gas
- 10 gallons of diesel
- 4 gallons of jet fuel
- 1.7 gallons of fuel oil
- 1.7 gallons of propane
- 7.6 gallons of various other products

If that doesn't quite pencil out, it is because as oil is refined, you actually end up with a couple gallons more of product. For the record, not all oil is created equal. For example, Venezuelan crude yields only 5 percent gasoline while sweet Arabian crude produces 30 percent.

One way to transition away from imported oil is to drill more here in the United States, and I support that. Another way is to use a substitute for oil. I support that as well. We currently do that by producing ethanol from corn. Ethanol production now makes up nearly 5 percent of the gasoline pool and is growing. Much has been made of the diversion of corn to fuel and the impact on world food supplies and food prices. But if one looks closer one sees that skyrocketing petroleum prices have raised input costs for the farmer. Fuel, pesticides, herbicides, and fertilizers all are derived from . . . *oil*! Worldwide drought and other adverse growing conditions have contributed far more to any shortages than the amount of corn grown for fuel in America. The drought in Australia may well have been related to global warming caused in great part by . . . *oil*!

Many well-meaning people are perpetuating a complete distortion of reality as it relates to U.S. agriculture. The shortage argument simply bears no relation to the facts. In 2007–2008, corn exports from the United States were 2.25 billion bushels, the highest since 1990!

Certainly, we can all agree that corn-based ethanol production is just a step on the way to producing ethanol from the cellulose of plants in the future. We are in a transition. As with all fledgling technologies, we will have growing pains, but we will get more and more productive.

Producing ethanol from plants such as switchgrass and other similar sources will be much more efficient. Some scientists predict cellulosic ethanol has the potential to *triple* production. It is still at the early stages of development, but I believe that is the future of the ethanol industry.

But there are some challenges with ethanol. We make ethanol from corn now, but we don't yet have the full infrastructure to transport and market it. That needs to be fixed soon. As of 2008, there are about two hundred ethanol refineries in the country, with another two hundred in planning stages.

It makes sense to me to grow our energy in our farm fields year after year instead of relying on the goodwill of the members of OPEC to supply our oil at an affordable price. When it comes right down to it, I would rather see the American farmer make a buck than OPEC oil sheiks.

## RUDOLF DIESEL'S DREAM
## OF SELF-SUFFICIENCY

A close relative of ethanol is biodiesel—essentially vegetable oil—burned in diesel engines. When Rudolf Diesel developed the engine that carries his name over one hundred years ago, he envisioned self-sufficient farmers using the fuels they grew and produced. The first diesel engine ran on peanut oil. Indeed, when you recall the way farmers harnessed the wind with windmills to pump water before

Rural Electric Cooperatives brought electricity to farms, you can see a return to the common sense and innovation of that era.

As an aside, no one knows for sure, but Diesel's invention may have led to his death. He disappeared from a steamer headed to London in 1913. History's sleuths have blamed coal industrialists, who lost a lot of money when diesel engines shoved aside coal-burning contraptions. Other speculation is that Diesel was done in by the Germans who capitalized on the new technology to create a diesel-powered submarine fleet that created great difficulties for the Allies in World War I. Or maybe Rudolf just decided to go for a dip in the ocean. At any rate, Rudolf Diesel was a man with a vision of self-sufficiency that is as important today as it was then.

In 2001 the late Dwight Baumann, a North Dakota native and professor at MIT, lobbied the North Dakota Legislature to approve tax incentives for biodiesel production. This was before energy prices went through the roof. Baumann, too, was ahead of his time when he converted his 1984 Volvo to run on vegetable oils and drove it from Pittsburgh to Bismarck to make his case. Even then, vegetable oil at 90 cents a gallon was cheaper than diesel. It's still cheaper today. Baumann started and ran the car on diesel first to warm it up and then switched to a tank with vegetable oil in it. Mileage was as good as with diesel.

Because diesel engines are 40 percent more efficient than gasoline engines, this country could cut the amount of fuel burned for transportation by that amount simply by going completely diesel. We all know Willie Nelson has a tour bus that runs on biodiesel. God bless him, some news reports suggest Willie used to run on other organic material, too. But his bus is green, and that sends an important message about the viability of the fuel.

America has been slow out of the gate, while Europe produces and consumes 80 percent of the world's biodiesel.

Let there be no arguments about its viability. Emerging Markets Online (EMO), an energy strategy company, says American biodiesel consumption galloped from 25 million gallons per year in 2004 to over 250 million gallons in 2006. Ten times as much in two years!

The upside is tremendous. As of early 2008, just 1 percent of all diesel consumed in the United States was biodiesel. But with eighty new plants projected in 2008, biodiesel consumption will continue to increase.

EMO projects, "It is possible that biodiesel could represent as much as 20% of all on-road diesel used in Brazil, Europe, China and India by the year 2020." What is particularly exciting is that other nations are working to diminish their own addictions to oil. In the end, nations will be helping each other to minimize the sway the Middle East has held over global politics in recent decades.

After the crippling OPEC embargo of the 1970s, Brazil embarked on a quest for energy independence and has achieved it due in great part to ethanol production from sugarcane.

## WE HAVE SEEN THE FUTURE AND IT MAY BE POND SCUM

While biodiesel now comes from soybeans and other oilseed plants, there is promising research on algae. Using algae to produce biodiesel would be an advantage, because it would not be subject to the criticism of affecting the price or availability of food, as has been the case with corn-based ethanol.

The federal government discontinued its research on algae about fifteen years ago. When I became chairman of the appropriations panel that funds energy issues, I restarted the algae research at one of our national research laboratories.

Michael Briggs of the University of New Hampshire has written a brilliant paper on the prospect of using fast-growing, oil-rich algae-based biodiesel to replace all of the fuels currently used for transportation. It's an audacious vision of the future that would make us self-sufficient and greener.

Algae is the single-celled pond scum that we see in wastewater ponds. It grows with water, sunlight, and $CO_2$. There's nothing very fancy about growing algae. And it increases its bulk in hours.

While we are trying to decide how to limit the $CO_2$ emissions from coal plants in order to protect our planet, some are telling us that we can put the $CO_2$ to beneficial use by producing algae with it. Feed the $CO_2$ to algae farms, a process that would consume the $CO_2$ and grow algae at the same time. In addition, the prize at the end of the process is that the algae can be harvested to produce biodiesel. And even more important, projections are that an acre of algae can produce up to eight to ten times the amount of fuel as an acre of corn.

There are demonstration projects under way in the United States and elsewhere, and I am excited that this new technology might someday soon help our country three ways:

1. Give us one more renewable energy option.
2. Make us less reliant on OPEC.
3. Decrease our dependence on less-green fuels and protect our environment by minimizing $CO_2$ emissions.

Fighting the OPEC cartel with pond scum! That's innovation and, some might say, redundant.


## A DRIVE-BY SOLUTION

Two-thirds of the oil we consume goes into our gas tanks. Now, let's suppose we got real serious and decided to hit those oil sheiks where it hurts—right in their gold bullion. We just have to make our vehicles more efficient. It's called conservation. And finally the country seems willing to bite the bullet and demand it.

In 1908 Henry Ford's Model T got 25 miles per gallon. In 2004, according to the Environmental Protection Agency, average auto mileage was less than 21 mpg. That makes no sense at all.

In 2007, for the first time in twenty-seven years, Congress required the automakers to build more efficient automobiles. The new law requires that automakers increase gas mileage of vehicles by a modest 10 mpg over the ten years beginning in 2010 and ending in 2020. The increases are mandated for all classes of vehicles.

The automakers complained and moaned, but this time it didn't do any good. Unlike the old Corporate Average Fuel Economy (CAFE) standards, this new system requires that appropriate standards and attributes are applied to each class of vehicle, ensuring that all of them, including the heavier vehicles, will get better fuel efficiency.

This approach also ensures that manufacturers are not penalized for producing a wide range of vehicles. It is good public policy. No one likes seeing his financial future going into a gas tank. The bill will raise the CAFE standards to 35 mpg by 2020. But that is still miles behind China, which in 2008 mandated that cars get 43 mpg and heavier trucks 21 mpg. We can do better.

America loves its automobiles. And no one I know is predicting a future without them. But we not only have to make them more efficient; we need to find other power sources for the future, too.

Little things and big things can contribute to reducing our reliance on foreign oil. Requiring more efficient vehicles, that's a big thing. But if we planned our trips better, carpooled, took a bus, and just drove smarter, could we cut our consumption by 5 percent in a year? Easy. Just keeping your engine tuned up can save 4 percent. Energy-conserving motor oil (look for the label) can save 2 percent. You can gain up to 15 percent in mileage just by keeping your tires properly inflated (I know, real men don't keep checking their tires . . . but maybe it's time to start). Parking in the shade decreases gas evaporation from your tank. Drive slower when you can.

During the 2008 presidential campaign, Barack Obama was mocked by his opponents for endorsing such commonsense and effective approaches to conservation. But he was right on. What if everyone tackled this like the folks back home did during World War II, because they knew conservation was a life-and-death matter? You want to support the troops? Conserve. You want to support your country? Conserve.

In the near term, battery-powered or hybrid vehicles will become more popular and affordable. They are more efficient. The most common hybrids on the market use battery power to help boost the internal combustion engine at critical times to improve mileage. The vehicles recharge their batteries as they go, so they don't need to be plugged in. It's progress—one step closer to freeing ourselves from OPEC's grip. Battery technology continues to advance and batteries are getting smaller, lighter, and more efficient.

One of the real bright spots in the energy arena is the leadership of T. Boone Pickens, a legendary oilman and noted conservative. I have disagreed strongly with him in the past, as he sent big checks to the swift boat group that attacked Senator John Kerry. I thought it was disgusting. But, as the old saying goes, "even a stopped clock is right twice a day." Pickens's plan that encourages immediate expansion of wind energy and solar energy to power the electric grid makes sense to me. I agree with him that we should build a national transmission grid just as we built an interstate highway system. Then we can produce wind energy and solar energy where it is most advantageous, and using smart grid technology, move it to be used where it is needed.

Pickens says simply that we have an energy crisis and "we can't drill our way out of this problem." To have a man like Pickens endorse green energy with such vigor will have a powerful impact and is a reminder of the strength and innovation of the private sector.

Pickens wants a portion of our vehicle fleet (eighteen-wheelers on our highways and fleets such as garbage trucks) to be converted to being powered by natural gas. It makes some sense to me. I don't know whether that will happen, but in the longer run I believe we will see our major vehicle fleet converted to hydrogen and fuel cells. The amazing thing about hydrogen is that it is everywhere. It can even be extracted from water through the process of electrolysis.

Hydrogen holds great promise, but it will take time to produce affordable hydrogen/fuel cell vehicles and the infrastructure to support them. And someday when we reach that point, we will drive hydrogen-powered cars that provide more power to the wheel even as they emit water vapor from the tailpipe. That can be our future. Unlimited energy and a cleaner environment! And that will be a giant step toward being able to tell the Saudis and others that we don't need their oil.

So far, I have concentrated on the automobile because becoming more efficient on our highways is the key to energy independence. Remember, nearly 70 percent of our energy consumption is used for transportation.

But we can also become much more efficient elsewhere, too.

## ONE BUILDING AT A TIME

We can have major conservation progress in our homes and commercial buildings. The good news is we have already made huge gains. According to Dr. Marilyn Brown, director of the renewable energy program at the Oak Ridge National Laboratory (quoted by John Schoen of MSNBC), "We are using 27 percent less energy per person for residential uses—home heating, cooling and lighting—than we did in the 70s, even though new homes have increased in size by 50 percent over the past 30 years. That's a phenomenal improvement."

About 8 percent of the homes in America are heated by using heating oil. The average home consumes about eight hundred to one thousand gallons a year. Just lowering the thermostat one degree would save 3 percent. Tuning up your furnace can save as much as 10 percent. Better insulation in our buildings also saves energy. In fact, retrofitting buildings is the most immediately effective source of savings from conservation.

Home owners have other alternatives, too. Many have switched to electricity. I think we'll see solar and wind energy incorporated into more new homes to the point that it will be the norm within a decade. We will also see smart grid technology so that home owners and utilities will work together to use electricity more effectively.

We should find a way to cut in half the number of homes heated by fuel oil in the next five years. Solar energy, wind energy, energy-saving lighting . . . there are so many ways to improve our use and choice of energy that will make us less dependent on OPEC oil.

To do this our country has to make a commitment to renewable energy. Consider this: about ninety years ago our country enacted generous, long-term incentives to facilitate the exploration for oil and gas. These incentives have lasted nearly a century.

Contrast that with what we have done for renewable energy. In 1992 Congress enacted tax incentives for renewable energy. The Production Tax Credit was designed to stimulate development of wind and other renewable energy sources.

The renewable energy tax incentives were temporary and modest. *In the next sixteen years they were allowed to expire three times, and they were extended for short periods five times. It has been a pathetic weak-willed effort to get renewable energy started in the United States.* Naturally, some fossil fuel companies in years past have sought to undermine the new green competition with disinformation and political pressure. Recently that has diminished somewhat.

I believe we should have at least a ten-year commitment to these renewable energy tax incentives. We need to tell investors and developers that this is the direction America is headed for the next decade. Only then will everyone understand we are serious about developing renewable energy.

## GO BACK, JACK, USE IT
## AGAIN . . . RECYCLE!

Recycling is one of the most important keys to saving energy and reducing greenhouse gases. In this area, America has come a long way. It's a good thing, too, because each American generates 4.6 pounds of waste per day. Sweden and Germany generate about 2 pounds per person.

Today there are nearly eighteen hundred plastic recycling companies in America, so we have an infrastructure that recycled more than a million tons of plastic bottles in 2005, according to the American Chemistry Council. When you consider that *each ton of recycled plastic saves eleven barrels of oil* and that only 25 percent of plastic bottles are recycled, you can see there is a great upside.

According to the Environmental Protection Agency, better than half of paper—which takes up the most space in our landfills—is now recycled, as well as 45 percent of aluminum cans, 63 percent of steel packaging, and two-thirds of major appliances. That's remarkable progress. It is estimated that we are saving more than 900 trillion BTUs—equal to the energy use in *9 million homes.*

According to the EPA, about 4 percent of the 26.7 million tons of plastic generated in the United States was recycled in 2003. While recycling percentages are increasing, we know we can do better. One of the newest uses for recycled plastic is for lumber. Hey, save a tree, some oil, and the backbreaking labor of staining a deck each year to keep it in shape. A friend of mine used recycled plastic boards when he replaced his aging wooden deck. It looks great and is very sturdy, and he loves the fact that it doesn't need to be treated.

EPA involvement in helping set up recycling programs where there are none and helping solve the logistics in more remote areas could help kick-start tremendous growth in recycling. We need to set aggressive national recycling goals. It is a painless way for us to save thousands of barrels of oil a day.

Another commonsense way to have an impact is to stop buying water in plastic bottles. Seriously, is anything sillier than that? Tap water is better for you, because some plastic bottles may be leaching chemicals into the water. Get a travel mug, and remember, it's environmentally sound, doesn't fund terrorism, and saves you money. As Emeril Lagasse would say, *"Bam!"*

## CAN COAL REDUCE OUR DEPENDENCE ON FOREIGN OIL?

Most of the oil is *over there* and much of the coal is *here.* So, can we use coal to replace some of the foreign oil that we now import? And more important, can we do it while addressing the greenhouse gas problem that contributes to climate change?

We have hundreds of years of coal supplies available. But given the environmental problems associated with burning coal, can we continue to use it in the same or increasing quantities as we have used it in the past? I believe that if we make the effort, we can find the technology to allow us to use our most abundant resource and do it in a way that protects our environment.

It's possible to turn coal into a synthetic fuel that is a substitute for natural gas. The knowledge to do that has been around for eighty years. Germany produced 124,000 barrels of synthetic fuel a day from coal toward the end of World War II. The process converts coal into a gas and then into synthetic fuels.

Today South Africa produces 150,000 barrels of synthetic fuel a day, supplying 28 percent of that country's needs. There is one example of synthetic fuel production in the state of North Dakota. Basin Electric Power Cooperative has a major project that turns lignite coal into synthetic natural gas. It has been a very successful plant. It also ships the $CO_2$ from the plant to Canada to use in an enhanced oil recovery program.

There are tax incentives now in place to encourage synthetic fuel plants in the United States, which were passed in the Democrats' First 100 Days in 2006, but it takes years to build a plant.

According to Patrick Barta in his 2006 *Wall Street Journal* article:

In the U.S., the Defense Department is studying coal-to-oil technology as a way to reduce the American military's dependence on Middle Eastern crude oil. And the National Coal Council, an industry association, is pushing for government incentives to help generate some 2.6 million barrels of liquid fuel a day from coal by 2025. That would satisfy some 10% of America's expected oil demand that year. The plan would require 475 million tons of coal a year, which represents more than 40% of current annual U.S. production. Industry officials believe America's coal reserves are big enough to allow for the extra production.

But the major question is whether coal can be used to produce synthetic fuels without causing serious problems as a result of the $CO_2$ emissions that come from these plants. The answer is: not now. But I think technology can and will solve that problem.

I believe science and technology can find a way to capture and sequester the $CO_2$ emissions from coal plants and that will allow us to continue to use our most abundant resource as a part of the replacement for foreign oil.

As I have described earlier in this chapter, some promising research is under way on $CO_2$ capture:

- I described the algae projects in which the $CO_2$ is fed to algae ponds and the algae consumes the $CO_2$ and is then harvested for diesel fuel.
- Another company in Texas has developed a process to capture the stream of $CO_2$ coming from the stack of a coal plant and chemically turn it into three products: hydrogen, chloride, and baking soda. The baking soda contains the $CO_2$ that otherwise would have been emitted from the plant. Then they simply put the baking soda in a landfill.
- Still another company has told me of a new patented process by which they turn the $CO_2$ into a new product that is used as a substitute for cement.
- Dr. Craig Venter, a renowned scientist, is creating synthetic microbes that would consume coal and turn it into methane gas. That would be game changing. Coal is our most abundant resource.

I am convinced that in the near future we will have the ability to capture the $CO_2$ and put it to beneficial use even as we continue to use coal to meet our energy needs.

Exciting research is being done to create a coal plant in the future that is a zero-emission plant. If we can achieve that (and I believe we will), we will then be able to use our vast coal resources while at the same time protecting our environment.

In addition to continuing to use our coal resources, I believe that our country will begin to construct some additional nuclear power plants. In an age when there is concern about global warming, the production of energy from nuclear power plants has a major advantage in that it does not release $CO_2$ into the atmosphere.

Yes, there are still unresolved issues surrounding the storage of the nuclear waste, but even in that area there are beginning to be some technological advances that can reduce the amount of waste and safeguard the waste. There are nonproliferation issues that attend to the world's increasing use of nuclear power as well. And the Bush administration's nuclear power agreement with India doesn't bode well for our making sure that nuclear power plants overseas won't be used to produce the material needed for nuclear weapons.

Still, I think there will be some more nuclear power plants built in our country in the years ahead and it is our obligation to address storage and other related issues.

## OIL EXPLORATION

Even as we work on a range of other energy issues, such as renewable energy and conservation, we still will need to produce more oil and gas here at home in the coming years.

Some have tried to reduce the issue of domestic production to shouting about whether we are going to open for drilling the Arctic National Wildlife Refuge (ANWR). But we set that aside many decades ago as a wildlife refuge (President Eisenhower signed that legislation), and I think it is foolish to decide to produce in a pristine area that we have set aside for future generations.

The seasoned analysts understand that an area with some of the greatest potential future oil development is in the Gulf of Mexico, where experts believe the greatest opportunity for successful oil drilling exists. The second and third most promising areas, respectively, are off the West Coast and in Alaska.

A substantial portion of our domestic oil now comes from the

Gulf of Mexico. But we are limited in our ability to produce because so much of it has been put off-limits.

Hurricane Katrina caused massive damage in the gulf region, but through it all the offshore oil drilling rigs survived without damage to the environment. I think this demonstrated that we can continue to produce on the outer continental shelf without major risk to the environment.

I and three other Senators developed the proposal that is now law to open up what is called Lease 181 in the Gulf of Mexico for oil and gas production. Although we got 8.3 million acres opened up, it was scaled back from the legislation we proposed. We need to make more of the area of the gulf available for production.

Earlier in this chapter I referenced the new 2008 study that I requested be done by the U.S. Geological Survey of the Baaken oil field in North Dakota, Montana, and parts of Canada. They estimated that up to 4.3 billion barrels of oil were recoverable using today's technology. But that is just a small fraction of the oil that exists. When technology improves, more will be accessible.

Producing more domestically is necessary as part of our inevitable transition toward less dependence on foreign oil. While I am confident of many energy breakthroughs and alternatives to oil for the next generation, I am just as sure that petroleum will be a part of our energy mix in the future. Our job now is to lessen our need for foreign oil and supplement it with other sources of energy.

The excitement of building a future of renewable energy sources is evident everywhere. For example, we are seeing major success in harnessing the energy from the wind. And finally, I believe we will see other major contributions coming from solar, geothermal, and more.

We'll see wind and solar energy contributing more to our electrical needs. We may well see a future of decentralization of energy transmission. Individual homes and communities may adopt technology and green energy to become energy self-reliant and then sell the excess energy they produce from their wind or solar energy plant back on the grid in a "smart grid" future.

In 2008 a Spanish company, Acciona, completed a wind farm straddling the borders of North and South Dakota that could power sixty thousand homes. The company utilizes existing transmission capacity to sell energy on the spot market. However, wind energy won't really take off until we can provide expansion of transmission capacity.

The transition toward less dependence on foreign oil and the development of energy alternatives here at home will require all of us to understand the need for a new approach to energy consumption and production.

As we take inspiration from our own history it will do us good to reconsider our perspectives as the Greatest Generation did. I grew up with that generation as mentors, and what strikes me is that they did not see those times as years of sacrifice as much as a time to act according to the simple notion that they had to live smarter, waste less, and recycle more. They *had* to be more independent. It always seemed to me that someone of that era could fix anything with baler twine and a little wire. They fixed instead of discarded. It was a sin to buy something new unless absolutely necessary. They walked two blocks to the store instead of driving.

There's a fine line between sacrifice and common sense, because both require doing what needs to be done. The sacrifice and common sense of that generation made America the greatest country on earth. Now, a new generation is called upon to overcome the current challenges and lead this country and world into a new era of common sense and smarter living.

# CHAPTER 10

. . .

# *Health Care: A Leading*
# *Cause of Stress*

EVEN AS OUR country battles to lift the economy out of a deep
recession, the increasing cost of health care is continuing to eat
away at family and business income every year. And it hurts our
economy.

It's astonishing. Here in America, a country known for a generous spirit, we have Americans stressed out over what I believe ought
to be a basic right of every American—affordable health care. According to *Time*, even an average healthy family able to afford insurance will spend $12,000 for a policy. And even the insured must fear
bankruptcy in the event of serious illness. It is estimated that nearly
one-half the bankruptcies in this country are related to health-care
expenses that people can't afford.

Our broken system is an incredible drain on both resources and
peace of mind, and I believe it is hurting our country in so many
different ways. Businesses that offer health-care benefits to their employees struggle to pay the bill. Federal and state governments watch

their budgets explode with steeply increasing health-care costs every year.

To me, the subject of health care will always take me back to a different time and place—a one-room drugstore on the street level with a doctor's examining room on the second floor. It belonged to Dr. Simon W. Hill, who practiced medicine for nearly sixty years in our town of several hundred people. He made house calls, delivered babies, and ran the drugstore, and no one in my hometown ever went without health care because they didn't have money.

Doc Hill treated everybody. If they had money, they paid by cash or check. If they were small-time farmers who didn't have any money to spare, they would give the doc a few fryer chickens or some meat from a hog or a steer when they butchered it. If they had nothing, they got free health care. It was a type of private-pay, Medicaid, and Medicare system all rolled into one, managed by a small-town doctor. And it worked.

Yes, he treated our neighbor's son for an abscessed tooth once and pulled the wrong tooth. But it was an honest mistake. After all, Doc Hill wasn't a dentist. He was just doing the best he could to relieve pain in a small town over an hour away from the nearest urban center of ten thousand people. And because my small town had no lawyer, I don't believe Doc Hill was ever sued.

That was long ago and far away, and in the intervening years things have changed in a big way and we now have medical care that has seen remarkable advances but also faces major challenges.

Even as we struggle to find a way to make sense of a health-care system that can be both unbelievably good and at the same time callously unavailable to someone in desperate need, I want to tell a fascinating story about a laboratory experiment that gives us just a glimpse of what the future holds as scientists search every day for health and medical advances. This story illustrates why if we can begin to fix the problem of cost and access in health care, there is great reason to have hope for the future. We will continue to see breathtaking advances in the science and technology of health care at an accelerated pace in the years to come.

## THE MONKEY AND THE RED BALL

Even today we are witnessing great advances in research to help restore functions for those who have lost an arm or a leg. The federal government is doing the research, and this is an example of both the substantial cost and the real dividends that come from medical science.

The research involves a monkey belonging to the Defense Advanced Research Projects Agency (DARPA). This recent experiment began with a monkey sitting in a chair with a computer joystick in front of him. The joystick was attached to a metal arm in front of the monkey that he could move back and forth and up and down. In front was a red ball that moved across horizontally on a wire.

The monkey was taught that if he used the joystick to cause the metal arm to touch the red ball when it moved across in front of him, he got a treat. It was learned behavior that he repeated over and over. The monkey became expert at touching the red ball and getting his treat.

Then the researchers implanted electrodes in the monkey's brain and attached the electrodes to a type of sophisticated computerized electronic artificial arm that they had designed and built. They located the artificial arm next to the monkey and continued the experiment.

They removed the joystick. When the red ball moved across in front of the monkey, he had no joystick and no way to touch it and get his treat. But he had not forgotten what he wanted to do. The monkey's thoughts were then transmitted from his brain through the electrodes to the bionic artificial arm, and the artificial arm reached up and touched the ball.

The researchers were incredulous. They had thought that with luck they might be able to intercept the monkey's memory with the experiment. But they actually used the electrodes to capture the monkey's thoughts. It was a stunning breakthrough.

Dr. Tony Tether, the head of DARPA, was at Walter Reed Hospital in Washington, D.C., one day visiting with Iraq war veterans who had lost arms and legs in the war. He told one young man who had lost an arm in an explosion in Iraq about the experiments with the monkey and that it could lead someday to the soldier having a new arm that functions much like his real one did. A sophisticated artificial new arm could move as a result of thoughts from the brain.

The researcher cautioned the soldier that it could be five years, ten years, or more before something like that might be available.

"That's okay," the soldier said. "I'm only twenty-two. Just keep working to get it done."

If you are as wide-eyed with hope as I am about such medical advances, you must have a deep-seated belief that we can unlock the mysteries of some of our dread diseases and afflictions and advance the cause of healing those who are sick or injured. But despite all of the excitement about new medical breakthroughs, we face daunting challenges with day-to-day care in America.

## THE SICK-CARE SYSTEM

We hear a lot of talk about our "health-care system," but in fact we really don't have such a thing. We have a "sick-care system."

If you get sick and are headed toward an expensive acute-care hospital bed, your insurance policy (if you have one) is going to kick in and start paying the bills for your hospital stay. This approach to health care pays when you get sick but won't cover the much smaller bill to keep you well. It doesn't make much sense, but it is what we have to understand if we are going to understand "common sense," or the lack of it, as it relates to health care. Common sense in a health-care system always begins with our memory of our first primary care giver—in most cases, a mother. Long before families recognized the terms "primary care physician" and "home health care" there was a mother (occasionally a father) at home doing primary and home health care. You will no doubt remember the constant prodding and sometimes downright relentless nagging of your mother. It was all about health.

"Put on your coat. It's cold outside!"

"Did you brush your teeth?"

"Have some fruit. It's good for you."

"Make sure you wash your hands."

"Quit fooling around before someone pokes an eye out!"

"Are you wearing clean underwear?" Okay, maybe that's not health care specific, but every young boy remembers that question. And the answer was always, "Yes, Mom, I am."

All of that motherly advice was intended to keep you safe and well.

Nowadays all of the emphasis of our health-care system is on preparing yourself for when you get sick. The focus is on making sure you have good health insurance to take care of you when you fall ill and good nursing home insurance to take care of you when your body and/or mind breaks down. There is much less emphasis on what to do to avoid getting sick.

Today's health-care system is about money—big money—and is reactive instead of proactive. It is about treating you when you are sick. So, the money in the system is to support a "sick-care system." And it makes very little sense.

According to *Reader's Digest*, George Halvorson, CEO of Kaiser Foundation Health Plan, notes that diabetes, asthma, heart trouble, and depression account for 75 percent of our health-care spending. These are not exotic maladies but entirely treatable and preventable in most cases if we get serious about prevention. Diabetes is the fastest-rising disease in the country and yet it is something that can often be prevented through proper nutrition and exercise.

## KEEPING PEOPLE WELL COSTS LESS THAN TREATING THEIR ILLNESSES LATER

It is a fact that most of the money spent in our health-care system is expended in support of treating sickness rather than encouraging wellness. I don't suggest that we shouldn't spend money to help people when they are sick. But I think it makes a lot more sense to spend less money up front keeping them well rather than spending more money later when they are lying in an expensive acute-care hospital bed.

How did we lose the common sense that had been the foundation of good health in almost every home when we grew up? And how do we change the system and our way of thinking to emphasize health and begin paying for preventive measures in order to stop paying more later for failing health?

In many ways, health care is a big success story of this generation, and we have some of the best in the world. Not too many Americans, facing a serious health challenge, get busy looking for options of treatment in a foreign country. It is here in our country where we have seen world-class medical centers develop with state-of-the-art equipment and care. The problem is, not everyone can afford that treatment. The cost of health care is galloping out of sight and out of reach for tens of millions of our citizens.

The miracle drugs, breathtaking surgeries, and ability to look inside the body without making an incision are all wonderful changes in health care. But such things cost a fortune, and because of these escalating costs there are now over 46 million Americans who have no health-care insurance coverage.

According to the Institute of Medicine, the hidden cost of having that number of uninsured totals somewhere between $75 and $205 billion a year. The *Reader's Digest* article quoted earlier says the cost of the uninsured to the average family amounts to a $700 a year "hidden tax." It just stands to reason that regular health care and early treatment save both lives and money. When a condition becomes chronic, it is far more expensive to treat.

A new study by researchers for the American Cancer Society shows that patients without health coverage are twice as likely to die within five years of diagnosis as those with private insurance coverage. The study's conclusion makes sense. Those Americans who don't have health insurance are less likely to get recommended cancer-screening tests. When the patients finally do get diagnosed, their cancer is likely to have spread.

Every day, 46 million Americans are spinning a roulette wheel, hoping to avoid illness and hospitalization that could bankrupt them. In the end, that just ends up costing the system more.

## MEDICAL BILLS FORCE EVEN THE INSURED INTO BANKRUPTCY

Today, the motivation for not getting sick is something entirely different. If you revisit our entire history as a country, have we ever been more concerned about health care than we are now? With all the advances in medicine, why is that?

It's because most people understand they are one big illness away from bankruptcy. The cost of a catastrophic illness can wipe out the family savings in a heartbeat, and an Associated Press story from February 2, 2005, revealed that illnesses trigger about half of all personal bankruptcies. So, the reason for those big bankruptcy numbers is because there are over 46 million Americans who have no health insurance, right? Wrong! *Most* of those who filed for bankruptcy because of medical bills did so even though they *were* insured! According to "Medical Bills Make Up Half of Bankruptcies: Study Finds Most Bankruptcy Filers Had Health Insurance":

> Researchers from Harvard's law and medical schools said the findings [from a Harvard University study] underscore the inadequacy of many private insurance plans that offer worst-case catastrophic coverage, but little financial security for less severe illnesses.

"Unless you're Bill Gates, you're just one serious illness away from bankruptcy," said Dr. David Himmelstein, the study's lead author . . . "Most of the medically bankrupt were average Americans who happened to get sick."

In 2001 there were *1.46 million* personal bankruptcies, an estimated 730,000 Americans filing because of expenses relating to illness.

I think Americans accept that sometimes business decisions go awry or personal mismanagement can lead to bankruptcy, but I believe most people feel there is an inherent unfairness in a system that punishes the sick just for not being well-heeled enough to pay the rocketing cost of health care.

A whole new industry has sprung up to prey on those with delinquent medical bills. Brian Grow and Robert Berner of *Business-Week* tell the story of April Dial, a twenty-three-year-old truck-stop waitress who makes $17,000 a year plus tips. She suffers from diabetes, but when her hospital grew disenchanted with the $100 monthly payments she was making to pay off four emergency room visits, she soon discovered her debt had been "transferred" and the company called Complete Care was demanding $455 a month.

What is happening is that hospitals that are typically able to recover only about 10 cents on the dollar on delinquent debt through traditional methods are turning accounts over to finance experts, banks, credit card companies, and private equity firms. Sometimes interest can be as high as 27 percent. The days of paying what you can to your hospital are over.

Dial told *BusinessWeek* that after she pays for rent, food, and other doctor visits, there isn't enough left over to pay the bill. "Every extra dime I have [already] goes to paying medical bills."

The increase in fine print means patients often don't know their debts are being "transferred" to companies like GE Money Bank and its CareCredit company. The same *BusinessWeek* article tells the story of Alice Diltz, sixty-eight, a part-time hospital aide, who needed two extractions and five implants at a cost of $7,450 at Hillside Dental Care in Queens, New York. Her retired husband's dental policy covered only $200 for the two extractions.

Grow and Berner report:

Diltz paid $250 from her pocket and signed up for what she says she thought was an installment plan directly with the clinic. In fact, she signed an application for CareCredit, which was labeled as such, but in small print. Diltz says neither [her] . . . dentist . . . nor his staff mentioned a credit card.

While having her teeth pulled, Diltz began to bleed heavily. She got scared and left the dental office after the extractions. Four days later she canceled the implants, assuming her dealings with Hillside were over. But several weeks later she received a bill from CareCredit for $7,000. Hillside had transferred that amount to the credit-card company, which in turn paid the clinic about $6,300 up front. Diltz says she called CareCredit to dispute the charge, but bills kept arriving. Several weeks later, she says she called again and objected in writing. But GE told her she had missed a 60-day deadline and couldn't reverse the charge.

The author of *This Land Is Their Land: Reports from a Divided Nation*, Barbara Ehrenreich, says, "In general, the great accomplishment of the private health insurance industry has been to overturn the very meaning of insurance, which is risk-sharing: I once tried to explain to a Norwegian woman why it was so hard for me to find health insurance. I'd had breast cancer, I told her, and she looked at me blankly. But then you really *need* insurance, right? Of course, and that's why I couldn't have it."

Ehrenreich continues, "This is not because health insurance executives are meaner than other people, although I do not rule that out." She says it's just that they're running a business, the principal purpose of which is not health care but profits.

She tells the story of Dr. Prem Reddy, who owns eight hospitals in Southern California, which have helped him amass a $100 million fortune: "His hospitals are infamous for refusing to treat uninsured patients, like a patient with kidney failure and a 16-month-old baby with a burn. The *Los Angeles Times* quoted him as saying, 'Patients may simply deserve only the amount of care they can afford.'" Furthermore, he derides the "entitlement mentality" that everyone should have access to high-quality health care.

That is the root of the problem and what causes me to wonder what happened to the common sense we learned about health care when we were growing up.

## A SYSTEM ONLY A SCROOGE COULD LOVE

And one of the problems with the high cost of health care is that no one is watching the till. The last time you went to see a doctor, did you ever see a full accounting of the cost, or did you just get a bill for your share? In many cases where there is a health insurance payment or a Medicare payment to a doctor or a hospital, the patient is not the one who reviews the bill and says, "Yes, those are the services the hospital provided and I certify that the bill is correct."

You can't have a car repaired or even get groceries without an itemized list, but health-care billing is a mystery to most of us. That's pure folly. Medicare did a pilot project evaluating Medicare claims from sixteen hundred health-care providers in South Florida. It turns out that *over 30 percent* of the Medicare claims submitted to the federal government for payment were fraudulent! That wouldn't have happened if the patient had been a part of the billing process to certify that the services that were being billed were the only ones rendered. Obviously, that has to change. Many things must change. I suppose that Medicare will argue that the patient does see the itemization of services, but when I saw some of the statements my parents received it seemed to me as if they were written in some strange foreign language.

The first thing we have to do to fix things is embrace the proposition that the current system has to change. It is so flawed, bloated, clogged with paper, and, in some cases, greed ridden that it defies belief. The for-profit health-care industry and its political enablers have successfully frightened Americans about alternatives, yet twenty-eight industrialized nations already guarantee access to health care as a right of citizenship, with health-care coverage for everyone. It's not as if it can't be done. Other countries are doing it and so should we.

## GET OFF THE COUCH

Before we talk about a system for health-care reform, let's discuss personal responsibility. Get off the couch! You can read this while on the exercise bike.

The people who know will tell you that your odds of living a long life will be improved if you do three things. Wear a seat belt. Stop smoking. And lose weight. It's that simple. So, if we are talking about health care and its costs, let's look at obesity and the fact that we are wearing out both our remote controls and our living room couches. Don't even think about reining in health-care costs if you aren't willing to talk about improving your own fitness.

Preventive medicine requires two things. The first is easy if we have the will. You take your car in every three thousand miles for an oil change and a checkup, but most Americans never bother to get a regular checkup on themselves. We must commit ourselves to getting routine checkups.

The second thing we need to do is a bit more complicated but necessary. We have to focus on the nearly unbelievable sedentary lifestyles of Americans, our bad nutrition habits, and the general environment in which we live, all of which contribute to obesity, diabetes, heart disease, cancer, and more.

Today we are told that two-thirds of Americans are either overweight or obese. That's unbelievable. A study by Johns Hopkins University predicts that at this rate 75 percent of Americans won't need padding to fill out a Santa suit by the year 2015—they will be fat but, I'll bet, not jolly about it. And more startling, 41 percent of the American people will be statistically obese.

It isn't rocket science to fix this. One key is to restore focus on physical fitness in our schools. If students must meet educational standards, why shouldn't they be required to meet some standards on fitness? English, math, and science are important. But all of those brilliant minds need some exercise if they are going to live long enough to contribute to a better society.

By having schools invest more in physical fitness and teach life-long fitness habits, we will save lives and untold trillions in the future. And it's long past the time to get rid of the soft-drink machines and the high-fat nacho chips in the school hallways.

How did America's parents allow our schools to contract with Coke, Pepsi, and Frito-Lay to compete for our kids' loose change in our school buildings? Were we sleeping? Who decided that we would ignore the growing childhood obesity if we could just get a fat contract from the companies that sell the soda and junk food to shore up our school funding?

How about raising the money for our schools the old-fashioned way, through taxes? Putting junk food in our schools is a deal with the devil and is a disservice to our kids. And I know, even when we clear the school hallways of those machines, the students will stop at the local McDonald's or Burger King after school and buy a double bacon cheeseburger, a large order of fries, and a thirty-gallon keg of Coke. Where is the fruit and vegetable aisle?

In the workplace, new federal regulations allow employers to penalize employees up to 20 percent of the cost of a health insurance policy for being overweight. It's the right instinct to be concerned about those who are overweight, but how about using rewards rather than penalties? It would be a whole lot more effective.

Better to *reward* employees for meeting certain fitness standards— like quitting smoking, lowering cholesterol, achieving cardiovascu- lar fitness. Instead of coffee breaks, allow employees to work out for half an hour. Buy them health club memberships. Pay them for sick days not used.

One of the heroes in the workplace is Jim Hagedorn, the CEO of Scotts Miracle-Gro. In an effort to promote healthier lifestyles and make his company more efficient, he created a $5 million wellness center that includes a free clinic, a physical therapist, and free generic prescriptions. Annual operating costs are $4 million to serve six thousand employees, but he believes it will save money and increase productivity.

Ultimately, we have to take personal responsibility and change our bad habits. Some experts have hypothesized that man has a primal urge to gorge, as his cave-dwelling ancestors must have done, not knowing when the next woolly mammoth might come along. But it seems to me that is just more psychobabble. We are well past the primal-urge days. These days it has more to do with the well-advertised prepackaged, precooked, unhealthy foods that have become the norm in our lives.

We take in far more empty calories than our bodies need and we burn off fewer. The plain fact is, there is no health-care plan that will work unless we make some real changes about the way we eat and exercise.

## WHY THE URGENCY ABOUT HEALTH-CARE COSTS?

The cost of health care is running far ahead of both inflation and wage increases. *It's not sustainable*, and it is an indication that something is terribly wrong with our system.

According to the National Coalition on Health Care, our health-care spending is over $2 trillion annually. America now spends 16 percent of its gross domestic product on it, and this is estimated to grow to 20 percent by 2015. That means for every dollar produced in America, 20 cents will be spent on health care. By contrast, health-care spending in those countries with universal coverage is 10.9 percent of the GDP in Switzerland, 10.7 percent in Germany, 9.7 percent in Canada, and 9.5 percent in France, according to the Organisation for Economic Co-operation and Development.

Those numbers don't mean much to a family or a business. It is the monthly business cost or the outlay each month for the family health insurance plan that really matters. And that continues to increase at a rapid pace. The cost of health insurance and health care, combined with other adverse economic conditions, means that most Americans are losing ground.

Clearly, we need some sort of a national health-care system in order to get the escalating costs under control. Opponents would frame this debate as an argument of capitalism versus "socialism." But that's not the choice. We can develop a national system using the private sector and retaining the choice of doctors. But with 46 million people uninsured and many Americans struggling to pay their increasing health insurance bill each month, we need change, and soon.

To continue employing a system in which the availability of health care depends upon your ability to pay is reprehensible. The New Testament tells us that Jesus didn't ask the sick whether they had coverage. He just healed them. So should we.


## PUTTING THE BRAKES ON DRUG PRICE INCREASES

One of the fastest-growing areas of health care is the cost of prescription drugs. That is because the pharmaceutical companies have a virtual monopoly in pricing their drugs.

A special provision in U.S. law allows only the drug manufacturers themselves to import prescription drugs into the United States. That means that U.S. consumers are a captive market—not allowed to purchase prescription drugs from other countries. And because the pharmaceutical industry charges lower prices for most prescription drugs in nearly every other country, the only way they can stop the American consumer from shopping abroad for the best prices on FDA-approved drugs is to have this sweetheart deal preventing the consumers from importing drugs.

The United States is virtually the only country that does not have some kind of price controls on prescription drugs. So, the pharmaceutical industry sells most of the brand-name prescription drugs in other countries for a fraction of the price they charge in the United States and charges the highest prices in the world to the American consumer.

There isn't a delicate way to say it. Big Pharm's pricing policies are gouging sick Americans. The drug companies simply charge what the market will bear.

Here's what John McCain said about it: "Drug companies want to keep your drug prices high." McCain pointed out, as I have been doing for years, that the price we pay for a drug is much higher than the price paid for the identical drug in other countries. In many cases the pharmaceutical companies produce the drug in the United States and export it to other countries and sell it for far lower prices in those countries. Then they jack up their prices in the United States and refuse to allow American consumers to buy the cheaper drugs abroad.

The biggest-selling drug in the world is Lipitor, a cholesterol-lowering medication. It is made in Ireland and sold around the world. In Canada a bottle of Lipitor costs one-half the price of the identical bottle purchased in the United States by American consumers. And the same is true for most of the brand-name prescription drugs.

The simple solution is to allow the American consumer to take advantage of the global economy. If the big corporations want a free market so they can buy and sell anywhere, why should the American consumer be prevented from equal access to this market? I'm talking about allowing access to FDA-approved drugs produced in FDA-approved plants overseas. The same pill put in the same bottle. How can that be unsafe?

With prices 60 to 70 percent cheaper in Canada and the downward pressure reimportation would put on domestic prices, I believe consumers could save $50 billion over ten years. I, along with thirty other members of the U.S. Senate from both parties, have worked for several years on legislation that would allow American citizens to import FDA-approved drugs that are sold in other countries for a fraction of the price that they are required to pay in the United States. The pharmaceutical industry has blocked it with its allies in Congress who apparently have no qualms about charging Americans the highest prices in the world for prescription drugs.

You would think these rascals in the pharmaceutical industry would blush and begin acting more responsibly. Instead, I have no doubt they are working on anti-blush medicine.

The immediate effect of allowing Americans to import lower-priced prescription drugs will be to save consumers money, but there is a more important effect. It will force the drug companies to reprice their drugs being sold in our country. And that's the real reason the drug companies are waging an aggressive battle to prevent consumers from benefiting from the same global economy they enjoy themselves.

The drug industry has spent millions trying to convince people that allowing the import of lower-priced drugs would be unsafe for the consumers. But that's nonsense. The fact is, Europe has been allowing the importation of prescription drugs among European countries for over two decades without any safety issues at all. The European system is called Parallel Trading and has worked for twenty years without a hitch.

The pharmaceutical industry needs to be reined in. I recognize it is a vital industry and it does need to stay profitable and productive. The advancements in medicine and science we have seen in a generation tell us that there is much that is right with that industry as well. But greed has become commonplace, in my judgment, and stains what should be a noble industry.

One complaint by the drug industry is worth considering. When they spend billions for research and discover an important new drug, the timeline for their exclusive patent protection starts even before clinical trials for the drug. Clinical trials and FDA approval can often take many years. There are times when a company will have only a seven- or ten-year patent protection by the time they get their drugs to the market.

The current limited window for profit may well put pressure on the FDA to move things along too soon, before the long-term effects of a new drug are known. And it also might be putting pressure on the drug companies to overprice their drugs to capture what they can before the patent period runs out.

I would like to see a task force working with the FDA devise a formula that establishes reasonable drug prices based on the true expenditures of the company. And the company that discovers and produces a drug should have a reasonable time for exclusive sale of it after it is put on the market.

And part of that evaluation should consider how much of the development of the drug has come from public financing through the National Institutes of Health (NIH), whose research is used by the pharmaceutical companies to produce new drugs as well.

And while I am talking about change, I think it is time to complain about the television advertising for drugs that you can only get with a doctor's prescription. I'm of the mind that a doctor, not a television commercial, ought to be suggesting the right medicine for me. Encouraging Americans without medical degrees to lobby their doctor for a certain brand of pills for a malady they probably don't have isn't healthy. Plus, the cost of all that advertising gets passed on to the consumer.

I'm tired of television commercials that tell me to ask my doctor "whether the purple pill is right for me." I don't even know what the purple pill is designed to cure. I'm sure not going to ask my doctor to cure anything that doesn't ache or pain. So let's leave prescription medicine to those who prescribe it—the doctors.

It's time to tell the pharmaceutical industry they should either end or tone down the television advertising and give us fair pricing. Is this a free-speech issue? Some may make the case, but as long as taxpayer dollars are paying for much of the research, I think it is reasonable that as partners in the venture we have oversight of the marketing of powerful and sometimes addictive drugs.

## HEALTH-CARE COSTS MAKE AMERICAN BUSINESSES LESS COMPETITIVE

In my last book, I wrote about American corporations that moved their jobs overseas in search of cheap labor. I'm interested in helping American companies keep their jobs in the United States and compete successfully around the world. Author Thomas L. Friedman might be enthralled by seeing what used to be good American jobs being performed by low-income foreign workers, but I'm not.

In this new global economy described by and applauded by Friedman and others it is hard for American companies to compete if they offer decent wages, health-care benefits, and retirement plans to their American workers. So, we can either give up, like Friedman, and describe the new world order as one in which we see wages and benefits collapsing or begin to help American business with a system that starts to put the brakes on increasing health-care costs.

It stands to reason that if we can help American businesses be more competitive we should. General Motors, for example, estimates that $1,500 of each vehicle's cost is attributed to health-care expenses. So when General Motors competes with foreign car companies it starts out with a big disadvantage because it is paying more for its workers. American businesses aren't just crying wolf. This is a real and growing problem. It is estimated, for example, that the price for American-produced steel is 10 percent higher due to health-care costs.

Combine one-sided trade agreements and the lure of cheap overseas labor, coupled with dramatically higher health-care costs in the United States, and you have a recipe for the exodus of American jobs.

Much of our health-care coverage in the United States is employment based. That is, it becomes part of the compensation package, and business pays most of the cost of the employee health insurance for over half of the American workforce.

That has been a major increasing burden for business in recent years. Businesses have had to face an average of a *73 percent increase in premiums* just since 2000, according to Katherine Swartz of the Harvard School of Public Health. Smaller businesses have seen their costs *double.*

As we try to develop a new health-care system, some think we should abandon the employment-based system. I don't! I think we should keep it and build on it. But that will require that we rein in costs and provide some incentives for businesses to continue to provide health insurance coverage.

## AND WHAT ABOUT HEALTH SAVINGS ACCOUNTS?

The Bush administration touted Health Savings Accounts as the answer to health-care reform. While HSAs may be an attractive option for the young and healthy or in some cases for the very ill, the problem is, they don't answer the question—if families cannot afford to pay monthly premiums as it is, how can they afford to build up meaningful funds in an HSA?

The idea is to save money in an Individual Retirement Account (IRA) with pretax dollars to pay for all but catastrophic medical costs, which would be covered by a high-deductible and lower-cost insurance policy. The maximum allowable contribution is $2,850 for an individual and $5,650 for a family. Some HSA plans offer preventive care, and that is a good thing.

Medical expenditures may be paid for out of the account with no tax consequences. This includes some expenditures such as dental and vision, which may not otherwise be covered by a policy. That especially makes sense for those in the retirement years, when there will almost certainly be more health-related costs.

This plan has been widely derided from the left and perhaps too wholeheartedly embraced from the right. But this option works for some who have the financial wherewithal to make it work.

Tax breaks offered by an HSA don't mean much to a low-income family with fewer tax obligations. And the evidence shows that high deductibles keep people from going to the doctor. Since early detection is critical to saving lives and lowering medical expenses, HSAs appear to have the opposite effect and therefore can be counterproductive for good health.

The Commonwealth Fund Biennial Survey found that 44 percent of privately insured adults with deductibles of $1,000 or more avoided getting necessary health care or prescriptions because of the cost, compared with 25 percent of adults with deductibles under $500. There is also evidence that rising cost exposure leads people to accumulate medical debt, take on credit card debt, and reduce their savings. The Commonwealth Fund survey found that 40 percent of privately insured adults with deductibles of $1,000 or more had problems paying medical bills or had accumulated medical debt, compared with 23 percent of adults with deductibles of $500 or less.

Clearly, this option does not solve the problem of those families who cannot currently afford health coverage, but HSAs have the potential to benefit some of those who are already insured. And one of the benefits is that HSAs put the consumers in the position of seeing what is being charged for health-care services and being informed consumers. And that is a good thing. In their fledgling state, HSAs have not had much of an impact, but they have the potential to drive prices down for consumers.

## STARTING WITH THE KIDS

Congress did take an important step toward addressing part of the health-care crisis in America in late 2007 when it presented a $60 billion (over five years) bipartisan bill to expand the State Children's Health Insurance Program, or SCHIP, from enrollment of 6.6 million children to more than 10 million.

Building on the current federal program to provide health-care coverage to children who do not have any makes good sense to me.

If we can't make sure that we have health care available for everyone, let's at least start with the most vulnerable—our kids.

Unfortunately, that sounded too much like federalized health care to President Bush and he vetoed it. Even some of his Republican supporters were critical.

"Unfortunately, I believe that some have given the President bad advice on this matter," said Senator Orrin G. Hatch, Republican of Utah. He said supporting the health bill "is the morally right thing to do."

Senator Charles E. Grassley, Republican of Iowa, said that contrary to what Mr. Bush said about his own vision for the insurance plan, "It won't even cover kids on the program today, much less reach out to cover more kids."

Under the SCHIP program, all that happens is money is set aside to buy health insurance on the open market for families caught between the cracks, who can't afford coverage but don't qualify for Medicaid. States match a portion of the federal dollars. This isn't a program that should threaten the sensibilities of those who don't like government. I think it is the type of thing that should be a priority for government.

In February of 2009 Congress once again enacted a bill to expand the Children's Health Insurance program and President Obama signed it into law.


## THE WAGES OF SIN TAXES?

You can't talk about health without mentioning smoking. The quality of our health has much to do with what we put in our bodies. And cigarettes lead the list of things that can kill us.

Smoking is horribly addictive, I know. And despite the claim of a lot of smokers, "I can quit any time I want," it is just not the case. If you're in the Minneapolis–St. Paul Airport someday in January when the temperature is twenty below zero and the wind is howling at twenty miles an hour, walk over to door six and look outside.

You'll see people huddled up, shivering in bitter cold subzero wind-chills, smoking cigarettes. It seems to me those people have pretty much given up the ability to claim, "I can quit any time I want to."

One of the ways we have dealt with the health dangers of smoking is through what is called a sin tax. According to people who track these things, it appears to work. Heck, if higher prices have kept people from buying health insurance, it should work with cigarettes. But it's probably not quite a parallel case because of the addiction. Still, it is true that higher prices make more people seriously consider stopping smoking.

The biggest cigarette "tax" ever came in 1998, with the settlement of a $250 billion lawsuit (over twenty-five years) by the states against the tobacco industry. The problem was, many state governments applied the largess to wholly unrelated budget items. It became a convenient way to heist billions from a bunch of people no one will feel sorry for. State legislators took the money, and instead of investing in health matters related to smoking cessation and other health issues, many of them diverted it to a range of other unrelated matters.

The decades of education and increased out-of-pocket cost of smoking have made a difference, however. Fewer people are smoking, but the 20 percent of adults who now smoke equates to 44 million Americans merrily puffing away.

But smoking is a killer. It is blamed for 435,000 premature deaths annually in the United States and $75 billion in health-care costs a year, according to the federal Centers for Disease Control and Prevention.

When you measure society's cost of smoking against the tobacco settlement, the industry made out all right. They're still managing to stay in business in a big way (especially by targeting the cigarettes to international markets), and even if we have been successful in shrinking the number of smokers, who, let's face it, are going to keel over sooner than most, the tobacco companies have a world full of eager young smokers to target. We have to get to them before the tobacco companies reach them.

Alcohol is also subject to the so-called sin tax. Used in moderation by adults, alcohol is in a different category than tobacco. But alcohol can become an addictive product that kills.

But there are many other killers as well. Pork rinds plugs up the arteries. Cheetos, too. Twinkies. We know they are unhealthy and possibly dangerous. One San Francisco murderer claimed it was the Twinkies that made him do it.

So, do we slap Twinkies with a sin tax? Maybe not. Maybe just warning labels. It will be the Nanny State saying: "Warning: This Twinkie, along with being filled with things no one can pronounce, when consumed in excess may plump you up so much it impacts your gas mileage."

In the end, my conclusion is that there is a place for "sin taxes," but they are far from a cure. Education and personal responsibility can play a large part in improving the health of America.

But we have to support personal efforts. A compassionate approach with counseling and other treatments covered under a universal plan could begin to address addictions and other health-related issues, including obesity. I'm not ready to punish people addicted to anything by restricting health care based on the conclusion that they are weak willed. Let's heal, not punish.

## A REALITY CHECK ON HOW WE TREAT DRUG ADDICTS

They used to burn witches at the stake in America. We don't do that anymore. While some in the last administration might not have agreed that burning at the stake constitutes torture, most other people agree—it's barbaric and would contribute to global warming. (Okay, I'm exaggerating!)

There was a time when we prosecuted homosexuals, too. We don't do that anymore, either. We've evolved and understand how wrong some of our actions were. But we've still not learned much about how to deal with those who suffer from a drug addiction.

These days we still throw most of them in prison, which is part of the reason America's prison population is larger per capita (751 per 100,000) than any other country's, including China and Russia. There are 2.3 million imprisoned in America. We have 5 percent of the global population and one-fourth of all prisoners!

Drug addiction is a serious health problem in America and it's time to take a realistic and compassionate look at how we deal with addicts. It's your brother, mother, and friend we're talking about. It's Betty Ford. It's even Rush Limbaugh.

The health consequences of a drug addiction are devastating. But rather than working to treat the addiction, our country has poured billions annually into a "War on Drugs" that we've not been winning. In some ways it is a war on people who are already victims of their addiction.

I'm not saying we should give up on the effort. I just think we need to be smarter. To succeed in the drug war we have to shut down demand. That means we have to worry not just about those who are dealing (and we should throw the book at them) but also about those who are using. And instead of simply throwing those who are using into jail at a time when they are addicted to drugs, we should be trying to treat the addiction.

The focus in dealing with drug addiction has been on prosecution, which clogs court systems and jail cells and in the long term does nothing about solving the underlying cause of the drug problem. Prosecution is appropriate in some cases and I support the police and the prosecutors. But it seems to me the only way we can really deal with the drug problem is through prevention and care, including addiction treatment.

It's time to ask what really makes sense. Should we continue to spend less on prevention and education than we do on jail cells? Of course not! Can't we fight the scourge of meth, cocaine, and other hard-core drugs while considering that many addicts are sick people in need of treatment more than jail? I believe we can and should.

No one is willing to talk much about this on a national level. But if we are going to address the health of Americans, shouldn't we gather experts from health, social services, and prisons and rethink our approach and focus on health rather than punishment?

My main point is that there are crimes that harm others and those must be punished. But harm to one's self because of an addiction should be reconsidered. Such enlightenment will not cause the sky to fall or the saints to weep. Societies must evolve and reconsider the way things are done.

I have based my case purely on ethics. But it makes economic sense, too. In California, after six years of Proposition 36, which gave nonviolent first- and second-time drug offenders the option of treatment, the number of people jailed for drug possession has gone down by 32 percent (2007 figures). That kept five thousand people out of jail and saved $1.7 billion by canceling construction of a men's prison and closing a women's facility. The $120 million annual budget has proved too little, however. A study by UCLA indicates that $230 million is required to provide minimal adequate treatment. Critics argue for more of an investment. Measured against $1.7 billion in savings, it seems the money would be well spent.

## SO WHAT IS THE ANSWER TO A NATIONAL HEALTH PLAN?

How do we solve the health-care crisis in America? I don't think the experience of our country with a fee-for-service system in which people are free to choose their own doctor will or should ever be changed.

But we must develop a national health-care system that will make sure every American has health insurance. The only way to control costs is to develop a program that makes sure health care is available to all Americans. There are a number of ways that this can be done, but in the end it will require federal legislation to create a program that can work to provide broad coverage and control health-care costs.

Even with all the challenges of a system that works well for some but doesn't work at all for others, I believe we can fix our health-care system. This is not some mysterious illness for which we don't have a cure.

To those who have done well in America and don't need Social Security or Medicare or a national health-care program, I say, "Good for you. You've benefited from the American marketplace and lived the dream. Of those who are given much, much is expected."

As for health care for the rest of America, change is coming. With a little give-and-take from those who have and those who don't and some cooperation between private industry and government and, ultimately, between Republicans and Democrats, I believe the generosity of spirit, of necessity, will still be found in America. But in the search for health-care reforms that work it will be sorely tested.

The policies I have discussed in this chapter could guide our country toward better health for all Americans. First and foremost we need a national program that covers all Americans. That program should include the following simple commonsense solutions that will dramatically cut health-care costs.

BEGIN EMPHASIZING HEALTH CARE FIRST. When sick care is needed we should make sure that it's available to all in a national health-care plan. But if we emphasize the less costly things that can keep people well, much less costly sick care will be necessary.

GET THE SODA POP AND HIGH-FAT NACHO SNACK MACHINES OUT OF OUR SCHOOLS. Stop pushing sugar and fat at our kids while they are in school and start once again requiring physical education in a serious way.

PUT THE BRAKES ON SKYROCKETING DRUG PRICES. We can do that by allowing Americans to buy FDA-approved drugs from other countries if necessary. That will force the pharmaceutical industry to reduce its prices here in the United States.

PUT PRESSURE ON THE PHARMACEUTICAL INDUSTRY TO DUMP OR TONE DOWN THE TELEVISION ADVERTISING OF PRESCRIPTION DRUGS THAT ONLY A DOCTOR CAN PRESCRIBE. It drives up the cost and demand of prescription drugs. Let's put the medicine decisions back in the hands of doctors, not advertising firms.

LET'S SHAME STATE GOVERNMENTS THAT RECEIVED LARGE CASH SETTLEMENTS FROM THE TOBACCO INDUSTRY INTO SPENDING THAT MONEY ON AN INFORMATION CAMPAIGN TO PERSUADE KIDS NOT TO START SMOKING. Many of the states took the money and used it for other purposes. Protecting kids from tobacco should be the first priority for these billions of dollars.

These suggestions aren't new and they aren't radical. They represent the common sense we should expect from a policy that really cares about improving the health of the American people while controlling the costs of health care.

As we fuss over and fix the administrative and economic issues in health care, let's not lose sight of the exciting new advances in our midst. There are breathtaking changes in health care ahead of us. One of the most important reasons for this is that for the first time in human history, following the completion of the Human Genome Project, we now have an owner's manual for the human body. It is already paving the way for breakthrough changes in how we prevent illness and disease and how we treat them. Stay tuned! There is so much good news ahead!

# CHAPTER 11

• • •

## *Cheap Labor*

ONE OF THE significant, unresolved economic issues in our country is the one dealing with immigration policy. It is controversial, difficult, and important.

When my previous book about outsourcing, *Take This Job and Ship It*, was published, some readers expressed surprise that I had not included a chapter on immigration. In retrospect, I believe those readers were right. Immigration and the outsourcing of American jobs are really two sides of the same coin. Both have the potential to undermine workers' wages and job security in the short run and undermine our economy and strength as a nation in the long run.

It is interesting to me that the same corporate interests that have been pushing to outsource American jobs in search of cheap labor are pushing to import low-cost labor through the back door to keep costs down on those jobs that remain here at home. That is why there is a connection between immigration and trade. Both have an impact on the availability of jobs here at home for our citizens.

I'm not one of those who think that all immigration is bad for our country. Most of us come from immigrant ancestors. And immigrants have made major contributions to the building of our country.

Our current immigration laws are generous. We allow several million people to come to this country to live legally each and every year. Some of them come here to stay permanently and others are allowed in for shorter durations, such as agricultural workers. But the fact remains, we are a generous country with respect to immigration.

Immigration legislation considered in Congress in recent years recognizes that there has been a flood of immigrants coming to this country illegally and something needs to be done to respond to it.

The estimated 12 million people who have entered the country without legal authorization often are forced to live and work in the shadows. They take low-wage jobs, often paying well below the minimum wage. They have little ability to complain about it for fear of being deported. So they work for substandard wages, which not only takes jobs away from Americans but puts downward pressure on other wages as well. So, the proponents of comprehensive immigration legislation make the case that we have to do something to resolve the status of these 12 million who are here illegally.

I agree that we will have to find a way to resolve the status of those who are already here. And the fact is, no one thinks it is a wise or achievable policy to try to round up 12 million people and deport them. It just isn't going to happen. So we do need to find thoughtful policies that will distinguish between those who have lived here for many years, raised a family here, worked hard, and been model citizens and those who have just come across the border in the last couple of years. The policies we develop should steer us toward compassion and common sense in dealing with people and families, many of whom are our neighbors, coworkers, and fellow parishioners.

But first things first! Before we try to resolve the status of the illegal immigrants, we have to get control of our borders. Otherwise the problem of illegal immigration will just continue to grow.

I was one of only a handful of Democrats to vote against the Senate immigration bill in 2006. The bill contained the "guest worker" program requested by President Bush and the U.S. Chamber of Commerce. As it was introduced, it would have not only established a path to legalization for about 12 million illegal aliens living in the United States but also allowed up to 4.7 million additional workers who aren't *yet* here to come here and assume low-wage jobs. The Chamber of Commerce managed to get that included as a requirement for its support for the legislation. It would have done all of this without resolving the issue of how to provide the kind of border security that would stop the flood of immigrant labor crossing our borders illegally.

## SUPPORTING AMERICAN JOBS
## FOR AMERICAN WORKERS

The strategy of hiring guest workers instead of qualified Americans is employed every day in America. Moira Herbst reported in *BusinessWeek* on a YouTube video that exposes the sham: It's a group of lawyers openly discussing strategies for helping their clients pretend that they're trying to recruit American workers—as required by law—while they, in fact, hire cheaper foreign workers. In the video, Lawrence Lebowitz, director of marketing for the Pittsburgh law firm Cohen & Grigsby, says flat-out, "Our goal is clearly *not* to find a qualified and interested U.S. worker." Lebowitz advises going through the motions of hiring Americans without doing so.

I know there are some strident opponents of illegal immigration whose concerns are rooted in bigotry. That is a response we should all reject. But the real issue remains the economic harm that unlimited immigration by low-wage workers does to American workers who are looking for jobs.

The mantra is that these illegal aliens are doing jobs no one else will do. No, many of them are doing jobs *paying less* than Americans workers can afford to live on. The solution is to pay a decent wage. The implication is that America's workers have gotten too soft to do the tough jobs. Tell that to the steelworker, the farmer and rancher, and the shipbuilder.

Besides, according to Steven Camarota of the Center for Immigration Studies, "There is little evidence that immigrants take only jobs Americans don't want. Even those occupations with the highest concentrations of new immigrants still employ millions of native-born workers. *The decline in native employment was most pronounced in states where immigrants increased their share of workers the most* [emphasis added]. Occupations with the largest immigrant influx tended to have the highest unemployment rates among natives."

As illustrated by the U.S. Chamber of Commerce support for the Amnesty Bill, it is clear this is about businesses looking for ways to keep salaries low and profits high. This is a convenient way to bust unions. And it's working. The illegal immigrant worker is pitted against the American worker, and the standard of living of American workers is driven down by layoffs and stagnant wages because illegal workers will work for lower wages.

With many U.S. corporations shipping American jobs overseas, loose immigration policies are a calculated effort to import cheap foreign labor to do the jobs that are left. But the resulting disintegration of the middle class is bound to weaken the country. Why would our leaders allow that to happen?

The fact is, during this deep recession, many American families are struggling to meet the mortgage and shoulder the cost of health care and college educations on wages that are not keeping up with the cost of living. Bob Seger famously sang the worker's anthem "Feel Like a Number," and the sentiment never held truer than it does today:

I take my card and I stand in line
To make a buck I work overtime

We are experiencing a great philosophical divide in America today. To some, labor is a commodity on the spreadsheet. Just numbers! They want to get as much labor as cheap as they can. No questions asked. But the minute we start distancing ourselves from the reality that these are real human beings with real families, we start to lose cohesiveness as a country. It becomes *us versus them*. By *them*,

I mean institutions like the U.S. Chamber of Commerce and the powers in government that support and reward outsourcing. Parse it any way you wish, but when it comes right down to it, it is an attack on working people. And yes, I understand that the same description holds true for immigrant families. Immigrants are real human beings with real families. They have hopes and dreams as well. But our *first* responsibility is to our citizens who are looking for decent jobs that pay well. There is no social program in this country as important as a good job that pays well when it comes to being able to take care of a family.

There are some who make the point that it is just mostly manual labor jobs that we are losing, as if that alone weren't a serious problem. But that is not accurate.

The thought is that with a good education and/or retraining, we can put Americans back to work again. And for the most part education does make a difference. According to 2007 U.S. Census figures, college graduates averaged $51,000 a year while high-school graduates made $28,000 a year. Those who did not graduate from high school made less than $19,000.

But in this global economy, even that is changing. Molly Hennessy-Fiske reported in the *Los Angeles Times* in 2006:

> Offshoring, which has shifted manufacturing and call-center jobs to . . . Mexico and India, is increasingly affecting white-collar sectors such as engineering and software design.
>
> And companies have continued their long effort to replace salaried positions with lower-paid, nonsalaried jobs, including part-time and freelance positions without benefits.

Lawrence Mishel, president of the Economic Policy Institute, told the *L.A. Times* reporter:

> "The [Bush] administration is saying the only reason people are not sharing in the recovery is they don't have the right

skills." . . . But if college graduates are not doing well, Mishel said, "what does that say?"

What it says is we are witnessing the erosion of the strongest economy in history into something much less.

We haven't seen CEO jobs outsourced yet, but the day that starts happening, you can bet there will be an impassioned demand for action.

## WHO GETS A FREE RIDE AND WHO PAYS THE TOLL?

Who benefits from illegal immigration? First of all, illegal immigrants benefit even if they are taking low-wage jobs. They are, in most cases, working, struggling to pull their families out of poverty. Employers benefit, too. It could be big business or an agricultural business employing illegal workers to get tomatoes picked.

Of course, the tomatoes would still get picked if there were no illegal workers. But without a glut of workers willing to work cheap, it would certainly cost more to get the tomatoes picked. That could impact consumers. The price of tomatoes might rise. So, you see, as a consumer, you receive a tangible benefit from illegal labor. Or so it would seem. But there are hidden costs to consider.

A hard fact of economics is that it costs a certain amount to produce a product and make a profit. However, reality is altered by passing expenses on to taxpayers and subsidizing profits. But there is no free lunch. At the end of the day, somebody pays, and when it comes to this shell game with American jobs, that somebody is you, whether it is through tax dollars to support the added stress to social programs by immigrants or through the actual loss of your job or suppression of your wages. You may not notice the subtle creep, but it's happening.

## IF NAFTA WORKED, WHY DO WE HAVE SO MANY IMMIGRANTS FROM MEXICO?

In 1994, when the North American Free Trade Agreement went into effect over my many documented protests, global economists cited the agreement as one that would be good for all three countries. Well, we know many major American industries set up shop across the border—and that wasn't good for American workers. The irony is, it hasn't been good for many exploited Mexican workers, either. Otherwise, why would they be looking for work in America?

*Washington Post* columnist Harold Meyerson explained in 2006 that market conditions drove 2 million Mexican farmers from their land and

> the experience of Mexican industrial workers under NAFTA hasn't been a whole lot better. With the passage of NAFTA, the *maquiladoras* on the border boomed. But the raison d'etre for these factories was to produce exports at the lowest wages possible, and with the Mexican government determined to keep its workers from unionizing, the NAFTA boom for Mexican workers never materialized. In the pre-NAFTA days of 1975 . . . Mexican wages came to 23 percent of U.S. wages; in 1993–94, just before NAFTA, they amounted to 15 percent; and by 2002 they had sunk to a mere 12 percent.
>
> The official Mexican poverty rate rose from 45.6 percent in 1994 to 50.3 percent in 2000. And that was before competition from China began to shutter the *maquiladoras* and reduce Mexican wages even more.

In America, since NAFTA, we have lost 3.1 million manufacturing jobs while our trade deficit with Mexico and Canada has risen to $138.5 billion in 2007 from $9.1 billion in 1993. And they call that success?

# THE SOLUTION IS NOT ROCKET SCIENCE

When it comes to stemming the tide of illegal workers, all we have to do is penalize those who hire them. If the jobs dry up, the flood of illegal immigrants across the border will slow to a trickle. (More than half of the illegal immigrants in the United States come from Mexico.) We just need the political will to do so. Can we compromise to accommodate those already here, including many with children born on American soil? Sure we can, and we will. But it is important to get this right. We can't put the cart before the horse. We must have a workable plan to secure our borders first. Then we can address the remaining important immigration issues.

The connection between the immigration debate and the outsourcing of American jobs in the global economy is one that will continue. We cannot and should not wall ourselves off from the rest of the world. But our immigration policies must be smart and effective. That means controlling our borders while at the same time developing policies that recognize that there is a need for imported labor in some areas. Those policies have to be developed in concert with a set of goals that respond to the needs of American workers first. That is the way we will continue to build and strengthen a middle class in America. And the growth of that middle class is what has allowed our American economy to prosper over the years.

In my previous book I said that in order for American workers to obtain their fair share of the income that comes from their labor, they need to be able to unite and bargain collectively. Labor unions have been effective at negotiating to increase the wages of working people. In recent years union membership has been on the decline. During the same period, worker productivity has been increasing, but workers' wages have remained stagnant. In my previous book I said that stronger unions would help. By that, I didn't mean that the union organizations themselves should be stronger. I meant that the rights of workers who wish to collectively bargain should be strengthened. It is the rights of the workers, not the structure of labor organizations, that matters.

My reference to unions is rooted in my connection during my youth to the North Dakota Farmers Union, which I believe has been a positive force in allowing farmers to organize to achieve better farm policies.

While workers have benefited by being able to form unions in our country, there have been times long past when the labor unions have gained so much strength that they could force work rules and other provisions that undermined common sense. When that happens, it rewards inefficiency, reduces productivity, and makes us less competitive.

But that has not been the case in recent years. Most of what has happened in recent years has resulted in worker concessions in contracts on wages and benefits as they have had to compete in a global economy with a couple of billion people willing to work for very low wages.

Still, it is important to recognize that the right to organize unions has been very beneficial to American workers and was a major contributor to building an affluent middle class in the United States in the last century. Many employers will state that it has been beneficial to their company as well when they can access a trained, quality workforce that belongs to a first-rate labor union.

## FOREIGN STUDENTS

One area that I believe warrants special attention in the immigration debate is a set of policies that recognize the value of allowing those foreign students who receive their advanced degrees at our colleges and universities to stay and work in this country. It makes little sense to me to host those students from other countries who come here to get their college degrees in math, science, engineering, and other critical disciplines and then send them back to their countries when they are ready to contribute in the workforce, especially when we need people with their skills here.

Inviting them to stay and become a part of our future is an area of immigration that would strengthen our country. It makes sense to me. Some call this idea elitist. I don't think so. We are desperately behind in training the number of the next generation of engineers, scientists, and people in other disciplines with critical skills that our country is going to need. I don't know why we shouldn't strengthen our country by inviting some of the brightest students from abroad to come to study and then allow them to stay and work here after they have attained the kind of skills that could help our country.

If you wonder about the value of this type of policy, go visit one of our major college campuses or perhaps one of our premier national laboratories and see some of the best and brightest from abroad who have attained their advanced degrees here and who will be required to leave our country after they have finished their education or a short work period. I say those are the very people who can meet some important needs in our country and after we educate them, we should do our best to keep them here when we are short of the skills they possess.

# CHAPTER 12

• • •

# *Hope*

As this book is being completed at the end of 2008, I know there are powerful reasons for the American people to lack confidence in their future. The fatigue of a long war in Iraq, the rising unemployment caused by a deep recession, a record number of home foreclosures, the collapse of some of America's largest financial institutions, big federal budget and trade deficits—all of these events created a near-perfect economic storm that has hurt every American citizen. Millions have lost their homes. Millions more have lost their jobs. And many more have lost hope.

But I believe there is still great reason to have hope. This is a great country with a bright future if we can fix the things that are wrong here in America. And we will do that.

In the 2008 presidential election, a record number of voters expressed that hope and determination by waiting in long lines to cast their votes for change.

And with their votes they caused that change. They elected a new President.

It will be a hard road. These big, difficult problems didn't happen overnight and they can't be solved in a day by this new President or any President.

But ours is a country that has a resilient spirit. We work hard. We are strong. And have always felt we could do nearly anything.

The story of the tough-minded patriots who insisted on their independence in the early days of our country is inspiring. They faced great odds, but they prevailed. When George Washington was asked to command the Continental Army in the fight against the British, his army of only five thousand soldiers was made up of shopkeepers, farmers, and other regular citizens. They were up against fifty thousand well-trained British soldiers. Yet somehow those brave colonists and soldiers won. And the new American citizens were free to create their own country here and live their dream of liberty, freedom, and self-government.

Many decades later, our country overcame the devastation of a civil war. It was a time when Americans were killing Americans. And a new leader named Abraham Lincoln emerged to lead this country through its darkest hours.

In a century our citizens fought successfully in two world wars, survived a depression, and created the largest expansion of the middle class in the history of the world. Average Americans built a country unlike any other on earth. We invented the telephone, television, computers, and the Internet even as we found cures or preventions for horrible diseases. And we just kept going, building and creating.

We've achieved nearly unbelievable success in every area of endeavor. In science, education, medicine, engineering.

So, mindful of the serious challenges we face today (and they are big and serious), I'm not a bit pessimistic about our future. On the contrary, I am convinced we will prevail.

In this book, I described how we got off track. And now we are suffering through the harsh results of bad business, bad judgment, and bad politics.

The lessons we are learning are some of the same lessons that were learned leading up to and during the Great Depression. In the years following, new rules and regulations were created to prevent it from ever happening again. But as I have described in this book, in recent years, at the urging of the big financial interests, and with the help of both political parties, those rules, regulations, and protections were dismantled, exposing our country to the risks of the type of financial and economic crisis we experienced beginning in late 2008.

Now we live in a complicated world that is interconnected with information flowing at the speed of light twenty-four hours a day. What happens in one corner of the planet can have a major impact on the rest of the planet. That is what has happened with the financial crisis.

The period ahead is going to require innovative, courageous leadership to steer us back to economic health. We can do this. But it will require a national commitment from all of us to be a part of something bigger than ourselves.

Over the relatively short life of our democracy, there have been many predictions that our form of self-government will fail. But it hasn't and it won't. Because it is based on an idea! And that idea is rooted in the understanding that every citizen should be free to choose their own destiny and that people are able through self-government to make the best decisions about their future.

America has always been a place where anything and everything is possible for all of its citizens most of the time. It comes from the freedom spelled out in the document that begins with "We the People"!

And that freedom of opportunity is what Ralph Waldo Emerson described when he wrote: "I had an almost intolerable awareness that every morning began with an infinite promise. Any book may be read, any idea thought, any action taken. Anything that has ever been possible to human beings is possible to most of us every time the clock says six in the morning. On a day no different than the one now breaking, Shakespeare sat down to begin *Hamlet*."

All of that is true in America. It is why, despite all of our challenges, I have a deep reservoir of optimism about the future of our country. The extraordinary spirit of the American people to demand and expect more of themselves and their government has always provided the garden for growth and progress in nearly every area of human endeavor.

I remember over the years both watching and hearing Ray Charles sing the song "America the Beautiful." Nobody sang that song quite like Ray Charles. He sang, "O beautiful for spacious skies, for amber waves of grain, for purple mountain majesties above the fruited plain." But he never saw any of that. He was blind.

But that wasn't the point. The passion of that song—"and crown thy good with brotherhood"—was for the "idea" of America. The idea of our common bond and our commitment to one another!

Now, more than ever, as we face these new challenges, we need to understand that common bond and renew that commitment. And I have an abiding faith that we will. These challenges require all of us to respond to that call to take action to strengthen our great country.

# BIBLIOGRAPHY

Anderson, Jenny. "Wall Street Winners Get Billion-Dollar Paydays." *New York Times*, April 16, 2008.
———— and Julie Creswell. "Top Hedge Fund Managers Earn Over $240 Million." *New York Times*, April 24, 2007.
Anderson, Sarah, et al. *Executive Excess 2007: The Staggering Social Cost of U.S. Business Leadership*, fourteenth annual CEO compensation survey. Institute for Policy Studies, August 29, 2007. Online at http://www.ips-dc .org/reports/070829-executiveexcess.pdf.
Baker, David R. "Enron's Early Gaming: Transcripts Reveal Manipulation Started in 1998." *San Francisco Chronicle*, February 4, 2005.
Barr, Alistair. "Simons, Griffin, Lampert Earn Over $1 Bln in 2006: Top 25 Hedge Fund Managers Took Home $570 Mln on Average Last Year." *MarketWatch*, April 24, 2007. Online at http://www.marketwatch.com.
Barta, Patrick. "South Africa Has a Way to Get More Oil: Make It from Coal." *Wall Street Journal*, August 16, 2006.
Brennan, Arthur. "Have Bush Administration Reconstruction and Anti-Corruption Failures Undermined the U.S. Mission in Iraq?" Senate Democratic Policy Committee Hearing transcript. Online at http://www .ethicsworld.org/publicsectorgovernance/PDF%20links/brennan.pdf.
Briggs, Michael. "Widescale Biodiesel Production from Algae." University of New Hampshire, Physics Department, revised August 2004. Online at http://www.unh.edu/p2/biodiesel/article_alge.html.
Browning, Lynnley. "Offshore Tax Breaks Lure Money Managers." *New York Times*, July 1, 2007.
Burman, Leonard. "Capital Gains: What Is the Effect of a Lower Tax Rate?" Tax Policy Center, January 30, 2008. Online at http://www.taxpolicycenter .org/briefing-book/key-elements/capital-gains/lower-rate.cfm.

Camarota, Steven A. "A Jobless Recovery? Immigrant Gains and Native Losses." Center for Immigration Studies, October 2004. Online at http://www.cis.org/articles/2004/back1104.html.

"CEO Compensation: Special Report." *Forbes*, May 3, 2007. Online at http://www.forbes.com.

Chandrasekaran, Rajiv. *Imperial Life in the Emerald City: Inside Iraq's Green Zone*. New York: Knopf, 2006.

Chivers, C. J. "Supplier Under Scrutiny on Arms for Afghans." *New York Times*, March 27, 2008.

Conry, Tara, et al. "18 Big Ideas to Fix Health Care Now." *Reader's Digest*, November 2008.

Davis, Ann. "Where Has All The Oil Gone?" *Wall Street Journal*, October 6, 2007.

Democratic Policy Committee. "Major Findings: DPC Oversight Hearings on Waste, Fraud, and Corruption in Iraq." September 26, 2008. Online at http://dpc.senate.gov/dpc-new.cfm?doc_name=sr-110-2-155.

Dreyfuss, Barbara T. "What Hedge Funds Risk." *The American Prospect*, June 17, 2007.

Ehrenreich, Barbara. *This Land Is Their Land: Reports from a Divided Nation*. New York: Macmillan, 2008.

Equilar, Inc. "SEC Approves Potential Changes to Executive Compensation Disclosure Requirements." Press release, January 18, 2006. Online at http://www.equilar.com/press_20060118.pdf.

Financial Policy Forum, Derivatives Study Center. *Primer Derivatives*. Washington, D.C. 2000, updated in 2002. Online at http://www.financialpolicy.org/dscprimer.htm.

Fisher, Daniel. "A Dangerous Game." *Forbes*, October 16, 2006.

Flintoff, Corey. "Iraqi Watchdog Official Alleges High-Level Corruption." *All Things Considered*, NPR, September 7, 2007.

Gates, William H., Sr., and Chuck Collins. *Wealth and Our Commonwealth*. Boston: Beacon Press, 2004.

Greenspan, Alan. *The Age of Turbulence: Adventures in a New World*. New York: Penguin, 2007.

Grow, Brian, and Robert Berner. "Fresh Pain for the Uninsured." *BusinessWeek*, November 21, 2007.

"Harvey Pitt: Accounts Angel Who Supped with the Devil." *The Independent*, August 11, 2002.

Hedgpeth, Dana. "KBR Faulted on Water Provided to Soldiers." *Washington Post*, March 11, 2008.

Hennessy-Fiske, Molly. "That Raise Might Take 4 Years to Earn as Well." *Los Angeles Times*, July 24, 2006.

Herbst, Moira. "Americans Need Not Apply." *BusinessWeek*, June 22, 2007.

Institute for the Analysis of Global Security. "Fueling Terror." Online at http://www.iags.org/fuelingterror.html.

Johnston, David Cay. "Income Gap Is Widening, Data Shows." *New York Times*, March 29, 2007.

Kaplan, David E. "The Saudi Connection." *U.S. News and World Report*, December 7, 2003.

Kelley, Matt. "Largest Iraq Contract Rife with Errors." *USA Today*, July 17, 2007.

Kirkland, Rik. "The Real CEO Pay Problem." *Fortune*, June 30, 2006.

Kristof, Kathy M. "CEO Sold as Stock Dropped." *Los Angeles Times*, September 29, 2007.

Lynch, David J. "Debate Brews: Has Oil Production Peaked?" *USA Today*, October 16, 2005.

McIntyre, Robert. "Tax Me If You Can: Interview Transcript." *Frontline*, February 19, 2004. Online at http://www.pbs.org/wgbh/pages/front line/shows/tax/interviews/mcintyre.html.

Meyerson, Harold. "NAFTA and Nativism." *Washington Post*, February 8, 2006.

Morley, Jefferson. "Halliburton Doing Business with the 'Axis of Evil.'" *Washington Post*, February 3, 2005.

Nader, Ralph. *The Good Fight: Declare Your Independence and Close the Democracy Gap.* New York: Regan Books, 2004.

Pelofsky, Jeremy. "US Sent Billions in Cash on Pallets to Baghdad." Reuters, February 7, 2007.

Quaghebeur, Marc. "Belgium Confirms Status of Cross-Border Leases with U.S. Companies." *Tax Notes Today*, March 2, 2004.

Reckard, E. Scott, and Annette Haddad. "A Rush to Pull Out Cash." *Los Angeles Times*, August 17, 2007.

Sahadi, Jeanne. "CEO Pay: 364 Times More Than Workers." August 29, 2007. Online at http://money.cnn.com/2007/08/28/news/economy/ceo_pay_workers/index.htm.

Schoen, John W. "Why High Oil Prices Haven't Cut Demand." October 14, 2004. Online at http://www.msnbc.msn.com/id/6249750/.

Smith, Hedrick, writer, correspondent, and senior producer. "Tax Me if You Can." *Frontline*, February 19, 2004.

Smith, Jack Z. "This Is Like a Highway with No Cops and No Speed Limit." *McClatchy Newspapers*, November 1, 2007. Online at http://www.herald extra.com/content/view/241974/.

Stannard, Bruce. "Clyde Prestowitz in *The Australian*: Dumping of U.S. Dollar Could Trigger 'Economic September 11.'" Economic Strategy Institute. August 29, 2005. Online at http://www.econstrat.org.

Stiglitz, Joseph E., and Linda J. Bilmes. *The Three Trillion Dollar War: The True Cost of the Iraq Conflict.* New York: W. W. Norton, 2008.

Stockman, Farah. "Shell Firms Shielded U.S. Contractor from Taxes: Defense Outfit May Have Saved Millions." *Boston Globe*, May 4, 2008.

———. "Top Iraq Contractor Skirts US Taxes Offshore." *Boston Globe*, March 6, 2008.

Swartz, Katherine. "Universal Health Care: No Sick Joke." *BusinessWeek*, the Debate Room blog, June 2007. Online at http://www.businessweek .com/debateroom/archives/2007/06/universal_healt.html.

Tabb, William K. "Wage Stagnation, Growing Insecurity, and the Future of the U.S. Working Class." *Monthly Review* 59, no. 2, June 2007.

Tucker, Neely. "A Web of Truth: Whistle-Blower or Troublemaker, Bunny Greenhouse Isn't Backing Down." *Washington Post*, October 19, 2005.

Weinberg, Neil, and Bernard Condon. "The Sleaziest Show On Earth." *Forbes*, May 24, 2004.

Wirtz, Ronald A. "Goldilocks in the Corner Office." *Fedgazette*, Federal Reserve Bank of Minneapolis, December 2006.

Wolfe, Thomas. *You Can't Go Home Again.* New York: Harper Perennial Modern Classics, 1998.

Wolff, Edward N. *Recent Trends in Household Wealth in the United States: Rising Debt and the Middle-Class Squeeze.* The Levy Economics Institute of Bard College and Department of Economics, New York University, June 2007. Online at http://www.levy.org/pubs/wp_502.pdf.

Zuckerman, Gregory. "Trader Made Billions on Subprime: John Paulson Bet Big on Drop in Housing Values; Greenspan Gets a New Gig, Soros Does Lunch." *Wall Street Journal*, January 15, 2008.

# INDEX

hedge funds. *See also* derivatives
  derivative trading and, xii, 3, 34,
    40, 51, 57–58, 73–78, 83–87,
    114
  income of managers in, 12,
    78–80, 94–96, 110–11, 113–14,
    124
  Madoff scandal and, 60–61
  margin requirements for, 87–88
  market manipulation and,
    80–84
  oil futures market and, 84–88,
    184
  pension investments in, 81–82
  registration of, 80, 82
  regulation of, 40, 51, 57–58, 72,
    73, 75, 78, 81–88
  returns on, 79–80, 114
Hennessy-Fiske, Molly, 240
Herbst, Moira, 238
Hewlett-Packard, 120
Hill, Simon W., 210
Himmelstein, David, 216
Home Depot, 120
Homestead Act, 23, 26
Honest Leadership and
  Accountability in Contracting
  Act, 178
*Houston Chronicle*, 168
H & R Block, 50
HSAs. *See* Health Savings Accounts
Human Genome Project, 235
Hunter, Brian, 82–84
Hussein, Saddam, 143, 145
  assets of, 151, 157
  intelligence information on,
    134–39, 141
hybrid vehicles, 199–200
hydrogen power, 188, 200

ICE. *See* Intercontinental Exchange
immigrant labor, 243

economy influenced by, 29,
    236–45
  foreign students as, 244–45
  guest worker program for,
    237–38, 239
  NAFTA's impact on, 242
  standard of living's relation to,
    238–41
*Imperial Life in the Emerald City*
  (Chandrasekaran), 175
income
  of Americans, average, 27–28, 57,
    62, 79, 110–11, 113
  of CEOs/executives, xiii–xiv, 3,
    8, 12, 48, 57–58, 110, 112–13,
    116–26
  via earning dividends, 92
  of hedge fund managers, 12,
    79–80, 110–11, 113–14, 124
  imbalance in, 27–28, 57, 62–63,
    79, 110–11, 113–17, 125–26
  performance's relation to, 119–23,
    125
  of private equity firms, 114–17,
    124
  regulation, federal, of, 27–30,
    122–26
  retirement, 117–18, 120
  severance pay, 117, 119, 120
  tax rate variances related to, 12,
    90, 91–96, 100
*The Independent*, 59
India, 186, 197, 206
Individual Retirement Accounts,
  227
Institute for Policy Studies, 124
Institute for the Analysis of Global
  Security, 193
Institute of Medicine, 214
insurance, health
  claim itemization and, 218–19,
    228